The Entrepreneurial State

The Entrepreneurial State

Debunking Public vs. Private Sector Myths

Mariana Mazzucato

ANTHEM PRESS
LONDON · NEW YORK · DELHI

Anthem Press
An imprint of Wimbledon Publishing Company
www.anthempress.com

This edition first published in UK and USA 2013
by ANTHEM PRESS
75–76 Blackfriars Road, London SE1 8HA, UK
or PO Box 9779, London SW19 7ZG, UK
and
244 Madison Ave #116, New York, NY 10016, USA

British Library Cataloguing-in-Publication Data
A catalogue record for this book is available from the British Library.

Library of Congress Cataloging-in-Publication Data
Mazzucato, Mariana, 1968–
The entrepreneurial state : debunking public vs. private sector myths / Mariana
Mazzucato.
pages cm
Includes bibliographical references and index.
ISBN 978-0-85728-252-1 (pbk. : alk. paper)
1. Entrepreneurship–Government policy.
2. Technological innovations–Government policy.
3. Research, Industrial. 4. Diffusion of innovations. I. Title.
HB615.M372797 2013
338'.04–dc23
2013017536

ISBN-13: 978 0 85728 252 1 (Pbk)
ISBN-10: 0 85728 252 2 (Pbk)

This title is also available as an eBook.

This book is dedicated to my mother Alessandra, whose spirit continues to influence all those who met her – affecting our willingness and ability to understand and transform the world with firmness, generosity and grace. And to my father whose battle to survive without her has not diminished his nearly life-long pursuit of perhaps the only really renewable source of energy – nuclear fusion.

As a matter of fact, capitalist economy is not and cannot be stationary. Nor is it merely expanding in a steady manner. It is incessantly being revolutionized from within by new enterprise, i.e., by the intrusion of new commodities or new methods of production or new commercial opportunities into the industrial structure as it exists at any moment.

Joseph Schumpeter (1942 [2003], 13)

The important thing for Government is not to do things which individuals are doing already, and to do them a little better or a little worse; but to do those things which at present are not done at all.

John Maynard Keynes (1926, xxx)

It is a popular error that bureaucracy is less flexible than private enterprise. It may be so in detail, but when large scale adaptations have to be made, central control is far more flexible. It may take two months to get an answer to a letter from a government department, but it takes twenty years for an industry under private enterprise to readjust itself to a fall in demand.

Joan Robinson (1978, 27)

Where were you guys [venture capitalists] in the '50s and '60s when all the funding had to be done in the basic science? Most of the discoveries that have fuelled [the industry] were created back then.

Paul Berg, 1980 Nobel Prize in Chemistry winner
(quoted in Henderson and Schrage 1984)

CONTENTS

LIST OF TABLES AND FIGURES

Tables

Figures

LIST OF ACRONYMS

AEIC	American Energy Innovation Council
ARPA-E	Advanced Research Projects Agency – Energy (US Department of Energy)
ARRA	American Recovery and Reinvestment Act
ATP	Advanced Technology Program
BIS	Department of Business, Innovation and Skills (UK)
BNDES	Banco Nacional de Desenvolvimento Econômico e Social (Brazilian Development Bank)
CBI	Confederation of British Industries
CBO	Congressional Budget Office (UK)
CERN	European Organization for Nuclear Research, Geneva
DARPA	Defense Advanced Research Projects Agency (USA)
DECC	Department of Energy and Climate Change (UK)
DEMOS	UK think tank
DoD	US Department of Defense
DoE	US Department of Energy
DRAM	Dynamic random-access memory
EC	European Commission, Brussels
EPA	Environmental Protection Agency (USA)
EPRI	Electric Power Research Institute
FDA	Food and Drug Administration (USA)
FINNOV	FINNOV EC FP7 project (www.finnov-fp7.eu)

FIT	Feed-in tariff
GDP	Gross domestic product
GE	General Electric
GMR	Giant magnetoresistance
GPS	Global positioning system
GPT	General purpose technology
GW	Gigawatt
GWEC	Global Wind Energy Council
HM Treasury	Her Majesty's Treasury (UK)
IP	Intellectual property
IPO	Initial public offering on stock market
IPR	Intellectual property rights
MIT	Massachusetts Institute of Technology
MITI	Ministry of International Trade and Industry (Japan)
MRC	Medical Research Council (UK)
MW	Megawatt
NAS	National Academy of Sciences (USA)
NBER	National Bureau of Economic Research (USA, non-profit)
NESTA	National Endowment for Science, Technology and the Arts (UK)
NIH	National Institutes of Health (USA)
NIST	National Institute of Standards and Technology (USA)
NME	New molecular entity
NNI	National Nanotechnology Initiative (USA)
NSF	National Science Foundation (USA)
NYT	*New York Times* (USA)
OECD	Organisation for Economic Co-operation and Development
OSTP	Office of Science and Technology Policy (USA)
OTA	Office of Technology Assessment (USA)

OTP	Office of Tax Policy (USA)
PhRMA	Pharmaceutical Research and Manufacturers of America (trade association)
PIRC	Public Interest Research Centre (USA, non-profit)
PV	Photovoltaic
R&D	Research and development
S&P 500	Standard & Poor's (S&P) stock market index, based on the market capitalizations of 500 leading companies publicly traded in the US
SBIC	Small Business Investment Company (USA)
SBIR	Small Business Innovation Research (USA)
SITRA	Suomen itsenäisyyden juhlarahasto (Finnish Innovation Fund)
SMEs	Small and medium enterprises
SRI	Stanford Research Institute (USA, non-profit)
SST	(American) Supersonic Transport project
TFT	Thin-film transistor
TFP	Total factor productivity
TW	Terawatt
VC	Venture capital
WIPO	World Intellectual Property Organization

ACKNOWLEDGEMENTS

The book could not have been written without the intellectual stimulus and hard work of many colleagues and friends.

First and foremost were inspirational exchanges with two of the world's best economic historians: Carlota Perez and Bill Lazonick. Carlota's work, and our constant discussions, on the role of the State in different phases of technological revolutions, has challenged me to think hard about the changing role of different types of 'capital' – finance and production – over time. And the role of the State in guiding both for *productive* rather than purely speculative ends. But of course innovation requires some speculation – which Bill has been very careful to distinguish from 'manipulation'. Bill's incisive analysis leaves no words untouched, careful for example to distinguish business from the market, what most of us confuse when we use the term 'private sector'. Bill's work on the changing structure of capitalist production, and its relationship to labour markets and financial dynamics should be required reading for all students interested in the theory of the firm, and all policymakers interested in reforming finance to make capitalist production more inclusive and sustainable.

I also thank Bill for introducing me to two of his most brilliant master's students: Oner Tulum and Matt Hopkins, who provided me with the best possible research assistance one can get. Oner applied his surgical methods of studying company reports to get to the bottom of how much the State provided to Apple, both in terms of the underlying technologies as well as early stage financing; Chapter 5 could not have been written without him. And Matt applied his sharp and passionate understanding of clean technology – something he is both academically an expert on but also politically committed to; Chapters 6 and 7 could not have been written without him.

I'm also grateful to Caetano Penna and Caroline Barrow, who provided laborious editorial assistance. Caetano's background in both heterodox economics (and 'the Other Canon' framework) and in innovation studies – and his ground-breaking PhD on the 'transition' required in automobiles – made him a unique and stimulating sounding board and proofreader. Caroline, who found herself drowning in the editing and formatting the manuscript immediately after joining the Science and Technology Policy Research Unit (SPRU) at Sussex University, never lost her patience, and even provided interesting insights on the role of the public sector in the arts, from her experience as a professional dancer.

Finally, I am grateful for funding which allowed me to take some time off to write the manuscript. A grant from the Ford Foundation's *Reforming Global Finance* initiative, led by Leonardo Burlamaqui, was not only helpful but useful due to Leonardo's own work on understanding ways in which 'knowledge governance' can 'shape' markets. It was indeed Leonardo's work with Ford that inspired the first meetings and work that led to another research project, funded by the Institute for New Economic Thinking (INET), in which Randy Wray and I are today banging heads: a project on how to bring together the thinking of Joseph Schumpeter on innovation and Hyman Minsky on finance, to understand the degree to which finance can be turned into a vehicle for creative destruction rather than its current obsession with Ponzi-like destructive creation.

Amongst other friends and colleagues who have provided inspiration through interaction and feedback, I want to mention Fred Block, Michael Jacobs, Paul Nightingale and Andy Stirling, the latter two from SPRU, my new academic home. SPRU, founded by Chris Freeman, is one of the most dynamic environments in which I have worked – a place where innovation is understood to be at the core of capitalist competition, and where rather than mythologizing the process, it is studied 'critically' – in both its rate and its direction.

Lastly, over the last two years I have had the fortune to work closely with different policymakers around the world, who rightly yearn to hear 'different' voices in economics. In the UK I have found particular inspiration working with Secretary of State David Willetts, Shadow Business Secretary Chuka Umunna, Shadow Science Minister Chi Onwurah (now in the Cabinet Office) and Andrew Adonis. In the European Commission, working with Peter Droell (head of the Innovation Unit of the DG RTD) on how to think about public sector innovation (both 'within' and 'through') has provided me with motivation to not only talk about the potential 'entrepreneurial' role of government but to think concretely about how to build 'entrepreneurial' organizations within the public sector.

Of course none of the people listed here bear any responsibility for my own errors, exaggerations, provocations and sometimes too passionate opinions expressed in this book.

FOREWORD

By Carlota Perez

Debunking myths is never easy. Swimming against the tide requires determination, a serious commitment to the truth and massive evidence. That is what Mariana Mazzucato displays in this book, which successfully challenges the widespread idea that the State cannot pick winners, that it is clumsy, bureaucratic and incapable of entrepreneurial risk taking.

Her analysis is not just Keynesian; it is also Schumpeterian. The role of the State is not limited to interventions into the macroeconomy as a 'market fixer' or as for the passive financer of public R&D. The State is also seen as entrepreneur, risk taker and market creator. Mazzucato's argument goes well beyond the role played by government in the countries that recently forged ahead (Japan in the 1980s or South Korea in the 1990s) to focus on the role played by the public sector agencies of the United States – the wealthiest country in the world and an active promoter of 'free markets' – in making risky investments behind the Internet and in funding most of the crucial elements behind the 'stars' of the information revolution, companies such as Google and Apple. Indeed, an illuminating chapter on Apple computers shows how each of the technologies that make the iPhone so 'smart' can be traced back to State investments, from the Internet itself, to the touch-screen display, to the new voice-activated SIRI personal assistant. Mazzucato also analyses the crucial role of the German, Danish and other governments (including China, of course) in recent attempts to develop and diffuse clean energy technologies.

Her key point is that the most radical new technologies in different sectors – from the Internet to pharmaceuticals – trace their funding to a courageous, risk-taking State. Her account of the US government's investment in the Internet provides evidence for the complex set of actions that make such wide-ranging innovations happen. She highlights the importance of mission-oriented funding and procurement; of the bringing together of multiple agencies; and also of the creation of incentives for multiple sectors and the multiple financing tools deployed to make it happen.

Successful efforts do not stop at basic and applied research but carry out the work of achieving commercialization. Companies like Apple, Compaq, Intel and many others received early stage financing through government funding programmes like the SBIR (Small Business Innovation Research). For example, the infrastructure of the ICT revolution, laying the basis for the Internet, was lavishly funded by the State from its beginning stages until it was installed and fully functional and could be turned over for commercial use. As Mazzucato argues, no private investors or market forces could have done that job on their own.

Her more recent examples concerning investments in 'green' technologies show the significance of long-term, committed 'patient' finance. In the advanced world this funding has been provided by State agencies such as the US ARPA-E (the energy version of DARPA, the Defense Advanced Research Projects Agency, which developed the Internet) or by State investment banks such as KfW in Germany. In the emerging world, funds have come from BNDES, the national development bank of Brazil, or the Chinese Development Bank. In all cases and in all contexts – as Mazzucato convincingly shows – major innovations require time and patience. Private finance has become too short-termist and is increasingly dependent on government labs that engage in high-risk portions of the innovation chain before committing its own funds.

This is another myth that this book debunks: the much celebrated role of venture capital (VC). Mazzucato demonstrates how VC has depended on government for the more expensive and uncertain research, before entering and cashing in when the uncertainty of investing in new innovations have been significantly reduced. She even reveals that the much-vaunted failure of the Obama administration's support for Solyndra was equally, if not more, a result of venture capitalists withdrawing funding at a critical moment in the company's development.

In the course of the analysis, Mazzucato manages to establish a strong connection with the literature of 'industry dynamics'. This is a major contribution. Most of the arguments in favour of State intervention for growth and development forget to mention innovation, taking it as a natural companion of growth, a sort of manna from heaven. What Mazzucato does is to link the government directly to technology, innovation and entrepreneurship, while examining the key issues in the economics of innovation such as R&D and growth, the role of patents, and the role of SMEs and large firms acting as innovators and other related aspects.

Hence, this book appears with perfect timing. The stubborn economic crisis is not likely to be overcome with austerity measures or the expectation that 'business as usual' can return by saving the banks. This is a crisis like that of the 1930s, which requires measures as bold and as imaginative as those of the welfare state and Bretton Woods, but geared to the need for sustainable global development lead by today's knowledge society. It is to be hoped that the politicians in the advanced world will come around to understanding this, and that when they look for guidance they will discover the value of Mazzucato's ideas and arguments.

It is a good sign that the much shorter and earlier 'report' version of the current book was immediately recognized as relevant by the European Union and is being increasingly cited by top policy officials. In the United Kingdom also, the ideas have been highlighted in the media and both ministers and shadow ministers have been including them in their declarations and projects. There has also been growing attention to Mazzucato's work in other European countries at very high levels. It is to be expected that this complete version, with the path-breaking chapters on green technology and on the real story of the iPhone will be received with even greater interest.

There are at least three lessons vital for effective institutionalization of innovation that stem from Mariana Mazzucato's analysis. There is a need to strengthen the funding sources of public R&D; a need to increase public commitment to 'green' technology innovation and direction setting; and a need to update the Keynesian responses to modern economic crises.

If State investment in R&D is a necessary first condition in generating private innovation later, then guaranteeing a steady flow of funds for such purposes is in everybody's interest. Her account of the Apple story shows that, apart from 'staying foolish' as Steve Jobs recommended, what many successful entrepreneurs have done – including him   is to integrate State-funded technological developments into breakthrough products. Given the massive returns generated by their success, shouldn't entrepreneurs then return some of the rewards to the government, so it can continue taking the big risks that can later be turned into market game-changers? One could indeed hold that the reward is created in new tax revenues. Yet, globalization and information technology have enabled profits to migrate to low tax regions or even within tax havens. It is clear that innovation is needed in the tax system to ensure that high-risk public spending can continue to guarantee future private innovation. Mazzucato's analysis provides a framework for thinking about ways to reform the current model to achieve that.

The other direction for public sector innovation relates to 'green' technology. It is my own conviction that other than saving the planet, the green direction can, if properly supported, save the economy. By transforming consumption and production patterns and revamping existing structures and infrastructures, green technology can generate economic growth and long-term environmental sustainability. 'Green growth' can have an impact equivalent to what suburbanization and postwar reconstruction did to unleash the golden age in the West on the basis of the 'American way of life'. It is impossible for the new millions of consumers being incorporated into the global economy to find wellbeing following the energy- and materials-intensive path exploited in the past. The limits to resources plus the threat of global warming could either become a powerful brake against the globalization process or the most powerful driver of growth, employment and innovation in a generation.

Mazzucato holds that the 'green revolution' will depend on proactive governments. She shows, with ample illustration from the experience of the last decades in Europe, the US, China and Brazil, that success along the green direction has followed where clear, committed and stable government support has been available. As in the case of the US with information technology, it is those countries that are willing to accept the high risks and that are determined to support their entrepreneurs that are likely to lead the world markets in green technologies. Market uncertainty is unavoidable in the context of innovation, but policy uncertainty – as experienced in the US and UK with respect to all things 'green' – is deadly. Her analysis suggests that success is met by those countries that have been able to reach a strong national consensus and can therefore maintain the level of funding and sustained policy support through the ups and downs of the economy.

This brings us to the third lesson: we need the economic insights of both Keynes and Schumpeter. As Keynes rightly argued, government must become the investor of last resort when the private sector freezes. But in the modern knowledge economy it is not enough to invest in infrastructure or to generate demand for the expansion of production. If innovation has always been – as Schumpeter said – the force driving growth in the market economy, it is even more critical in the information age to continue to direct public resources into catalysing innovation. In her book, following the success of the mission-oriented experience of the United States for public R&D and innovation procurement, Mazzucato argues for the government to overcome recession by intensifying innovation efforts. It would now be crucial for governments to combine traditional infrastructures with modern technologies and to become active in the creation of the new markets through directly promoting and preparing the way for radical innovation.

This is one of those books that should be read by everybody: by those in the public sector that hope to solve the major issues of today; by those in the private sector aware that it is better to engage in a positive-sum game; by economists that need to abandon the narrow understanding of market forces promulgated in conventional economics texts; by academics that seek to do more research into these issues; by students that must realize that widely shared ideas are not necessarily true; by the general public frequently asked to view the State as a burden; and by politicians that need to overcome their fear of government action and design the bold policies that can unleash growth and restore wellbeing to all.

Carlota Perez

Author of *Technological Revolutions and Financial Capital: The Dynamics of Bubble and Golden Ages*

Technological University of Tallinn, Estonia; London School of Economics, University of Cambridge and University of Sussex, UK

February 2013

INTRODUCTION

DO SOMETHING DIFFERENT

...our disability is discursive: we simply do not know how to talk about things anymore.

Tony Judt (2010, 34)

A Discursive Battle

Never more than today is it necessary to question the role of the State in the economy – a burning issue since Adam Smith's *An Inquiry into the Nature and Causes of the Wealth of Nations* (Smith, 1776). This is because in most parts of the world we are witnessing a massive *withdrawal* of the State, one that has been justified in terms of debt reduction and – perhaps more systematically – in terms of rendering the economy more 'dynamic', 'competitive' and 'innovative'. Business is accepted as the innovative force, while the State is cast as the inertial one – necessary for the 'basics', but too large and heavy to be the dynamic engine.

The book is committed to dismantling this false image. In the same way that Mexico was stolen from California and Texas through the purposeful fabricated image of the 'lazy Mexican' under a palm tree (Acuña 1976), the State has been attacked and increasingly dismantled, through images of its bureaucratic, inertial, heavy-handed character. While innovation is not the State's main role, illustrating its potential innovative and dynamic character – its historical ability, in some countries, to play an *entrepreneurial* role in society – is perhaps the most effective way to defend its existence, and size, in a proactive way. Indeed, in *Ill Fares the Land*, Tony Judt (2010) describes that the attack on the welfare state, over the last three decades, has involved a 'discursive' battle – changing the ways we talk about it – with words like 'administration' rendering the State less important and adventurous.

The book seeks to change how we talk about the State, dismantling the ideological stories and images – separating evidence from fiction.

This work is based on a revised and significant expansion of a report I wrote for DEMOS, a UK-based think tank, on *The Entrepreneurial State*. Unlike a more traditional academic piece of writing – that can take years from start to finish – I wrote the DEMOS work in a style similar to the political pamphlets of the 1800s: quickly, and out of a sense of *urgency*. I wanted to convince the UK government to change strategy: to not cut State programmes in the name of making the economy 'more competitive' and more 'entrepreneurial', but to reimagine what the State *can* and must do to ensure a sustainable post-crisis recovery. Highlighting the active role that the State *has* played in the 'hotbeds' of innovation and entrepreneurship – like Silicon Valley – was the key to showing that the State can not only facilitate the knowledge economy, but actively create it with a bold vision and targeted investment.

This expanded version of the DEMOS report (more than double its size) builds on that initial research and pushes it harder, drawing out further implications at the firm and sectoral level. Chapter 5, dedicated entirely to Apple, looks at the whole span of State support that this leading 'new economy' company has received. After looking at the role of the State in making the most courageous investments behind the Internet and IT revolution, Chapters 6 and 7 look at the next big thing: 'green' technology. Unsurprisingly we find that across the globe the countries leading in the green revolution (solar and wind energy are the paradigmatic examples explored) are those where the State is playing an active role beyond that which is typically attributed to market failure theory. And the public sector organizations involved, such as development banks in Brazil and China, are not just providing countercyclical lending (as Keynes would have asked for), but are even 'directing' that lending towards the most innovative parts of the 'green' economy. Questions about whether such 'directionality' should raise the usual worries about the State's inability to 'pick winners' are confronted head on – demystifying old assumptions. The book also looks more explicitly at the collective group of actors that are required to create innovation-led growth and questions whether the current innovation 'ecosystem' is a functional *symbiotic* one or a dysfunctional *parasitic* one. Can a nonconfident State even recognize the difference? Chapters 8 and 9 go deeper into this question by asking how we can make sure that the distribution of the returns (rewards) generated from active State investments in innovation are just as social as the risks taken.

Indeed, some of the very criticisms that have recently been directed at the banks (socialization of risk, privatization of rewards) appear to be just as relevant in the 'real' innovation economy.

The reason I call, both the DEMOS report and the current book, the 'entrepreneurial' State is that entrepreneurship – what every policymaker today seems to want to encourage – is not (just) about start-ups, venture capital and 'garage tinkerers'. It is about the willingness and ability of economic agents to take on risk and real *Knightian* uncertainty: what is genuinely unknown.[1] Attempts at innovation usually fail – otherwise it would not be called 'innovation'. This is why you have to be a bit 'crazy' to engage with innovation... it will often cost you more than it brings back, making traditional cost–benefit analysis stop it from the start. But whereas Steve Jobs talked about this in his charismatic 2005 Stanford lecture on the need for innovators to stay 'hungry and foolish' (Jobs 2005), few have admitted how much such foolishness has been 'seriously' riding on the wave of State-funded and -directed innovations.

The State... 'foolishly' developing innovations? Yes, most of the radical, revolutionary innovations that have fuelled the dynamics of capitalism – from railroads to the Internet, to modern-day nanotechnology and pharmaceuticals – trace the most courageous, early and capital-intensive 'entrepreneurial' investments back to the State. And, as will be argued fully in Chapter 5, all of the technologies that make Jobs' iPhone so 'smart' were government funded (Internet, GPS, touch-screen display and the recent SIRI voice activated personal assistant). Such radical investments – which embedded extreme uncertainty – did not come about due to the presence of venture capitalists, nor of 'garage tinkerers'. It was the visible hand of the State which made these innovations happen. Innovation that would not have come about had we waited for the 'market' and business to do it alone – or government to simply stand aside and provide the basics.

Beyond Fixing Failures

But how have economists talked about this? They have either ignored it or talked about it in terms of the State simply fixing 'market failures'. Standard economic theory justifies State intervention when the social

---

1 'Knightian uncertainty' refers to the 'immeasurable' risk, i.e. a risk that cannot be calculated. This economic concept is named after University of Chicago economist Frank Knight (1885–1972), who theorized about risk and uncertainty and their differences in economic terms.

return on investment is higher than the private return – making it unlikely that a private business will invest. From cleaning up pollution (a negative 'externality' not included in companies' costs) to funding basic research (a 'public good' difficult to appropriate). Yet this explains less than one-quarter of the R&D investments made in the USA. Big visionary projects – like putting 'a man on the moon', or creating the vision behind the Internet – required much more than the calculation of social and private returns (Mowery 2010).

Such challenges required a vision, a mission, and most of all *confidence* about what the State's role in the economy is. As eloquently argued by Keynes in the *The End of Laissez Faire* (1926, xxx), 'The important thing for Government is not to do things which individuals are doing already, and to do them a little better or a little worse; but to do those things which at present are not done at all.' Such a task requires vision and the desire to *make things happen* in specific spaces – requiring not just bureaucratic skills (though these are critical, as pointed out by Max Weber)[2] but real technology-specific and sector-specific *expertise*. It is only through an exciting vision of the State's role that such expertise can be recruited, and is then able to map out the landscape in the relevant space. Indeed, a key part of DARPA's 'secret' – the agency that invented *and* commercialized the Internet within the US Department of Defense (examined in Chapter 4) – has been its ability to attract talent and create excitement around specific missions. And it is no coincidence that a similar agency in today's US Department of Energy, ARPA-E, is not only leading US green investments, but also having fun on the way (welcoming the trial and error process in energy research rather than fearing it) and attracting great brains in energy research (Grunwald 2012).

While many of the examples in the book come from the US – purposely to show how the country that is often argued to most represent the benefits of the 'free-market system' has one of the most interventionist governments when it comes to innovation – modern-day examples are coming more from 'emerging' countries. Visionary investments are exemplified today by confident State investment banks in countries like Brazil and China – not only providing countercyclical lending but also *directing* that lending to new uncertain areas that private

---

2 Evans and Rauch (1999) show, for instance, that a Weberian-type State bureaucracy that employs meritocratic recruitment and offers predictable, rewarding long-term careers enhances prospects for growth, even when controlling for initial levels of GDP per capita and human capital.

banks and venture capitalists (VCs) fear. And here too, like in DARPA, expertise, talent and vision matter. In Brazil, it is no coincidence that BNDES, the State investment bank, is run by two individuals whose background is Schumpeterian innovation economics – and it is their team of experts that have allowed the bold risk taking in key new sectors like biotech and cleantech to occur. The bank is today earning record-level returns in productive, rather than purely speculative, investments: in 2010 its return on equity was an astounding 21.2 per cent (reinvested by the Brazilian Treasury in areas like health and education) while that of the World Bank's equivalent organization, the International Bank for Reconstruction and Development (IBRD), was not even positive (−2.3 per cent). Equally, it is the Chinese Development Bank that is today leading the country's investments in the green economy (Sanderson and Forsythe 2012). While the usual suspects worry that these public banks 'crowd out' private lending (*Financial Times* 2012), the truth is that these banks are operating in sectors, and particular areas within these sectors, that the private banks fear. It is about the State acting as a force for innovation and change, not only 'de-risking' risk-averse private actors, but also boldly leading the way, with a clear and courageous vision – exactly the opposite image of the State that is usually sold.

From 'Crowding In' to 'Dynamizing In'

And this is the punchline: when organized effectively, the State's hand is firm but not heavy, providing the vision and the dynamic *push* (as well as some 'nudges' – though nudges don't get you the IT revolution of the past, nor the green revolution today) to make things happen that otherwise would not have. Such actions are meant to increase the courage of private business. This requires understanding the State as neither a 'meddler' nor a simple 'facilitator' of economic growth. It is a key partner of the private sector – and often a more daring one, willing to take the risks that business won't. The State cannot and should not bow down easily to interest groups who approach it to seek handouts, rents and unnecessary privileges like tax cuts. It should seek instead for those interest groups to work dynamically with it in its search for growth and technological change.

Understanding the unique nature of the public sector – as more than an inefficient 'social' version of the private sector   impacts the nature of the public–private collaborations that emerge, as well as the 'rewards' that the State feels justified to reap (an area I focus on in Chapter 9).

An entrepreneurial State does not only 'de-risk' the private sector, but envisions the risk space and operates boldly and effectively within it to make things happen. Indeed, when not confident, it is more likely that the State will get 'captured' and bow to private interests. When not taking a leading role, the State becomes a poor imitator of private sector behaviours, rather than a real alternative. And the usual criticisms of the State as slow and bureaucratic are more likely in countries that sideline it to play a purely 'administrative' role.

So it is a self-fulfilling prophecy to treat the State as cumbersome, and only able to correct 'market failures'. Who would want to work in the State sector if that is how it is described? And is it a coincidence that the 'picking winners' problem – the fear that the State is unable to make bold decisions on the *direction* of change – is discussed especially in countries that don't have an entrepreneurial vision for the State, i.e. countries where the State takes a backseat and is then blamed as soon as it makes a mistake? Major socioeconomic 'challenges' such as climate change and 'ageing' require an active State, making the need for a better understanding of its role within public–private partnerships more important than ever (Foray et al. 2012).

Images Matter

The cover of this book shows a face of a lion and a pussycat. Which one has 'animal spirits' (Keynes's famous expression) and which one is domesticated and 'lags' behind due to passivity? Which is the State? Which is business? This might be an exaggerated dichotomy but it is one that needs consideration because, as I will argue, we are continuously fed the image of just the opposite: a roaring business sector and purring bureaucratic State sector. Even Keynes, in discussing the volatility of private business investment, fed this contrast by talking about 'animal spirits' as guiding business investment – the image of a roaring lion. But in a secret letter to Roosevelt he also talked about business as 'domesticated animals':

> Businessmen have a different set of delusions from politicians, and need, therefore, different handling. They are, however, much milder than politicians, at the same time allured and terrified by the glare of publicity, easily persuaded to be 'patriots', perplexed, bemused, indeed terrified, yet only too anxious to take a cheerful view, vain perhaps but very unsure of themselves, pathetically responsive to a

kind word. You could do anything you liked with them, if you would treat them (even the big ones), **not as wolves or tigers, but as domestic animals by nature**, even though they have been badly brought up and not trained as you would wish. It is a mistake to think that they are more immoral than politicians. If you work them into the surly, obstinate, terrified mood, of which domestic animals, wrongly handled, are so capable, the nation's burdens will not get carried to market; and in the end public opinion will veer their way... (Keynes 1938, 607; emphasis added)

This view, of business not as tigers and lions, but as pussycats means that the State is not only important for the usual Keynesian countercyclical reasons – stepping in when demand and investment is too low – but also at *any* time in the business cycle to play the role of real tigers. Nowhere is this truer than in the world of innovation – where uncertainty is so high. Indeed, the green revolution that is taking off in the world, only happens to coincide with a crisis environment (and in fact the government's relevant investments reach much farther back in time). But even if today were a boom period, there would not be enough investments being made in radical green technologies were it not for the State. Even during a boom most firms and banks would prefer to fund low-risk incremental innovations, waiting for the State to make its mark in more radical areas. But as with all technological revolutions, green technology requires a bold government to take the lead – as this was the case with the Internet, biotech and nanotech.

Providing such leadership, the State makes things happen that otherwise would not have. But whether this role is justified given the characteristics of 'public good' and the role of 'externalities' (both critical to the market failure argument), or whether it is justified due to a broader understanding of the State as a courageous actor in the economic system makes all the difference. The former understanding leads to discussions about the possibilities of the State 'crowding out' (or 'crowding in') private investment, creating a narrow view of what the State is and what policy options are acceptable (Friedman 1979). The latter understanding leads to (more) exciting discussions about what the State can do to raise the 'animal spirits' of business – to get it to stop hoarding cash and to spend it in new path-breaking areas. This makes a big difference in how one imagines the policy 'space'. For a start, it makes the State less vulnerable to hype about what the business sector can (and does) do. It is indeed the weakest States that give in (the most) to the rhetoric that what is needed are different types of 'tax cuts' and elimination of regulatory 'red tape'. A confident government recognizes fully that the business sector might 'talk' about tax but 'walks' to where new technological and market opportunities are – and that this is strongly correlated with areas characterized by major public sector investments. Did Pfizer recently leave Sandwich, Kent (UK) to go to Boston in the US due to the latter's lower tax and lower regulation? Or was it due to the fact that the public sector National Institutes of Health (NIH) have been spending close to $30.9 billion per year in the USA funding the knowledge base on which private pharmaceutical firms thrive?

In economics, the 'crowding-out' hypothesis is used to analyse the possibility that increased State spending reduces private business investment, since both compete for the same pool of savings (through borrowing), which might then result in higher interest rates which reduces the willingness of private firms to borrow, and hence invest. While Keynesian analysis has argued against this possibility during periods of underutilized capacity (Zenghelis 2011), the point here is that *even in the boom* (when in theory there is full capacity utilization), there are in practice many parts of the risk landscape where private business fears treading and government leads the way. In fact, the spending that led to the Internet occurred mainly during boom times – as was the government spending that lead to the nanotechnology industry (Motoyama et al. 2001).

Thus a proper defence of the State should argue that it not only 'crowds in' private investment (by increasing GDP through the multiplier effect) – a correct but limited point made by Keynesians – it does something more. The way that I interpret Judt's challenge is that we must start using new words to describe the State. Crowding in is a concept that – while defending the public sector – is still using as a benchmark the negative: the possibility that government investment crowds out private investment, by competing for the same limited amount of savings. If we want to describe something positive and visionary, a word that is bolder and offensive, not defensive, should be used. Rather than analysing the State's active role through its correction of 'market failures' (emphasized by many 'progressive' economists who rightly see many failures), it is necessary to build a theory of the State's role in *shaping* and *creating* markets – more in line with the work of Karl Polanyi (1944) who emphasized how the capitalist 'market' has from the start been heavily shaped by State actions. In innovation, the State not only 'crowds in' business investment but also 'dynamizes it in' – creating the vision, the mission and the plan. This book is committed to explaining the process by which this happens.

The book tries to change the ways we talk about the State, in order to expand our vision of what it can do – it takes on Judt's 'discursive' battle. From an inertial bureaucratic 'leviathan' to the very catalyst for new business investment; from market 'fixer' to market shaper and creator; from simply 'de-risking' the private sector, to welcoming and taking on risk due to the opportunities it presents for future growth. Against all odds.

Structure of the Book

The book is structured as follows:

Chapter 1 begins by confronting the popular image of the State as a bureaucratic machine with a different image of the State as lead risk taker. The State is presented as an entrepreneurial agent – taking on the most risky and uncertain investments in the economy. Rather than understanding State risk taking through the usual lens of 'market failures' – with the State acting as an inert bandage for areas underserved by the market – the concept of its entrepreneurial risk taking is introduced. The State does not 'de-risk' as if it has a 'magic wand' that makes risks disappear. It *takes on* risks, shaping and creating new markets. The fact economists have no words for this role has limited our understanding of the role the State has played in the past – in areas like Silicon Valley – and the role that it can play in the future, in areas like the 'green revolution'.[3]

Chapter 2 provides background to the discussion by looking at how economists understand the role of innovation and technology in economic growth. Whereas a generation ago, technological advance was seen as something that was externally given in economic models, there is now extensive literature to show that actually it is the rate – and direction – of innovation that drives the ability for economies to grow. The chapter juxtaposes two very different frameworks for understanding the role of the State in innovation-led growth – both framed in terms of different types of 'failures' that the State corrects. The first is the 'market failure' approach, in which the State is simply remedying the wedge between private and social returns. The second is the 'systems of innovation' approach, which looks at R&D spending in a more holistic way, as part of a system in which knowledge is not only produced but also diffused throughout an economy.

---

3 Contemporary political economists, such as Chang (2008) and Reinert (2007), who specialize in the history of economic policy do of course talk about the role of the State in promoting a 'catching-up' process, or in actively acting countercyclically. Yet these are more in line with a view of the State not as an entrepreneurial risk taker (of *first* resort) but a more passive entrepreneur of last resort.

But even in this second approach the State is mainly fixing failures, this time 'system failures' – with the conclusion being that it is 'facilitating' innovation by 'creating the conditions' for it. These frameworks have provided the justification for increased government spending on innovation, while at the same time – due to the lack of attention on the State as lead risk taker – allowed certain myths to survive. These myths describe the relationship between innovation and growth; the role of SMEs; the meaning of patents in the knowledge economy; the degree to which venture capital is risk-loving; and the degree to which investment in innovation is sensitive to tax cuts of different kinds.

Chapter 3 presents a different view, of an entrepreneurial State acting as a lead risk taker and market-shaper. This is not a substitute for the view espoused in the other two frameworks, but a complement, and one that by being ignored has caused policies informed by the 'failures' approach to be limited in nature, and often more 'ideologically' driven. Examples are provided from the pharmaceutical industry – where the most revolutionary new drugs are produced mainly with public, not private, funds. I also examine the way in which venture capital has 'surfed the wave' of State investments in biotechnology.

Chapter 4 exemplifies the key points on the 'entrepreneurial State' by focusing on the recent industrial policy history of the US, and shows that despite common perceptions, there the State has been extremely proactive and entrepreneurial in the development and commercialization of new technologies. Entrepreneurship by the State can take on many forms. Four examples – the creation of the Defense Advanced Research Projects Agency (DARPA), the Small Business Innovation Research (SBIR) programme, the Orphan Drug Act of 1983, and recent developments in nanotechnology – are used to illustrate this point. It builds on the notion of the 'Developmental State' (Block 2008; Chang 2008; Johnson 1982) pushing it further by focusing on the type of risk that the public sector has been willing to absorb and take on.

While Chapters 3 and 4 look at sectors, Chapter 5 focuses on the history of one particular company – Apple – a company that is often used to laud the power of the market and the genius of the 'garage tinkerers' who revolutionize capitalism. A company that is used to illustrate the power of Schumpeterian creative destruction.[4] I turn this notion on its head.

---

4 Joseph Schumpeter (1942 [2003]) referred to 'creative destruction' as the process by which innovation changes the status quo, allowing the market shares of firms which introduce new products and processes to grow, and those of the firms that resist change to fall.

Apple is far from the 'market' example it is often used to depict. It is a company that not only received early stage finance from the government (through the SBIC programme, which is related to the SBIR programme discussed in Chapter 4), but also 'ingeniously' made use of publicly funded technology to create 'smart' products. In fact, there is not a single key technology behind the iPhone that has not been State-funded. Besides the communication technologies (discussed in Chapter 4), the iPhone is smart because of features such as the Internet, GPS, a touch-screen display, and the latest new voice activated personal assistant (SIRI). While Steve Jobs was no doubt an inspiring genius worthy of praise, the fact that the iPhone/iPad empire was built on these State-funded technologies provides a far more accurate tale of technological and economic change than what is offered by mainstream discussions. Given the critical role of the State in enabling companies like Apple, it is especially curious that the debate surrounding Apple's tax avoidance has failed to make this fact more broadly known. Apple must pay tax not only because it is the right thing to do, but because it is the epitome of a company that requires the public purse to be large and risk-loving enough to continue making the investments that entrepreneurs like Jobs will later capitalize on (Mazzucato 2013b).

Chapter 6 looks at the next 'big thing' after the Internet: the green revolution, which is today being led by the State, just like the IT revolution was. In 2012 China announced its plan to produce 1,000 GWs of wind power by 2050. That would be approximately equal to replacing the entire existing US electric infrastructure with wind turbines. Are the US and Europe still able to dream so big? It appears not. In many countries, the State is asked to take a back seat and simply 'subsidize' or incentivize investments for the private sector. We thus fail to build visions for the future similar to those that two decades ago resulted in the mass diffusion of the Internet. The chapter looks at which countries in the world are leading with a green vision, and the role of their States – and the 'patient' finance supplied by State development banks – in creating the 'catalytical' early, and risky, investments necessary to make it happen.

Chapter 7 focuses on the role of the 'entrepreneurial' risk-taking State in launching specific clean technologies, in this case wind turbines and solar PV panels. It was State funding and the work of particular State agencies that provided the initial push, early stage high-risk funding and institutional environment that could establish these important technologies. While Chapter 5 emphasized the role of the US entrepreneurial State in leading the IT revolution as well as in establishing the foundations of the biotech industry, this chapter emphasizes the role of countries like

Germany, Denmark and China in directing the green revolution as it spreads across more economies.

Chapters 8 and 9 argue that once we accept the role of the State as lead risk taker – beyond the usual 'market fixing' or 'creating conditions' approach – the question arises as to whether this role is represented in the risk–reward relationship. In so many cases, public investments have become business giveaways, making individuals and their companies rich but providing little (direct or indirect) return to the economy or to the State. This is most evident in the case of pharmaceuticals, where publicly funded drugs end up being too expensive for the taxpayers (who funded them) to purchase. It is also true in the case of IT, where the State's active risk-taking investments have fuelled private profits, which are then sheltered and fail to pay taxes back to the governments that supported them. Chapter 8 illustrates this point focusing in on Apple. Chapter 9 considers the points more generally, arguing that in a period of major cutbacks to reduce budget deficits, it is more critical than ever to engage in a discussion of how the State can ensure that its 'risk taking' earns back a direct return, beyond easily avoided taxation. Precisely because State investments are uncertain, there is a high risk that they will fail. But when they are successful, it is naïve and dangerous to allow all the rewards to be privatized. Indeed, criticism of the financial sector for launching the current economic crisis, reaping massive private returns and then socializing risk through unpopular bailouts is a general and unpopular feature of dysfunctional modern capitalism that should not become the norm.

Chapter 10 concludes by reflecting on how the core argument in the book – the State as an active, entrepreneurial, risk-taking agent – is not always a reality, but a possibility too often dismissed. The 'possibility' is only realized once key assumptions are overturned. From how we envision the State within its own organizations (encouraging departments in the public sector to be entrepreneurial, including the need to 'welcome' rather than fear failure), to the relationship between the State and other actors in the innovation system (e.g. by accepting itself as a more active agent, there will be many instances where the State's role is less about 'nudging' and 'incentivizing' and more about 'pushing'). The State's ability to push and direct is dependent on the kind of talent and expertise it is able to attract. And the irony is that the latter is more of a problem in countries where the State takes a back seat, only 'administering' and not leading with dynamic vision. Unless we challenge the numerous 'myths' of economic development, and abandon conventional views of the State's role in it, we cannot hope to address the structural challenges of the twenty-first century nor produce the technological and organizational change we need for long-term sustainable and equitable growth.

Taken as a whole, the book provides a fuller understanding of the public sector's centrality to risk-taking activities and radical technological change, essential to promote growth and development. It offers a very different description of the State from that envisaged by present economic policymakers, which tends to deny the State's leading role in innovation and production. It also challenges conventional industrial policy, which unduly downplays its scope for pioneering and promoting new technologies. In contrast, it describes scenarios where the State has provided the main source of dynamism and innovation in advanced industrial economies, by pointing out that the public sector has been the lead player in what is often referred to as the 'knowledge economy' – an economy driven by technological change and knowledge production and diffusion. From the development of aviation, nuclear energy, computers, the Internet, biotechnology, and today's developments in green technology, it is, and has been, the State – not the private sector – that has kick-started and developed the engine of growth, because of its willingness to take risks in areas where the private sector has been too risk averse. In a political environment where the policy frontiers of the State are now being deliberately rolled back, the contributions of the State need to be understood more than ever. Otherwise we miss an opportunity to build greater prosperity in the future by emulating the successful public investments of the past.

What is needed is a fully-fledged understanding of the division of innovative labour in capitalism (described in Chapter 1 below), and the role that both the private and public sector play in creating, producing and diffusing innovations. The book focuses on innovation not because this is the only or most important thing the State can invest in. The State's role in guaranteeing basic human rights for all citizens – from public healthcare to public education – as well as creating the necessary infrastructure, legal and justice system that allows the economy to function properly are equally if not more important activities. The focus on innovation is due in part to the fact that it is a point of discussion where the State is most frequently attacked for its role. While the role of the private sector has typically been hyped up, the public sector's role has been hyped down. The State is often being cast as the problem, whether it is investing in new technology or improving market function. A key aspect of the challenge is therefore to rebalance our understanding of how economies really work. Only once that is done can we begin to formulate the kinds of policies that work, rather than reproduce stereotypes and images which serve only ideological ends.

Chapter 1

FROM CRISIS IDEOLOGY TO THE DIVISION OF INNOVATIVE LABOUR

Governments have always been lousy at picking winners, and they are likely to become more so, as legions of entrepreneurs and tinkerers swap designs online, turn them into products at home and market them globally from a garage. As the revolution rages, governments should stick to the basics: better schools for a skilled workforce, clear rules and a level playing field for enterprises of all kinds. Leave the rest to the revolutionaries.

Economist (2012)

Across the globe we are hearing that the State has to be cut back in order to foster a post-crisis recovery. The assumption is that, with the State in the backseat, we unleash the power of entrepreneurship and innovation in the private sector. The media, business and libertarian politicians draw from this convenient contrast, and feed into the dichotomy of a dynamic, innovative and competitive 'revolutionary' private sector versus a sluggish, bureaucratic, inertial, 'meddling' public sector. The message is repeated so much so that it is accepted by the many as a 'common sense' truth, and has even made many believe that the 2007 financial crisis, which soon precipitated into a full blown economic crisis, was caused by public sector debt, rather than the truth.

And the language used has been forceful. In March 2011, UK prime minister David Cameron promised to take on the 'enemies of enterprise' working in government, which he defined as the 'bureaucrats in government departments' (Wheeler 2011). The rhetoric fits in with the UK government's broader theme of the Big Society, where responsibility for the delivery of public services is shifted away from the State to individuals operating either on their own or by coming together

through the third sector – with the justification that such 'freedom' from
the State's influence will reinvigorate such services. The terms used, such
as 'free' schools (the equivalent of charter schools in the USA) imply
that by freeing schools from the heavy hand of the State, they will be
both more interesting to students and also run more efficiently.

The increasing percentage of public services, across the globe,
that are being 'outsourced' to the private sector, is usually done using
precisely this 'efficiency' argument. Yet a proper look at the real cost
savings that such outsourcing provides – especially taking into account
the lack of 'quality control' and absurd costs that ensue – is almost never
carried out. The recent scandal where the security for London's 2012
Olympics was outsourced to a company called G4S, which then failed
due to utter incompetence to deliver, meant that the British Army was
called in to provide security during the Olympics. While the managers
of the company were 'reprimanded' the company today is still making
profits and outsourcing remains on the rise. Examples where outsourcing
is resisted, such as the BBC's choice to build the Internet platform for
its broadcasting, the iPlayer, in-house has meant that it has been able
to keep the BBC a dynamic innovative organization, that continues to
attract top talent, retaining its high market share in both radio and TV –
what public broadcasters in other countries can only dream of.

The view of the State as enemy of enterprise is a point of view found
constantly in the respected business press, such as the *Economist*, which
often refers to government as a 'Hobbesian Leviathan' which should
take the back seat (*Economist* 2011a). Their prescription for economic
growth includes focusing on creating freer markets and creating the
right conditions for new ideas to prosper, rather than taking a more
activist approach (*Economist* 2012). And in a recent special issue on the
green revolution, the magazine explicitly made the case, as quoted in
the beginning of this chapter, that while the government should 'stick
to the basics', such as funding education and research, the rest should
be left to the 'revolutionaries', i.e. businesses. Yet as will be argued in
Chapters 4–8, this revolutionary spirit is often hard to find in the private
sector, with the State having to take on the greatest areas of risk and
uncertainty.

When not lobbying the State for specific types of support, established
business lobby groups – in areas as diverse as weapons, medicine and
oil – have long argued for freedom from the long arm of the State,
which they see as stifling their ability to succeed through the imposition
of employee rights, tax and regulation. The conservative Adam Smith

Institute argues that the number of regulators in the UK should be reduced to enable the British economy to 'experience a burst of innovation and growth' (Ambler and Boyfield 2010, 4). In the USA, supporters of the Tea Party movement are united by a desire to limit State budgets and promote free markets. Big pharmaceutical companies, which, as we will see in Chapter 3, are some of the biggest beneficiaries of publicly funded research, constantly argue for less regulation and 'meddling' in what they claim is a very innovative industry.

And in the Eurozone

And, in the eurozone, it is today argued that all the ills of the 'peripheral' EU countries like Portugal and Italy come from having a 'profligate' public sector, ignoring the evidence that such countries are characterized more by a stagnant public sector which has not made the kind of strategic investments that the more successful 'core' countries, such as Germany, have been making for decades (Mazzucato 2012b).

The power of the ideology is so strong that history is easily fabricated. A remarkable aspect of the financial crisis that began in 2007 was that even though it was blatantly caused by excessive private debt (mainly in the US real estate market), many people were later led to believe that the chief culprit was public debt. It is true that public sector debt (Alessandri and Haldane 2009) rose drastically both due to the government-funded bank bailouts and reduced tax receipts that accompanied the ensuing recession in many countries. But it can hardly be argued that the financial crisis, or the resulting economic crisis, was caused by public debt. The key issue was not the amount of public sector spending but the type of spending. Indeed, one of the reasons that Italy's growth rate has been so low for the last 15 years is not that it has been spending too much but that it has not been spending enough in areas like education, human capital and R&D. So even with a relatively modest pre-crisis deficit (around 4 per cent), its debt/GDP ratio kept rising because the rate of growth of the denominator in this ratio remained close to zero.

While there are of course low-growth countries with large public debts, the question of which causes which is highly debatable. Indeed, the recent controversy over the work of Reinhart and Rogoff (2010) shows just how heated the debate is. What was most shocking, however, from that recent debate was not only the finding that their statistical work (published in what is deemed the top economics journal) was done incorrectly (and recklessly), but how quickly people had believed the core result: that debt above

90 per cent of GDP will necessarily bring down growth. The corollary became the new dogma: austerity will necessarily (and sufficiently) bring back growth. And yet there are many countries with higher debt that have grown in a stable fashion (such as Canada, New Zealand and Australia – all ignored by their results). Even more obvious is the point that what matters is surely not the aggregate size of the public sector, but what it is spending on. Spending on useless paperwork, or kickbacks, is surely not the same thing as spending on making a healthcare system more functional and efficient, or spending on top-quality education or ground-breaking research that can fuel human capital formation and future technologies. Indeed, the variables that economists have found to be important for growth – such as education and research and development – are expensive. The fact that the weakest countries in Europe, with high debt/GDP ratios, have been spending very little in these areas (thus causing the denominator in this ratio to suffer) should not come as a surprise. Yet the austerity recipes that are currently being forced on them will make this problem only worse.

And this is where there is a self-fulfilling prophecy: the more we talk down the State's role in the economy, the less able we are to up its game and make it a relevant player, and so the less able it is to attract top talent. Is it a coincidence that the US Department of Energy, which is the lead spender on R&D in the US government and one of the lead spenders (per capita) on energy research in the OECD, has been able to attract a Nobel Prize–winning physicist to run it? Or that those countries with much less ambitious plans for government organizations are more susceptible to crony-type promotions and little expertise within ministries? Of course the problem is not simply of 'expertise', but the ability to attract it is an indicator of the importance it is given within public agencies in a given country.

State Picking Winners vs. Losers Picking the State

We are constantly told that the State should have a limited role in the economy due to its inability to 'pick winners', whether the 'winners' are new technologies, economic sectors or specific firms. But what is ignored is that, in many of the cases that the State 'failed', it was trying to do something much more difficult than what many private businesses do: either trying to extend the period of glory of a mature industry (the Concorde experiment or the American Supersonic Transport project), or actively trying to launch a new technology sector (the Internet, or the IT revolution).

Operating in such difficult territory makes the probability of failure much higher. Yet by constantly bashing the State's ability to be an effective and innovative agent in society, not only have we too easily blamed the State for some of its failures, we have also not developed the accurate metrics needed to judge its investments fairly. Public venture capital, for example, is very different from private venture capital. It is willing to invest in areas with much higher risk, while providing greater patience and lower expectations of future returns. By definition this is a more difficult situation. Yet the returns to public versus private venture capital are compared without taking this difference into account.

Ironically, the inability of the State to argue its own position, to explain its role in the winners that have been picked (from the Internet to companies like Apple) has made it easier to criticize it for its occasional failures (e.g. the Supersonic Transport project). Or even worse, it has responded to criticism by becoming vulnerable and timid, easily 'captured' by lobbies seeking public resources for private gain, or by pundits that parrot the 'myths' about the origins of economic dynamism.

In the late 1970s capital gains taxes fell significantly following lobbying efforts on behalf of the US venture capital industry (Lazonick 2009, 73). The lobbyists argued before the government that venture capitalists had funded both the Internet and the early semiconductor industry, and that without venture capitalists innovation would not happen. Thus the same actors who rode the wave of expensive State investments in what would later become the dot.com revolution, successfully lobbied government to reduce their taxes. In that way the government's own pockets, so critical for funding innovation, were being emptied by those who had depended on it for their success.

Furthermore, by not being confident of its own role, government has been easily captured by the myths describing where innovation and entrepreneurship come from. Big Pharma tries to convince government that it is subject to too much regulation and red tape, while it is simultaneously dependent on government-funded R&D. Small business associations have convinced governments in many countries that they are underfunded as a category. Yet in many countries, they receive more support than the police force, without providing the jobs or innovation that helps justify such support (Hughes 2008; Storey 2006). Had the State better understood how its own investments have led to the emergence of the most successful new companies, like Google, Apple and Compaq, it would perhaps mount a stronger defence against such arguments.

But the State has not had a good marketing/communications department. Imagine how much easier President Barack Obama's fight for US national healthcare policy would have been if the US population knew the important role that the US government had in funding the most radical new drugs in the industry (discussed in Chapter 3). This is not 'propaganda' – it's raising awareness about history of technology. In health, the State has not 'meddled' but created and innovated. Yet the story told, and unfortunately believed, is one of an innovative Big Pharma and a meddling government. Getting the (complex) history right is important for many reasons. Indeed, the high prices charged for drugs, whether they are subsidized by the State or not, are justified by the industry with their alleged 'high R&D costs'. Uncovering the truth not only helps government policies to be better designed but also can help the 'market' system work better.

The emphasis on the State as an entrepreneurial agent is not of course meant to deny the existence of private sector entrepreneurial activity, from the role of young new companies in providing the dynamism behind new sectors (e.g. Google), to the important source of funding from private sources like venture capital. The key problem is that this is the *only* story that is usually told. Silicon Valley and the emergence of the biotech industry are usually attributed to the geniuses behind the small high-tech firms like Facebook, or the plethora of small biotech companies in Boston (US) or Cambridge (UK). Europe's 'lag' behind the USA is often attributed to its weak venture capital sector. Examples from these high-tech sectors in the USA are often used to argue why we need less State and more market: tipping the balance in favour of the market would allow Europe to produce its own 'Googles'. But how many people know that the algorithm that led to Google's success was funded by a public sector National Science Foundation grant (Battelle 2005)? Or that molecular antibodies, which provided the foundation for biotechnology before venture capital moved into the sector, were discovered in public Medical Research Council (MRC) labs in the UK? How many people realize that many of the most innovative young companies in the US were funded not by private venture capital but by *public* venture capital, such as that provided by the Small Business Innovation Research (SBIR) programme?

Lessons from these experiences are important. They force the debate to go beyond the role of the State in stimulating demand, or the worry of 'picking winners'. What we have instead is a case for a targeted, proactive, *entrepreneurial* State, one able to take risks and create a highly networked system of actors that harness the best of the private sector for the national good over a medium- to long-term time horizon. It is the State acting as lead investor and catalyst which sparks the network to act and spread knowledge. The State can and does act as creator, not just facilitator of the knowledge economy.

Arguing for an entrepreneurial State is not 'new' industrial policy because it is in fact what has happened. As Block and Keller (2011, 95) have explained so well, the industrial directives of the State are 'hidden' primarily to prevent a backlash from the conservative right. Evidence abounds of the State's pivotal role in the history of the computer industry, the Internet, the pharmaceutical-biotech industry, nanotech and the emerging green tech sector. In all these cases, the State dared to think – against all odds – about the 'impossible': creating a new technological opportunity; making the initial large necessary investments; enabling a decentralized network of actors to carry out the risky research; and then allowing the development and commercialization process to occur in a dynamic way.

Beyond Market Failures and System Failures

Economists willing to admit the State has an important role have often argued so using a specific framework called 'market failure'. From this perspective the fact that markets are 'imperfect' is seen as the exception, which means that the State has a role to play – but not a very interesting one. Imperfections can arise for various reasons: the unwillingness of private firms to invest in areas, like basic research, from which they cannot appropriate private profits because the results are a 'public good' accessible to all firms (results of basic R&D as a positive externality); the fact that private firms do not factor in the cost of their pollution in setting prices (pollution as a negative externality); or the fact that the risk of certain investments is too high for any one firm to bear them all alone (leading to incomplete markets). Given these different forms of market failure, examples of the expected role of the State would include publicly funded basic research, taxes levied on polluting firms and public funding for infrastructure projects. While this framework is useful, it cannot explain the 'visionary' strategic role that government has played in making these investments. Indeed, the discovery of the Internet or the emergence of the nanotechnology industry did not occur because the private sector wanted something but could not find the resources to invest in it. Both happened due to the vision that the government had in an area that had not yet been fathomed by the private sector. Even after these new technologies were introduced by government, the private sector still was too scared to invest. Government even had to support the commercialization of the Internet. And it took years for private venture capitalists to start financing biotech or nanotech companies. It was – in these and many such cases – the State that appeared to have the most aggressive 'animal spirits'.

There are many counterexamples that would characterize the State as far from an 'entrepreneurial' force. Developing new technologies and supporting new industries is not the only important role of the State, after all. But admitting the instances where it has played an entrepreneurial role will help inform policies, which are too often based on the assumption that at most the State's role is to correct market failures or facilitate innovation for the 'dynamic' private sector. The assumptions that all the State has to do is to 'nudge' the private sector in the right direction; that tax credits will work because business is eager to invest in innovation; that removing obstacles and regulations is necessary; that small firms – simply due to their size – are more flexible and entrepreneurial and should be given direct and indirect support; that the core problem in Europe is simply one of 'commercialization' – are all myths. They are myths about where entrepreneurship and innovation come from. They have prevented policies from being as effective as they could be in stimulating the kinds of innovation that businesses would not have attempted on their own.

The Bumpy Risk Landscape

As will be explained in more detail in the next chapter, innovation economists from the 'evolutionary' tradition (Nelson and Winter 1982) have argued that 'systems' of innovation are needed so that new knowledge and innovation can diffuse throughout the economy, and that *systems* of innovation (sectoral, regional, national) require the presence of dynamic links between the different *actors* (firms, financial institutions, research/education, public sector funds, intermediary institutions), as well as horizontal links *within* organizations and institutions (Lundvall 1992; Freeman 1995). What has been ignored even in this debate, however, is the exact role that each actor realistically plays in the 'bumpy' and complex *risk landscape*. Many errors of current innovation policy are due to placing actors in the wrong part of this landscape (both in time and space). For example, it is naïve to expect venture capital to lead in the early and most risky stage of any new economic sector today (such as clean technology). In biotechnology, nanotechnology and the Internet, venture capital arrived 15–20 years *after* the most important investments were made by public sector funds.

In fact, history shows that those areas of the risk landscape (within sectors at any point in time, or at the start of new sectors) that are defined by high capital intensity and high technological and market risk tend to be avoided by the private sector, and have required great amounts of public sector funding (of different types), as well as public sector vision and leadership to get them off the ground. The State has been behind most technological revolutions and periods of long-run growth. This is why an 'entrepreneurial State' is needed to engage in risk taking and the creation of a new vision, rather than just fixing market failures.

Not understanding the role that different actors play makes it easier for government to get 'captured' by special interests which portray their role in a rhetorical and ideological way that lacks evidence or reason. While venture capitalists have lobbied hard for lower capital gains taxes (mentioned above), they do not make their investments in new technologies on the basis of tax rates; they make them based on perceived risk, something typically reduced by decades of prior State investment. Without a better understanding of the actors involved in the innovation process, we risk allowing a symbiotic innovation system, in which the State and private sector mutually benefit, to transform into a parasitic one in which the private sector is able to leach benefits from a State that it simultaneously refuses to finance.

Symbiotic vs. Parasitic Innovation 'Ecosystems'

It is now common to talk about innovation 'systems' as 'ecosystems'. Indeed it seems to be on the tongue of many innovation specialists and policymakers. But how can we be sure that the innovation ecosystem is one that results in a *symbiotic* relationship between the public and private sector rather than a *parasitic* one? That is, will increased investments by the State in the innovation ecosystem cause the private sector to invest less, and use its retained earnings to fund short-term profits (via practices like 'share buybacks'), or more, in riskier areas like human capital formation and R&D, to promote long-term growth?

Usually a question like this might be framed in terms of the 'crowding-out' concept. Crowding out is a hypothesis in economics that says that the danger of State investment is that it uses up savings that could have been used by the private sector for its own investment plans (Friedman 1979). Keynesians have argued against the idea that State spending crowds out private investment, by emphasizing that this would only hold in a period of full resource utilization, a state that hardly ever occurs. However, the issues raised in this book present a different view: that an entrepreneurial State invests in areas that the private sector would not invest even if it had the resources. And it is the courageous risk-taking visionary role of the State which has been ignored. Business investment is mainly limited not by savings but by its own lack of courage (or Keynesian 'animal spirits') – the 'business as usual' state of mind. Indeed, firm-level studies have shown that what drives entry behaviour into industries (companies deciding to move into one particular sector) are not existing profits in that sector but projected technological and market opportunities (Dosi et al. 1997). And such opportunities are linked to the amount of State investment in those areas.

But what if that potentially courageous aspect of the private sector is diminished precisely because the public sector fills the gap? Rather than framing the question in terms of 'crowding out', I believe we must frame it in such a way that results in building private–public partnerships that are more symbiotic and less parasitic. The problem is not that the State has financed too much innovation, making the private sector less ambitious. It is that policymakers have not been ambitious enough to demand that such support be part of a more collaborative effort in which the private sector also steps up to the challenge. Instead big R&D labs have been closing, and the R of the R&D spend has also been falling, with BERD (business expenditure on R&D) falling in many countries like the UK (Hughes and Mina 2011). While State spending on R&D and business spending tend to be correlated (the former ups the game for the latter), it is important that policymakers be more courageous – not only in agreeing to 'fund' sectors but also in demanding that businesses in those sectors increase their own stakes and commitment to innovation. A recent study by MIT claims that the current absence in the US of corporate labs like Xerox PARC (which produced the graphical user interface technology that led to both Apple's and Windows' operating systems) and Bell Labs – both highly co-financed by government agency budgets – is one of the reasons why the US innovation machine is under threat (MIT 2013).

The problem is also evidenced in industries, like pharmaceuticals, where there is a trend of increasing public sector investments in

R&D, while private sector spending is decreasing. According to Lazonick and Tulum (2012), the National Institutes of Health (NIH) have spent more than $300 billion over the last decade ($30.9 billion in 2012 alone), and become more involved in the D component of R&D, meaning they absorb greater costs of drug development (such as through clinical trials), while private pharmaceutical companies[1] have been spending less on R&D overall, with many shutting down R&D labs altogether. Of course the total R&D spent may be increasing, because the development (D) part is getting increasingly expensive. But this hides the underlying issue. While some analysts have justified the decreasing expenditure on research in terms of low productivity of R&D (increased expenditures, not matched by increased discoveries), others, like Angell (1984, ex-editor of the *New England Journal of Medicine*), have been more explicit in blaming Big Pharma for not doing its share. She argues that for decades the most radical new drugs have been coming out of public labs, with private pharma concerned more with 'me too' drugs (slight variations of existing drugs) and marketing (see Chapter 3 for more details). And in recent years, CEOs of large pharma companies have admitted that their decision to downsize – or in some cases eliminate – their R&D labs is due to their recognition that in the 'open' model of innovation most of their research is obtained by small biotech firms or public labs (Gambardella 1995; *China Briefing* 2012). Big Pharma's focus is thus turned to working with such alliances, and 'integrating' knowledge produced elsewhere, rather than funding R&D internally.

Financialization

One of the greatest problems, which we return to in Chapter 9, has been the way in which such reductions in spending on R&D have coincided with an increasing 'financialization' of the private sector. While causality may be hard to prove, it cannot be denied that at the same time that private pharma companies have been reducing the R of R&D, they have been increasing the amount of funds used to repurchase their own shares – a strategy used to boost their stock price, which affects the price of stock options and executive pay

---

1 From now on 'pharma' will refer to pharmaceutical companies, and Big Pharma the top international pharma companies.

linked to such options. For example, in 2011, along with $6.2 billion paid in dividends, Pfizer repurchased $9 billion in stock, equivalent to 90 per cent of its net income and 99 per cent of its R&D expenditures. Amgen, the largest dedicated biopharma company, has repurchased stock in every year since 1992, for a total of $42.2 billion through 2011, including $8.3 billion in 2011. Since 2002 the cost of Amgen's stock repurchases has surpassed the company's R&D expenditures in every year except 2004, and for the period 1992–2011 was equal to fully 115 per cent of R&D outlays and 113 per cent of net income (Lazonick and Tulum 2011). The fact that top pharma companies are spending a decreasing amount of funds on R&D at the same time that the State is spending more – all while increasing the amount they spend on share buybacks, makes this particular innovation ecosystem much more parasitic than symbiotic. This is not the 'crowding out' effect: this is free-riding. Share buyback schemes boost stock prices, benefitting senior executives, managers and investors that hold the majority of company stock. Boosting share prices does not create value (the point of innovation), but facilitates its extraction. Shareholders and executives are thus 'rewarded' for riding the innovation wave the State created. In Chapter 9 I look more closely at the problem of value extraction and ask whether and how some of the 'returns' from innovation should be returned to the employees and State that are also key contributors and stakeholders in the innovation process.

Unfortunately the same problem seems to be appearing in the emerging clean technology sector. In 2010, the US American Energy Innovation Council (AEIC), an industry association, asked the US government to increase its spending on clean technology by three times to $16 billion annually, with an additional $1 billion given to the Advanced Research Projects Agency – Energy (Lazonick 2011c). On the other hand, companies in the council have together spent $237 billion on stock repurchases between 2001 and 2010. The major directors of the AEIC come from companies with collective 2011 net incomes of $37 billion and R&D expenditures of approximately $16 billion. That they believe their own companies' enormous resources are inadequate to foster greater clean technology innovation is indicative of the State's role as the first driver of innovation or of their own aversion to taking on risks – or both.

The problem of share buybacks is not isolated but rampant: in the last decade, S&P 500 companies have spent $3 trillion on share buybacks (Lazonick 2012). The largest repurchasers (especially in oil and pharmaceuticals) claim that this is due to the lack of new opportunities. In fact in many cases the most expensive (e.g. capital-intensive) investments in new opportunities such as medicine and renewable energy (investments with high market and technological risk) are being made by the public sector (GWEC 2012). This raises the question of whether the 'open innovation' model is becoming a dysfunctional model. As large companies are increasingly relying on alliances with small companies and the public sector, the indication is that large players invest more in short-run profit gains (through market gimmicks) than long-run investments. I return to this question in Chapters 9 and 10.

Now that 'new' industrial policy is back on the agenda, with many nations trying to 'rebalance' their economies away from finance and towards 'real' economy sectors, it is more important than ever to question exactly what this rebalancing will entail (Mazzucato 2012a). While some have focused on the need for different types of private–public partnerships that can foster innovation and economic growth, what I'm arguing here (and will focus on more in Chapters 8 and 9) is that we need to be more careful to build the type of partnerships which increase the stakes of all involved, and which do not lead to similar problems that the financialization of the economy led to: socialization of risk, privatization of rewards.

The work of Rodrik (2004) has been particularly important in highlighting the need to rethink public and private sector interactions, and to focus more on processes rather than policy outcomes. His focus is on the types of exploratory processes that allow the public and private sectors to *learn* from each other, especially the opportunities and constraints that each face (Rodrik 2004, 3). He takes this to mean that the problem is not which types of tools (R&D tax credits vs. subsidies) or which types of sectors to choose (steel vs. software), but how policy can foster self-discovery processes, which will foster creativity and innovation. While I agree with Rodrik's general point about the need to foster exploration and trial and error (and this is in fact a core tenet of the 'evolutionary theory of economic change', which I review in the next chapter), I believe that the history of technological change teaches us that choosing particular sectors in this process is absolutely crucial. The Internet would never have happened without it being forcefully 'picked' by DARPA, and the same holds for nanotechnology which was picked by the NSF and later by the National Nanotech Initiative (both discussed in Chapter 4). And, most importantly, the green revolution will not take off until it is firmly picked and backed by the State (as will be discussed in Chapters 6 and 7).

Coming back to Keynes's (1926) fundamental point about the essential role of government, what we need to ask is: how can horizontal and vertical tools and policies 'make things happen' that would not have otherwise? The problem with R&D tax credits is not that they are specific policy tools, but they have been designed wrongly and do not increase private investments in R&D. Evidence shows that targeting R&D labour rather than R&D income (through credits) is much better for that (Lockshin and Mohnen 2012). And the problems with throwing money at a particular area like life sciences is not that it was 'picked' but that it was not first transformed to be less dysfunctional before it was supported. When so many 'life science' companies are focusing on their stock price rather than on increasing their side of the R in R&D, simply subsidising their research will only worsen the problem rather than create the type of learning that Rodrik (2004) rightly calls for.

Chapter 2

TECHNOLOGY, INNOVATION AND GROWTH

You can see the computer age everywhere but in the productivity statistics.
Solow (1987, 36)

In a special report on the world economy, the *Economist* (2010a) stated:

> A smart innovation agenda, in short, would be quite different from the one that most rich governments seem to favor. It would be more about freeing markets and less about picking winners; more about creating the right conditions for bright ideas to emerge and less about promises like green jobs. But pursuing that kind of policy requires courage and vision — and most of the rich economies are not displaying enough of either.

This view is also espoused by some 'progressive' academics, who argue that the State is limited to creating the 'conditions for innovation':

> ...accepting that the state will have a vital role in ensuring that market conditions reach the 'just right' balance which will spur innovation and that adequate investment is available for innovators. (Lent and Lockwood 2010, 7)

This is the view that asks little of government other than correcting market failures – such as through investment in basic science, education and infrastructure. The 'appropriate' role of the State is not a new debate, but it is one that benefits from a broader understanding of the academic literature on the role of innovation in creating economic growth.

Over two hundred and fifty years ago, when discussing his notion of the 'Invisible Hand', Adam Smith argued that capitalist markets left on their own would self-regulate, with the State's role being limited to that of creating basic infrastructure (schools, hospitals, motorways) and making sure that private property, and 'trust' (a moral code) between actors, were nurtured and protected (Smith 1904 [1776]). Smith's background in politics and philosophy meant that his writings were much more profound than the simple libertarian economics position for which he is usually acknowledged, but there is no escaping that he believed that the magic of capitalism consisted in the ability of the market to organize production and distribution without coercion by the State.

The path-breaking work of Karl Polanyi (who had a doctorate in law but is considered an important economist) has instead shown how the notion of the market as self-regulating is a myth unsupported by the historical origins of markets: 'The road to the free market was opened and kept open by an enormous increase in continuous, centrally organized and controlled interventionism' (Polanyi 2001 [1944], 144). In his view, it was the State which imposed the conditions that allowed for the emergence of a market-based economy. Polanyi's work has been revolutionary in showing the myth of the State vs. market distinction: the most capitalist of all markets, i.e. the national market, was forcefully 'pushed' into existence by the State. If anything it was the more local and international markets, which have pre-dated capitalism, that have been less tied to the State. But capitalism, the system that is usually thought of being 'market' driven, has been strongly embedded in, and shaped by, the State from day one (Evans 1995).

John Maynard Keynes believed that capitalist markets, regardless of their origin, need constant regulation because of the inherent instability of capitalism. Keynes contended that the stability of capitalism was dependent on keeping all of the four categories of spending (aggregate demand) in GDP in balance with one another: business investment (I), government investment (G), consumption spending (C), and net exports (X−M). A key source of extreme volatility was found in private business investment. The reason it is so volatile is that far from being a simple function of interest rates or taxes,[1] it is subject to 'animal spirits' – the gut-instinct assumptions made about future growth prospects in an

---

1 The insensitivity of investment to taxes is the reason that the 1980s-style 'supply-side' economics had little effect on investment and hence GDP, and a large effect on income distribution (no 'trickle-down' effect).

economy or specific sector by investors (Keynes 1934). In his view, this uncertainty constantly creates periods of under- or overinvestment, causing severe fluctuations in the economy that are compounded by the multiplier effect. According to Keynes, unless private investment is balanced by increased government spending, declines in consumption and investment will lead to market crashes and depressions, which were indeed a frequent fact of life before Keynes's ideas found their way into post–Second World War economic policies.

Keynesians have argued forcefully for the importance of using government spending to boost demand and stabilize the economy. Economists, inspired by the work of Joseph Schumpeter (1883–1950), have gone further, asking that the government also spend on those specific areas that increase a nation's capacity for innovation (reviewed further below). Support for innovation can take the form of investments made in R&D, infrastructure, labour skills, and in direct and indirect support for specific technologies and companies.

On the left side of the political spectrum, investments into programme areas that increase productivity have been less fashionable than simple spending on welfare state institutions such as education or health. But welfare state institutions cannot survive without a productive economy behind it that generates the profits and tax receipts that can fund such entitlements (Nordhaus and Shellenberger 2011; Atkinson 2011). While progressive redistributional policies are fundamental to ensuring that the results of economic growth are fair, they do not in themselves cause growth. Inequality can hurt growth but equality does not alone foster it. What has been missing from much of the Keynesian left is a growth agenda which creates and simultaneously redistributes the riches. Bringing together the lessons of Keynes and Schumpeter can make this happen. This is why the last chapters of this book focus on the need to better understand why innovation and inequality can go hand in hand, and how this requires realigning the risks and rewards of economic growth to put a stop to one of the unfortunate consequences of modern-day capitalism: risks that are socialized and rewards that are privatized, not just in the financial sector but also in manufacturing.

In general, there has been a lack of connection between Keynesian fiscal spending and Schumpeterian investments in innovation. The lack of connection is due in no small part to Keynes advocating 'useless government'; that is, that State intervention into an economy was based primarily on temporary spending that could occur in any manner (even if it was hiring workers to dig up treasure hidden in an abandoned coal mine)[2]. Indeed, this is the micro–macro connection that is still missing in modern-day economics. Yet empirically the connection is there. Not only is it true that productive investments generate growth, but that when spending is more 'directed' towards, say, the IT revolution in the 1980s and 1990s, and perhaps the green revolution in the years to come, the Keynesian multiplier effect is stronger. As Tassey argues:

> …the highest order problem is the long-term inadequacy of productivity enhancing investments (technology, physical, human and organizational capital). Increasing the demand for housing does have a multiplier effect on that industry's supply chain, but this effect pales compared to the leverage from investment in technology for hardware and software that drive productivity in many industries. Equally important, the jobs created by a technology-driven supply chain are much higher paying – but, they must be sustained over entire technology life cycles. (2012, 31)

Keynes focused on the need for the State to intervene in order to bring stability and prevent crises, certainly a pressing issue in today's circumstances.[3] But in order to understand the dynamics of such

---

2 This refers to Keynes's provocative statement that: 'If the Treasury were to fill old bottles with bank-notes, bury them at suitable depths in disused coal-mines which are then filled up to the surface with town rubbish, and leave it to private enterprise on well-tried principles of laissez-faire to dig the notes up again (the right to do so being obtained, of course, by tendering for leases of the note-bearing territory), there need be no more unemployment and, with the help of repercussions, the real income of the community, and its capital wealth, would probably become a good deal greater than it actually is' (1936, 129). Keynes was referring to the fact that in times of underutilized capacity, even such apparently useless actions could get the economic engine going. However, the point of this book is to highlight how the State has, even in the boom periods such as the 1990s, provided important directionality in its spending, increasing the animal spirits of the private sector by investing in areas that the private sector fears.

3 Indeed, the application of Keynesian analysis to the theory of economic crises, with a proper understanding of finance in this dynamic, was developed by Hyman Minsky. Minsky (1992) focused on the *financial* fragility of capitalism by highlighting the way that financial markets cause crises to occur. Financial bubbles followed cycles of credit expansion, and exaggerated growth expectations were followed by retraction, causing bubbles to burst and asset prices to collapse. Like Keynes, he believed that the State had a crucial role in preventing this vicious cycle and stabilizing growth.

investments, it is fundamental to better understand different perspectives on the theory of economic growth first, and then to establish the role of technology and innovation in driving that economic growth.

Technology and Growth

While growth and the wealth of nations has been the lead concern of economists since Adam Smith, in the 1950s it was shown by Abramovitz (1956) and Solow (1956) that conventional measures of capital and labour inputs could not account for 90 per cent of economic growth in an advanced industrialized country such as the United States. It was assumed that the unexplained residual must reflect productivity growth, rather than the quantity of factors of production. And still today there is immense debate among economists over which factors are most important in producing growth. This debate is reflected in politics, where different views about growth are espoused with great vehemence, often ignorant of the underlying theoretical assumptions and origins driving those views.

For years, economists have tried to model growth. Neoclassical economics developed its first growth model in the work of Harrod and Domar (Harrod 1939; Domar 1946), but it was Robert Solow who won the Nobel Prize for his growth 'theory'. In the Solow growth model, growth is modelled through a production function where output (Y) is a function of the quantity of physical capital (K) and human labour (L), *ceteris paribus* – other things remaining equal. Included in 'other things' was technological change.

$$Y = F (K, L)$$

While increases in K and L would cause movements *along* the production function (curve), exogenous (unexplained) changes in technical change would cause an upward shift in the curve (allowing both K and L to be used more productively). When Solow discovered that 90 per cent of variation in economic output was not explained by capital and labour, he called the residual 'technical change'. Abramovitz, who knew much more about the social conditions that support technical change than Solow, famously called the residual a 'measure of our ignorance' (Abromovitz 1956).

If the underlying model was found to be so deficient that it could not explain 90 per cent of the dependent variable it was describing, then it should have been thrown out and a new model developed. This was indeed what many, such as Joan Robinson (Harcourt 1972) had been arguing for decades. Robinson and others were highly critical of the production function framework. Instead of getting rid of the bad old model, however, technical change was simply added into it. Solow's theory (1956) became known as 'exogenous growth theory' because the variable for technical change was inserted exogenously, as a time trend A (t) (similar to population growth):

$$Y = A\,(t)\,F\,(K,\,L)$$

As economists became more aware of the crucial role that technology plays in economic growth, it became necessary to think more seriously about how to include technology in growth models. This gave rise to 'endogenous' or 'new growth' theory, which modelled technology as the endogenous outcome of an R&D investment function, as well as investment in human capital formation (Grossman and Helpman 1991). Rather than assuming constant or diminishing marginal returns as in the Solow model (every extra unit of capital employed earned a smaller return), the addition of human capital and technology introduced *increasing returns to scale*, the engine of growth. Increasing returns, which arise from different types of dynamic behaviour like learning by doing, can help explain why certain firms or countries persistently outperform others – there is no 'catch-up' effect.

Although new growth theory provided a rational argument for government investment, it did not lead to it explicitly. This is because new ideas were treated as endogenous to the firm, not as part of the institutional organization required to transform ideas into products. Nevertheless, the increasing emphasis on the relationship between technical change and growth indirectly led government policymakers to focus on the importance of investments in technology and human capital to foster growth. The result was *innovation-led growth* policies to support the knowledge economy, a term used to denote the greater importance of investing in knowledge creation in promoting economic competitiveness (Mason, Bishop and Robinson 2009). Studies that showed a direct relationship between the market value of firms and their innovation performance as measured by R&D spending and patent success supported these policies (Griliches, Hall and Pakes 1991).

From Market Failures to System Failures

In their ground-breaking *An Evolutionary Theory of Economic Change*, Nelson and Winter (1982) argued that the production function framework (exogenous or endogenous) was in fact the wrong way to understand technological change. Building on the work of Joseph Schumpeter (1934, 1942 [2003]), they argued for an 'evolutionary theory' of production (and economic change), which delved inside the 'black box' of the production function in order to understand how innovation occurs and affects competition and economic growth. In this approach, there is no assumption of 'representative agents' (as in standard growth theory) but rather a constant process of differentiation among firms, based on their different abilities to innovate because of different internal routines and competencies. Competition in this perspective is about the coevolution of those processes that create constant differences between firms and the processes of competitive selection that winnow in on those differences, allowing only some firms to survive and grow.

Rather than relying on laws of 'diminishing returns', which lead to a unique equilibrium, and assumptions about the 'average' firm, this approach focuses on dynamic increasing returns to scale (from the dynamics of learning by doing, as well as the kind of 'path-dependent' dynamics described by David 2004), and on different types of processes that lead to persistent differences between firms that do not disappear in the long run. The question is then: which firms survive and grow? Selection does not always lead to 'survival of the fittest' both due to the effect of increasing returns (allowing first-mover advantages which then 'stick') and also to the effects of policies which might favour certain types of firms over others. It might also be that selection dynamics in product markets and financial markets are at odds (Geroski and Mazzucato 2002b).

But most importantly, in this perspective innovation is firm specific, and highly uncertain. The 'evolutionary' and Schumpeterian approach to studying firm behaviour and competition has led to a 'systems of innovation' view of policy where what matters is understanding the way in which firms of different type are embedded in a system at sectoral, regional and national levels. In this systems view, it is not the quantity of R&D that matters, but how it is distributed throughout an economy, often reflective of the crucial role of the State in influencing the distribution (Freeman 1995; Lundvall 1992). Schumpeterian economists criticize endogenous growth theory because of its assumption that R&D can be modelled as a lottery where a certain amount of R&D investment will create a certain probability for successful innovation. They argue that in fact innovation is an example of true Knightian uncertainty, which cannot be modelled with a normal (or any other) probability distribution that is implicit in endogenous growth theory, where R&D is often modelled using game theory (Reinganum 1984). By highlighting the strong uncertainty underlying technological innovation, as well as the very strong feedback effects that exist between innovation, growth and market structure, Schumpeterians emphasize the 'systems' component of technological progress and growth.[4] Systems of innovation are defined as 'the network of institutions in the public and private sectors whose activities and interactions initiate, import, modify and diffuse new technologies' (Freeman 1995), or 'the elements and relationships which interact in the production, diffusion and use of new, and economically useful, knowledge' (Lundvall 1992, 2).

The emphasis here is not on the stock of R&D but on the circulation of knowledge and its diffusion throughout the economy. Institutional change is not assessed through criteria based on static allocative efficiency, but rather on how it promotes technological and structural change. The perspective is neither macro nor micro, but more meso, where individual firms are seen as part of broader network of firms with whom they cooperate and compete. The system of innovation can be interfirm, regional, national or global. From the meso perspective the network is the unit of analysis (not the firm). The network consists of customers, subcontractors, infrastructure, suppliers, competencies or functions, and the links or relationships between them. The point is that the competencies that generate innovation are part of a collective activity occurring through a network of actors and their links or relationships (Freeman 1995).

The causation that occurs in the steps taken between basic science, to large-scale R&D, to applications, and finally to diffusing innovations is not 'linear'. Rather, innovation networks are full of feedback loops existing between markets and technology, applications and science. In the linear model, the R&D system is seen as the main source of innovation, reinforcing economists' use of R&D stats to understand growth. In this more non-linear view, the roles of education, training, design, quality control and effective demand are just as important. Furthermore, it is

---

4 The emphasis on heterogeneity and multiple equilibria requires this branch of theory to rely less on assumptions of representative agents (the average company) and unique equilibria, so dear to neoclassical economics. Rather than using incremental calculus from Newtonian physics, mathematics from biology (such as distance from mean replicator dynamics) are used, which can explicitly take into account heterogeneity, and the possibility of path dependency and multiple equilibria. See M. Mazzucato, *Firm Size, Innovation and Market Structure: The Evolution of Market Concentration and Instability* (Northampton, MA: Edward Elgar, 2000).

better able to recognize the serendipity and uncertainty that characterizes the innovation process. It is useful for understanding the rise and fall of different economic powers in history. For example, it explains the rise of Germany as a major economic power in the nineteenth century, as a result of State-fostered technological education and training systems. It also explains the rise of the United States as a major economic power in the twentieth century as a result of the rise of mass production and in-house R&D. The United States and Germany became economic powers for different reasons but what they had in common was attention to developing systems of innovation rather than a narrow focus on raising or lowering R&D expenditures.

The general point can be illustrated by contrasting the experience of Japan in the 1970s and 1980s with that of the Soviet Union (Freeman 1995). The rise of Japan is explained as new knowledge flowing through a more horizontal economic structure consisting of the Ministry of International Trade and Industry (MITI), academia and business R&D. In the 1970s Japan was spending 2.5 per cent of its GDP on R&D while the Soviet Union was spending more than 4 per cent. Yet Japan eventually grew much faster than the Soviet Union because R&D funding was spread across a wider variety of economic sectors, not just those focused on the military and space as was the case in the Soviet Union. In Japan, there was a strong integration between R&D, production and technology import activities at the enterprise level, whereas in the Soviet Union there was separation. Crucially, the Soviet Union did not have, or permit, business enterprises to commercialize the technologies developed by the State. Japan had strong user–producer linkages, which were nonexistent in the Soviet system. Japan also encouraged innovation with incentives provided to management and the workforce of companies, rather than focusing mainly on the ministries of science. Johnson (1982) argues that the 'Japanese miracle' was in essence the presence of a Developmental State,[5] or, the coordination of the Japanese

---

5 Chalmers Johnson (1982) was one of the first authors to conceptualize the 'Developmental State', when he analysed the State-led industrialization of Japan. Johnson argued that, in contrast to a (supposedly) hands-off, regulatory orientation in the US, the Japanese 'Developmental State' directly intervened in the economy, with strong planning promoted by a relatively independent State bureaucracy, which also promoted a close business–government relationship, whereby governmental support, protection and discipline resulted in a private elite willing to take on risky enterprises. Subsequent elaborations of the 'Developmental State' concept can be found in, among others, Wade (1990), Chang (1993), Evans (1995), Woo-Cumings (1999) and Chang and Evans (2000). Recently, contrary

economy through deliberate and targeted industrial policy instituted by MITI. Yet, Lazonick (2008, 27–8) adds that, 'the contribution of the developmental state in Japan cannot be understood in abstraction from the growth of companies' (such as Toyota, Sony or Hitachi); aside from the Japanese State's public support for industry, 'it was the strategy, organization, and finance, internal' to Japan's leading firms that transformed them 'from entrepreneurial firms into innovative firms' and that 'made them successful' in challenging the competitiveness of the world's most advanced economies. Equally important were the lessons learned by Japanese people that went abroad to study Western technologies for their companies, and relationships between those companies to US firms. These companies benefitted from the lessons of the US 'Developmental State', and then transferred that knowledge to Japanese companies which developed internal routines that could produce Western technologies and eventually surpass them. Japanese conglomerates were among the first foreign companies to license the transistor from AT&T (Bell Labs) in the early 1950s. As a result key connections were made with Western companies such as GE, IBM, HP and Xerox. Particular sectors like electronics were targeted forcefully, and the organizational innovation adopted by Japanese firms embodied a flexible 'just-in-time' and 'total quality' production system (which was a necessity to avoid unused capacity and waste, and deal with the lack of natural resources in Japan) that was applied to a wide variety of economic sectors with great success.

Table 1 compares the Japanese and Soviet systems of innovation. It is important in this context to highlight that the MITI's industrial policy was beyond the 'picking winners' idea that many opposed to industrial policy cite today. Japan's approach was about coordinating intra-industrial change, inter-sectoral linkages, inter-company linkages and the private–public space in a way that allowed growth to occur in a holistic and targeted manner. The Japanese model, which was an alternative to the more vertical 'Fordist' model of production in the US, characterized by rigidity and tense relations between trade unions and management, caused a more solid flow of knowledge and competencies in the economy that provided an advantage to the horizontally structured and flexible Japanese firms. While on opposite ends of the political spectrum, the

---

to Johnson's (1982) original view, Block (2008) showed the existence of an often 'hidden' Developmental State in the US, a view similarly espoused by Reinert (2007) and Chang (2008).

Table 1. Contrasting national systems of innovation: Japan and the USSR in the 1970s

Japan	USSR
High gross domestic expenditure on R&D (GERD)/GNP ratio (2.5%)	Very high GERD/GNP ratio (c. 4%)
Very low proportion of military or space R&D (<2% of R&D)	Extremely high proportion of military or space R&D (>70% of R&D)
High proportion of total R&D at enterprise level and company financed (approx. 67%)	Low proportion of total R&D at enterprise level and company financed (<10%)
Strong integration of R&D, production and technology import at enterprise level	Separation of R&D, production and technology import, weak institutional linkages
Strong user–producer and subcontractor network linkages	Weak or nonexistent linkages between marketing, production, and procurement
Strong incentives to innovate at enterprise level that involve management and workforce	Some incentives to innovate made increasingly strong in 1960s and 1970s but offset by other negative disincentives affecting management and workforce
Intensive experience of competition in international markets	Relatively weak exposure to international competition except in arms race

Source: Freeman (1995). Note: Gross domestic expenditures on research and development (GERD) are all monies expended on R&D performed within the country in a given year.

production model in the USSR and the USA were equally 'rigid', allowing the Japanese model to supersede both.

Regional systems of innovation focus on the cultural, geographical and institutional proximity that create and facilitate transactions between different socioeconomic actors. Studies focusing on innovative milieu such as industrial districts and local systems of innovation have demonstrated that conventions and specific socioinstitutional factors in regions affect technological change at a national level. Specific factors might include interactions between local administrations, unions and family-owned companies in, for example, the Italian industrial districts.

The State's role is not just to create knowledge through national labs and universities, but also to mobilize resources that allow knowledge and innovations to diffuse broadly across sectors of the economy. It does this by rallying existing innovation networks or by facilitating the development of new ones that bring together a diverse group of stakeholders. However, having a national system of innovation that is rich in horizontal and vertical networks is not sufficient. The State must also lead the process of industrial development, by developing strategies for technological advance in priority areas.

This version of the State's role has been accepted in a consensus between multiple countries that are attempting to catch up with most technologically advanced economies. There is a whole literature devoted to the role of the so-called 'Developmental State', where the State is active not only in Keynesian demand management but also in leading the process of industrialization. The most typical examples are the East Asian economies, which through planning and active industrial policy were able to 'catch up' technologically and economically with the West (Amsden 1989). In states that were late to industrialize, the State itself led the industrialization drive. It took on developmental functions, for example by targeting certain sectors for investment, placed barriers to foreign competition until such time as companies in the targeted sectors were ready to export, and then provided assistance finding new export markets for companies. In Japan, for example, Johnson (1982) illustrates how the MITI worked to coordinate Japanese firms in new international markets. This occurred through investments made in particular technologies (picking winners), and the creation of specific business strategies meant to win particular domestic and international markets. Furthermore, the Japanese State coordinated the finance system through the Bank of Japan as well as through the Fiscal Investment Loan Program (funded by the postal savings system).

Chang (2008) offers similar illustrations for South Korea and other recently emerged economies. China has engaged in a targeted industrialization strategy too, only joining the World Trade Organization once its industries were ready to compete, rather than as part of an International Monetary Fund–backed industrialization strategy. The Chinese strategy showed the weaknesses of the Washington Consensus on development, which denied the State the active role that it played in the development of major industrialized nations such as the United States, Germany and the United Kingdom.

If there is strong evidence that the State can be effective in pursuing targeted catch-up policies by focusing resources on being dominant in certain industrial sectors, why is it not accepted that the State can have a greater role in the development of new technologies and applications beyond simply funding basic science and having an infrastructure to support private sector activity?

Myths about Drivers of Innovation and Ineffective Innovation Policy

The fact that economics was putting so much emphasis on innovation in the growth process caused policymakers, since the 1980s, to begin paying much more attention to variables like R&D and patents as a predicator of innovation and therefore of economic growth. For example, the European Union's Lisbon Agenda (2000) and its current Europe 2020 strategy (EC 2010) set a target for 3 per cent of the EU's GDP to be invested in R&D, along with other policies meant to encourage the flow of knowledge between universities and business – and a stronger link between financial markets and innovative firms of different size.

While countries within the OECD continue to differ greatly in their R&D spending (Figure 1 below), what is interesting is that those European countries that have suffered the most from the financial crisis, which later turned into a sovereign debt crisis, were also countries that have the lowest R&D expenditures. This of course does not mean that it is their low R&D intensity that caused their problems, but it is surely related. In the case of Italy, in fact, its high debt/GDP ratio (120 per cent in 2011) was not due to too much spending but spending in the wrong places. Its deficit for many years was relatively mild, at around 4 per cent. But its lack of investment in productivity-enhancing R&D and human capital development meant that its growth rate remained below the interest rate that it paid on its debt, thus making the numerator of the debt/GDP ratio grow more than the denominator. The fact that EU countries spend so differently on areas that create long-run growth is one of the reasons that they were each affected so differently by the economic crisis. The numerous approaches to growth were a reason that there was such little solidarity when it came time to help each other out. German 'falks' feel that German tax money should not be used to bail out the Greeks. However, they err in thinking that the Greeks are spendthrifts. The reforms that are required to make the European project work require not only 'structural' reforms (increasing the propensity to pay tax, labour market reform etc.) but also, and especially, increases in public and private sector investment in research and human capital formation that produce innovation. Getting support for such policies is virtually impossible under the current new 'fiscal compact', which limits spending by European member states to 3 per cent of GDP without differentiating between the spending that, through innovation and capital investments, can lead to future growth.

While low spending on R&D is a problem throughout much of the European 'periphery', it is also true that if a country has lower than average R&D spending, this is not necessarily a problem if the sectors that the country specializes in are not sectors in which innovation occurs necessarily through R&D (Pierrakis 2010). For example, the UK specializes in financial services, construction and creative industries (such as music) – all with relatively low needs for basic R&D. And there are many industries, especially in the service sector, that do no R&D at all. Yet these industries often employ large numbers of knowledge workers to generate, absorb and analyse information. If, all other things equal, these industries represented a smaller proportion of GDP, it would be easier for an economy to reach the 3 per cent target for R&D/GDP (which characterized both the European Commission's Lisbon Agenda and the current EC 2020 agenda). But would the performance of the economy be superior as a result? It depends on how these industries contribute to the economy. Are these 'low-tech' industries providing important services that enhance the value-creating capabilities of other industries or the welfare of households as consumers? Or are they, as is often the case in financial services, focused on extracting value from the economy, even if that process undermines the conditions for innovation in other industries (Mazzucato and Lazonick 2010)?

One of the problems that such simple targets encounter is that they divert attention from the vast differences in R&D spending across industries and even across firms within an industry. They can also mask significant differences in the complementary levels of R&D investments made by governments and businesses that are also required to generate superior economic performance.

The National Systems of Innovation perspective described above highlights the important role of intermediary institutions in diffusing the knowledge created by new R&D throughout a system. An even greater problem with R&D-based innovation policies is the lack of understanding of the complementary assets that must be in place at the firm level that make it possible for technological innovations to reach the market, e.g. infrastructure or marketing capabilities.

Figure 1. Gross R&D spending (GERD) as a percentage of GDP in OECD, 1981–2010

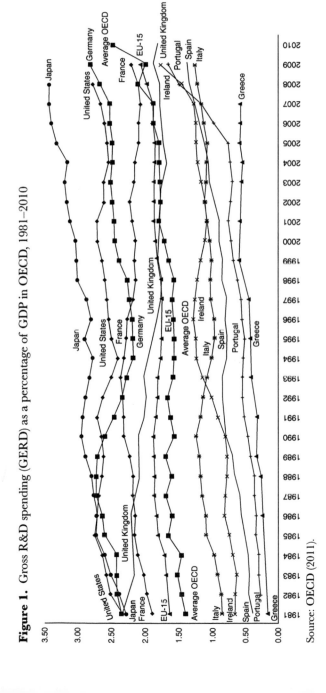

Source: OECD (2011).

There have been many myths created around innovation-led growth. These have been based on wrong assumptions about the key drivers of innovation, from R&D, to small firms, venture capital and patents. A brief discussion of these follows. I call them 'myths', though they are perhaps more clearly called false assumptions leading to ineffective innovation policy.

Myth 1: Innovation is about R&D

The literature on the economics of innovation, from different camps, has often assumed a direct causal link between R&D and innovation, and between innovation and economic growth. While the systems of innovation literature referred to above has argued strongly against the linear model of innovation, much innovation policy still targets R&D spending at the firm, industry and national levels. Yet there are very few studies which prove that innovation carried out by large or small firms actually increases their growth performance – that is, the macro models on innovation and growth (whether 'new growth' theory models or the 'Schumpeterian' models) do not seem to have strong empirical 'micro foundations' (Geroski and Mazzucato 2002a). Some company-level studies have found a positive impact of R&D on growth (Geroski, Machin and Toker 1992; 1996, Yasuda 2005) while others found no significant impact (Almus and Nerlinger 1999; Bottazzi et al. 2001; Lööf and Heshmati 2006). Some studies have found even a negative impact of R&D on growth, which is not surprising: if the firms in the sample don't have the complementary assets needed, R&D becomes only a cost (Brouwer, Kleinknecht and Reijnen 1993; Freel and Robson 2004).

It is thus fundamental to identify the company-specific conditions that must be present to allow spending on R&D to positively affect growth. These conditions will no doubt differ between sectors. Demirel and Mazzucato (2012), for example, find that in the pharmaceutical industry, only those firms that patent five years in a row (the 'persistent' patenters) and which engage in alliances achieve any growth from their R&D spending. Innovation policies in this sector must thus target not only R&D but also different attributes of firms. Coad and Rao (2008) found that only the fastest-growing firms reap benefits from their R&D spending (the top 6 per cent identified in NESTA's 2009 report 'The Vital 6%'). Mazzucato and Parris (2011) find that the relationship between R&D spending and fast-growing firms only holds in specific periods of the industry life-cycle, when competition is particularly fierce.

Myth 2: Small is Beautiful

Finding that the impact of innovation on growth is indeed different for different types of firms has important implications for the commonly held assumption that 'small firms' matter (for growth, for innovation and for employment), and hence that many different policies that target SMEs are needed to generate innovation and growth. Hughes (2008) has shown that in the UK SMEs received close to £9 billion in direct and indirect government support, which is more than the police force receives. Is this money well spent? The hype around small firms arises mainly from the confusion between size and growth. The most robust evidence available emphasizes not the role of small firms in the economy but to a greater extent the role of *young* high-growth firms. NESTA, for example, showed that the firms most important to growth in the UK have been the small number of fast-growing businesses that, between 2002 and 2008, generated the greatest employment increase in the country (NESTA 2011). And while many high-growth firms are small, many small firms are not high growth.[6] The bursts of rapid growth that promote innovation and create employment are often staged by firms that have existed for several years and grown incrementally until they reached a take-off stage. This is a major problem since so many government policies focus on tax breaks and benefits to SMEs, with the aim of making the economy more innovative and productive.

Although there is much talk about small firms creating jobs, and increasingly a focus of policymakers, this is mainly a myth. While by definition small firms will create jobs, they will in fact also destroy a large number of jobs when they go out of business. Haltiwanger, Jarmin and Miranda (2010) find that there is indeed no systematic relationship between firm size and growth. Most of the effect is from age: young firms (and business start-ups) contribute substantially to both gross and *net* job creation.

Productivity should be the focus, and small firms are often less productive than large firms. Indeed recent evidence has suggested that some economies that have favoured small firms, such as India, have in fact

---

6 Not to mention the statistical effect of being small: while a one-person micro-enterprise that hires an additional employee will display a 100 per cent growth in employment, a 100,000 person enterprise that hires 1,000 employees will show 'only' a 1 per cent increase in employment. And yet, it is obvious which of these hypothetical firms contributes more to a decrease in unemployment at the macro-level.

performed worse. Hsieh and Klenow (2009), for example, suggest that 40–60 per cent of the total factor productivity (TFP) difference between India and the United States is due to misallocation of output to too many small and low-productivity SMEs in India. As most small start-up firms fail, or are incapable of growing beyond the stage of having a sole owner-operator, targeting assistance to them through grants, soft loans or tax breaks will necessarily involve a high degree of waste. While this waste is a necessary gamble in the innovation process (Janeway 2012), it is important to at least guide the funding process with what we know about 'high growth' innovative firms rather than some folkloristic notion of the value of SMEs as an aggregate category – which actually means very little.

Bloom and Van Reenen (2006) argue that small firms are less productive than large ones because they are less well managed and subject to provincial family favouritism. Furthermore, small firms have lower average wages, fewer skilled workers, less training, fewer fringe benefits and higher instances of bankruptcy. They argue that the UK has many family firms and a poor record of management in comparison with other countries such as the US and Germany (2006). Among other reasons, this is related to the fact that the tax system is distorted by giving inheritance tax breaks to family firms.

Some have interpreted as a result that it is high growth rather than size that matters, and that the best that government can do is to provide the conditions for growth through policies that foster innovation. Bloom and Van Reenen (2006) argue that instead of having tax breaks and benefits target SMEs, the best way to support small firms is to 'ensure a level playing field by removing barriers to entry and growth, among firms of all sizes, enforcing competition policy, and strongly resisting the lobbying efforts of larger firms and their agents'. But as we will see in Chapters 3 and 5, often the most innovative firms are precisely those that have benefitted the most from direct public investments of different types, making the association between size and growth much more complex.

The policy implication is that rather than giving handouts to small companies in the hope that they will grow, it is better to give contracts to young companies that have already demonstrated ambition. It is more effective to commission the technologies that require innovation than to hand out subsidies in the hope that innovation will follow. In an era where budget deficits are constraining available resources, this approach could yield significant taxpayer savings if, for example, direct transfers to firms that are given just because of the size of a company were ended, such as small business rate relief for smaller companies and inheritance tax relief for family firms (Schmidt 2012).

Myth 3: Venture Capital is Risk Loving

If the role of small firms and R&D is overstated by policymakers, a similar hype exists in relation to the potential for venture capital to create growth, particularly in knowledge-based sectors where capital intensity and technological complexity are high.

Venture capital is a type of private equity capital focused on early stage, high-potential growth companies. The funding tends to come either as seed funding or as later-stage growth funding where the objective of venture capitalists is to earn a high return following a successful IPO, merger or acquisition of the company. Venture capital fills a funding void that exists for new firms, which often have trouble gaining credit from traditional financial institutions such as banks. Such firms thus often have to rely on other sorts of funding such as 'business angels' (including family and friends), venture capital and private equity. Such alternative funding is most important for new knowledge-based firms trying to enter existing sectors or for new firms trying to form a new sector.

Risk capital is scarce in the seed stage of firm growth because there is a much higher degree of risk in this early phase, when the potential of the new idea and its technological and demand conditions are completely uncertain (see Table 2). The risk in later phases falls dramatically.

Figure 2 shows that the usual place where it is assumed venture capital will enter is the stage of the invention-innovation process (second and third stage above). In reality the real picture is much more non-linear and full of feedback loops. Many firms die during the transition between a new scientific or engineering discovery and its successful transformation into a commercial application. Thus moving from the second to the third phase shown in Figure 2 is often referred to as the valley of death.

Figure 2 does not illustrate how time after time it has been public rather than privately funded venture capital that has taken the most risks. In the US, government programmes such as the Small Business Innovation Research (SBIR) programme and the Advanced Technology Program (ATP) within the US Department of Commerce have provided 20–25 per cent of total funding for early stage technology firms (Auerswald and Branscomb 2003, 232). Thus, government has played a

Table 2. Risk of loss for different stages at which investments are made (%)

Point at which investment made	Risk of loss
Seed stage	66.2%
Start-up stage	53.0%
Second stage	33.7%
Third stage	20.1%
Bridge or pre-public stage	20.9%

Source: Pierrakis (2010).

Figure 2. Stages of venture capital investment

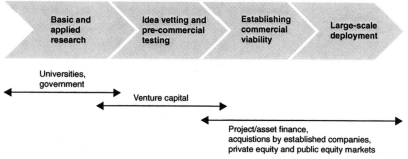

Source: Ghosh and Nanda (2010, 6).

leading role not only in the early stage research illustrated in Figure 2, but also in the commercial viability stage. Auerswald and Branscomb (2003) claim that government funding for early stage technology firms is equal to the total investments of 'business angels' and about two to eight times the amount invested by private venture capital.

Venture capital funds tend to be concentrated in areas of high potential growth, low technological complexity and low capital intensity, since the latter raises the cost significantly. Since there are so many failures in the high-risk stages of growth, venture capital funds tend to have a portfolio of different investments with only the tails (extremes) earning high returns – a very skewed distribution.

Although most venture capital funds are usually structured to have a life of ten years, they tend to prefer to exit much earlier than ten years because of the management fees and the bonuses earned for high returns. Early exits are preferred in order to establish a winning track record and raise a follow-on fund. This creates a situation whereby venture capital funds therefore have a bias towards investing in projects where the commercial viability is established within a 3-to-5-year period (Ghosh and Nanda 2010). Although this is sometimes possible (e.g. Google), it is often not. In the case of an emerging sector like biotech or green tech today, where the underlying knowledge base is still in its early exploratory phase, such a short-term bias is damaging to the scientific exploration process which requires longer time horizons and tolerance of failure. Venture capital has succeeded more in the US when it provided not only committed finance, but managerial expertise and the construction of a viable organization (Lazonick 2002).

The problem has been not only the lack of venture capital investment in the most critical early seed stage, but also its own objectives in the innovation process. This has been strongly evidenced in the biotech industry, where an increasing number of researchers have criticized the venture capital model of science, indicating that significant investor speculation has a detrimental effect on the underlying innovation (Coriat, Orsi and Weinstein 2003; Lazonick 2011; Mirowski 2011). The fact that so many venture capital backed biotech companies end up producing nothing, yet make millions for the venture capital firms that sell them on the public market is highly problematic. It creates a need to question the role of venture capital in supporting the development of science and also its effect on the growth process. The increased focus on patenting and venture capital is not the right way to understand how risky and long-term innovations occur. Pisano (2006) in fact claimed that the stock market was never designed to deal with the governance challenges presented by R&D-driven businesses. Mirowski (2011, 208) describes the venture capital–backed biotech model as:

...commercialized scientific research in the absence of any product lines, heavily dependent upon early-stage venture capital and a later IPO launch, deriving from or displacing academic research, with mergers and acquisitions as the most common terminal state, pitched to facilitate the outsourcing of R&D from large corporations bent upon shedding their previous in-house capacity.

The problem with the model has been that the 'progressive commercialization of science' seems to be unproductive, generating few products, and damaging to long-term scientific discoveries and findings over time.

An alternative view is presented in Janeway (2012) who argues that stock market speculation is necessary for innovation. However, what he describes as a semi-natural element of capitalism was instead a result of a hefty political process, of lobbying (Lazonick 2009). NASDAQ was put in place to provide a speculative market on which high-tech start-ups could be funded but also exit quickly. And without NASDAQ, launched in 1971, VC would not have emerged as a well-defined industry in the 1970s. The coevolution of VC and NASDAQ is a result of the policy space being 'captured'. Another element not emphasized in Janeway, is the degree to which the 'rewards' to VC have been disproportional to the risks taken. His own VC company, Warburg Pincus, made millions in a game that he admits was about entering after the State did the hard work. While he says that the period of speculation was necessary, he does not confront the issue of how VC was justified in capturing such high returns. And neither that VC is itself becoming one of its own worst enemies by being such adamant lobbyists for a lower public purse (via lower taxes), which will not be able to fund the future innovations for VC to piggyback on.

Myth 4: We Live in a Knowledge Economy – Just Look at all the Patents!

Similarly to the myth that 'innovation is about R&D', a misunderstanding exists in relation to the role of patents in innovation and economic growth. For example, when policymakers look at the number of patents in the pharmaceutical industry, they presume it is one of the most innovative sectors in the world. This rise in patents does not however reflect a rise in innovation, but a change in patent laws and a rise in the strategic reasons why patents are being used. In ICT there has been a shift in the use of patents from the development and protection of proprietary technologies, resulting from in-house R&D, to cross-licensing in open systems, with the purpose of buying in technology (and the related patents) produced elsewhere (Chesbrough 2003; Grindley and Teece 1997). This has caused the R&D budgets of large companies, such as IBM, to fall at the same time that their patent numbers rose (Lazonick 2009, 88–9). Not recognizing these dynamics cause a focus on the number of patents to be misguided.

The exponential rise in patents, and the increasing lack of relationship this rise has had with actual 'innovation' (e.g. new products and processes), has occurred for various reasons. First, the types of inventions that can be patented has widened to include publicly funded research, upstream research tools (rather than only final products and processes), and even 'discoveries' (as opposed to inventions) of existing objects of study such as genes. The 1980 Bayh–Dole Act, which allowed publicly funded research to be patented rather than remain in the public domain, encouraged the emergence of the biotechnology industry, as most of the new biotech companies were new spinoffs from university labs receiving heavy State funding. Furthermore, the fact that venture capital often uses patents to signal which companies to invest in means that patents have increased in their strategic value to companies seeking to attract financing. All these factors have caused the number of patents to rise, with most of them being of little worth (e.g. very few citations received from other patents), and with most not resulting in a high number of innovations, e.g. new drugs in pharma (see Figure 5 in Chapter 3). Thus directing too much attention to patents, rather than to specific types of patents, such as those that are highly cited, risks wasting a lot of money (as argued below for the patent box case).

Researchers have argued that many of the recent trends in patents, such as the increase in upstream patents for things like 'research tools' have caused the rate of innovation to fall rather than increase as it blocks the ability of science to move forward in an open exploratory way (Mazzoleni and Nelson 1998). The effect has been especially deleterious to the ability of scientists in the developing world to repeat experiments carried out in the developed world. Prevented from replicating results, they cannot build on those experiments with their own developments, thus hurting their ability to 'catch up' (Forero-Pineda 2006).

Notwithstanding the fact that most patents are of little value, and that patents play a controversial role in innovation dynamics, different government policies continue to assume that patents have a strong link to ongoing high-tech R&D and must be incentivized to create innovation-led growth. In October 2010, George Osborne (the UK's chancellor of the exchequer, a role equivalent of the minister of finance or secretary of the treasury in other countries) announced a 'patent box' policy beginning in 2013, which will reduce the rate of corporation tax on the income derived from patents to 10 per cent. This of course fits with the current government's belief that investment and innovation can be easily nudged through tax policy. The same policy has recently been introduced in the Netherlands.

The Institute for Fiscal Studies (IFS) has argued against this policy, claiming that the only effect it will have is to reduce government tax revenue (by a large amount) without affecting innovation (Griffith et al. 2010).

It is argued that R&D tax credits are enough to address the market failure issue around R&D, and that the patent box policy is instead poorly targeted at research, as the policy targets the income that results from patented technology, not the research or innovation itself. Furthermore, the authors maintain that the patent box policy will also add complexity to the tax system and require expensive policing to ensure that income and costs are being appropriately assigned to patents. They claim that the great uncertainty and time lags behind creating patentable technologies will counteract the incentives. Since international collaborations are increasingly common, there is no guarantee that the extra research that is incentivized will be conducted in the country introducing the policy.

Myth 5: Europe's Problem is all about Commercialization

It is often assumed that Europe's main disadvantage in innovation as compared to the US is its lack of capability for 'commercialization' (see Figure 2) which stems from problems with the 'transfer' of knowledge. In fact, EU problems don't come from poor flow of knowledge from research but from the EU firms' smaller stock of knowledge. This is due to the great differences in public and private spending on R&D. While in the US R&D/GDP is 2.6 per cent, it is only 1.3 per cent in the UK. In Italy, Greece and Portugal – the countries experiencing the worst effects of the eurozone crisis – R&D/GDP spending is less than 0.5 per cent (Mazzucato 2012b).

If the US is better at innovation, it isn't because university–industry links are better (they aren't), or because US universities produce more spinouts (they don't). It simply reflects more research being done in more institutions, which generates better technical skills in the workforce (Salter et al. 2000). Furthermore, US funding is split between research in universities and early stage technology development in firms. Getting EU universities to do both runs the risk of generating technologies unfit for the market.

Thus there is not a problem of research quality in universities in Europe, nor in the collaboration between industry and universities, which probably occurs more frequently in the UK than the US. Nor is there a problem in universities generating firms, which again occurs more frequently in Europe than in the US (although there are major concerns about the quality of the firms that are generated, Salter et al. 2000;

Nightingale 2012). If European firms lack the ability to innovate then technology transfer policies are like pushing a piece of string.

More generally, in the economics of innovation literature, there is often talk of the 'European Paradox' – the conjecture that EU countries play a leading global role in top-level scientific output, but lag behind in the ability to convert this strength into wealth-generating innovations. Dosi, Llerena and Labini (2006) support the points made above by providing evidence that the reason for European weakness is not, as is commonly claimed, the lack of science parks or interaction between education and industry. It is a weaker system of scientific research and the presence of weaker and less innovative companies. Policy implications include less emphasis on 'networking' and more on policy measures aimed to strengthen 'frontier' research or, put another way, a better division of labour between universities and companies, where universities should focus on high-level research and firms on technology development.

An alternative view – often voiced – is that Europe lacks sufficiently speculative stock markets to induce VC investment (Janeway 2012). While there are surely problems with the European venture capital industry (Bottazzi and Da Rin 2002), and there is perhaps not an equivalent to NASDAQ, this view ignores how the overly speculative US model undermines innovation. The problem is that the ideology surrounding both the role of VC, the role of the stock market and innovation, and the analysis of where innovation comes from, has prevented a 'healthy balance' of speculation and investment to be sustainable over time.

Myth 6: Business Investment Requires 'Less Tax and Red Tape'

While there is a research component in innovation, there is not a linear relationship between research and development, innovation and economic growth. While it is important that the frontiers of science advance and that economies develop the nodes and networks that enable knowledge to be transferred between different organizations and individuals, it does not follow that subsidizing the activity of R&D per se within individual firms is the best use of taxpayers' money. Although it is common sense that there is a relationship between a decision to engage in R&D and its cost (see Myth 1), qualitative surveys of the effectiveness of the R&D tax credit for both large and small firms provide little evidence that it has positively impacted on the decision to engage in R&D, rather than simply providing a welcome cash transfer to some firms that have already done so.[7] There is also a potential problem under the current R&D tax credit system, in many countries, that it does not hold firms accountable as to whether they have conducted new innovation that would not otherwise have taken place, or simply pursued routine forms of product development. In time, therefore, as the entrepreneurial State is built, it would be more effective to use some of the expenditure on R&D tax credits to directly commission the technological advance in question. Recently, the Netherlands has introduced an R&D tax credit that targets not the income from R&D (easily fudged) but R&D workers – and this has been found to be more effective, creating the kind of 'additionality' that income-based R&D tax credits don't (Lockshin and Mohnen 2012).

More generally, as Keynes emphasized, business investment (especially innovative investment) is a function of 'animal spirits', the gut instinct of investors about future growth prospects. These are impacted to a greater extent not by taxes but by the strength of a nation's science base, its system of credit creation, and its quality of education and hence human capital. Tax cuts in the 1980s did not produce more investment in innovation; they only affected income distribution (increasing inequality). For this same reason, 'enterprise zones' which are focused almost exclusively on tax benefits and weakened regulation are not *innovation* zones. It would be best to save that money or to invest it in properly run science parks for which there is better evidence that innovation will follow (Massey, Quintas and Wield 1992).

It is important for innovation policy to resist the appeal for tax measures of different kinds – such as the patent box discussed above, or R&D tax credits – unless they are structured in such a way that will lead to investments in innovation that would not have happened anyway, and real evidence confirms it. Most of all, it is essential for policymakers to be wary of companies that complain about 'tax and red tape', when it is clear that their own global actions reflect a preference for areas of the world where the State is spending precisely in those areas that create confidence and 'animal spirits' regarding future growth possibilities.

This chapter has argued that many of the assumptions that underlie current growth policy should not be taken for granted. Over the last decade or so, policymakers searching for proxies for economic growth

---

7 See HMRC, *An Evaluation of R&D Tax Credits* (2010) for an example of this.

have looked to things they can measure such as R&D spending, patents, venture capital investment, and the number of small firms that are assumed to be important for growth. I have attempted to demystify these assumptions and now turn to the largest myth of all: the limited role for government in producing entrepreneurship, innovation and growth.

Chapter 3

RISK-TAKING STATE: FROM 'DE-RISKING' TO 'BRING IT ON!'

During a recent visit to the United States, French President François Mitterrand stopped to tour California's Silicon Valley, where he hoped to learn more about the ingenuity and entrepreneurial drive that gave birth to so many companies there. Over lunch, Mitterrand listened as Thomas Perkins, a partner in the venture capital fund that started Genentech Inc., extolled the virtues of the risk-taking investors who finance the entrepreneurs. Perkins was cut off by Stanford University Professor Paul Berg, who won a Nobel Prize for work in genetic engineering. He asked, 'Where were you guys in the '50s and '60s when all the funding had to be done in the basic science? Most of the discoveries that have fuelled [the industry] were created back then.'

Henderson and Schrage, in the *Washington Post* (1984)

The debate about what type of research is best conducted by the public or private sector tends to come down to a discussion of two important characteristics of research. The first is the long time horizon necessary (e.g. for 'basic' research) followed by the fact that many investments in research contribute to the public good (making it difficult for businesses to appropriate returns). These issues provide the rationale for public sector funding and establish the classic market failure argument for research (Bush 1945).

What is less understood is the fact that public sector funding often ends up doing much more than fixing market failures. By being more willing to engage in the world of Knightian uncertainty, investing in early stage technology development, the public sector can in fact create new products and related markets. Two examples include its role in dreaming up the possibility of the Internet or nanotech when the terms did not even exist. By envisioning new spaces, creating new 'missions' (Foray et al. 2012), the State leads the growth process rather than just incentivizing or stabilizing it. And coming back to Judt's point about the 'discursive' battle, this courageous act is poorly reflected by the term 'de-risking'. The role of the State has been more about *taking on* risk with courage and vision – not simply *taking it away* from someone else who then captures the returns. As discussed at the end of Chapter 1, this is about the State investing on a bumpy risk landscape in a dynamic division of innovative labour. In order for us to avoid the myths discussed in Chapter 2, it is essential to map the types of risk we are talking about in better ways. Illustrating these better ways is the subject of this chapter.

What Type of Risk?

Entrepreneurship, like growth, is one of the least-well-understood topics in economics. What is it? According to the Austrian economist Joseph Schumpeter, an entrepreneur is a person, or group of people, who is willing and able to convert a new idea or invention into a successful innovation. It is not just about setting up a new business (the more common definition), but doing so in a way that produces a *new* product, or a *new* process, or a *new* market for an existing product or process. Entrepreneurship, he wrote, employs 'the gale of creative destruction' to replace, in whole or in part, inferior innovations across markets and industries, simultaneously creating new products including new business models, and in so doing destroying the lead of the incumbents (Schumpeter 1949). In this way, creative destruction is largely responsible for the dynamism of industries and long-run economic growth. Each major new technology leads to creative destruction: the steam engine, the railway, electricity, electronics, the car, the computer, the Internet. Each has destroyed as much as they have created but each has also led to increased wealth overall.

For Frank H. Knight (1921) and Peter Drucker (1970), entrepreneurship is about taking risk. The behaviour of the entrepreneur is that of a person willing to put his or her career and financial security on the line and take risks in the name of an idea, spending time as well as capital on an uncertain venture. In fact, entrepreneurial risk taking, like technological change, is not just risky, it is highly 'uncertain'. Knight (2002, 233) distinguished risk from uncertainty in the following way:

> The practical difference between the two categories, risk and uncertainty, is that in the former the distribution of the outcome in

a group of instances is known... While in the case of uncertainty that is not true, the reason being in general that it is impossible to form a group of instances, because the situation dealt with is in a high degree unique.

John Maynard Keynes (1937, 213–14) also emphasized these differences:

By 'uncertain' knowledge, let me explain, I do not mean merely to distinguish what is known for certain from what is only probable. The game of roulette is not subject, in this sense, to uncertainty... The sense in which I am using the term is that in which the prospect of a European war is uncertain, or the price of copper and the rate of interest twenty years hence, or the obsolescence of a new invention... About these matters there is no scientific basis on which to form any calculable probability whatever. We simply do not know!

Technological change is a good example of the truly unique situation. R&D investments that contribute to technological change not only take years to materialize into new products, but most products developed fail. In the pharmaceutical sector, for example, innovation from an R&D project can take up to 17 years from its beginning to its end. It costs about $403 million per drug, and the failure rate is extremely high: only 1 in 10,000 compounds reach the market approval phase, a success rate of just 0.01 per cent. When successful, often the search for one product leads to the discovery of a completely different one, in a process characterized by serendipity.[1] This of course does not mean that innovation is based on luck, far from it. It is based on long-term strategies and targeted investments. But the returns from those investments are highly uncertain and thus cannot be understood through rational economic theory (as was discussed above, this is one of the critiques that modern day Schumpeterians make of

---

1 In numerous historical instances scientific theory and explanations have emerged after the technologies they were seeking to explain. The Wright brothers flew before aerodynamics was developed and the steam engine was operational before thermodynamics was understood. Technology often advances slightly ahead of science, and industrial innovation provides problems for academics to solve. See P. Nightingale, 'Technological Capabilities, Invisible Infrastructure and the Un-social Construction of Predictability: The Overlooked Fixed Costs of Useful Research', *Research Policy* 33, no. 9 (2004).

Figure 3. Sources of funding for R&D in the USA in 2008

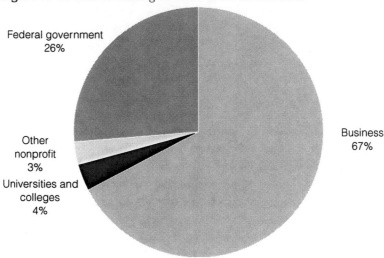

Source: National Science Foundation (2008).

'endogenous growth theory', which models R&D as a game-theoretic choice). Furthermore, the ability to engage in innovation differs greatly between companies and is one of the main reasons that firms are so different from each other, and why it is nearly impossible to find firms distributed 'normally' around an 'optimal-size firm' (the 'representative' agent), a concept so dear to neoclassical microeconomic theory.

The high risk and serendipitous characteristic of the innovation process is one of the main reasons why profit-maximizing companies will invest less in basic research; they can receive greater and more immediate returns from applied research. Investment in basic research is a typical example of a 'market failure': an instance where the market alone would not produce enough basic research so the government must step in. This is why there are few people, on all sides of the political spectrum, who would not agree that it should be (and is) the State that tends to fund most basic research. For the US economy, for example, Figures 3 and 4 show that while government spending on R&D makes up only 26 per cent of total R&D,[2] with the private sector making up 67 per cent,

2 It is also important to note that in the US, some public R&D funding is awarded with the expectation that it will be matched by business funds, or used to attract other funding, meaning that much of the 'private' R&D has been publicly induced.

Figure 4. Sources of funding for basic research R&D in the USA in 2008

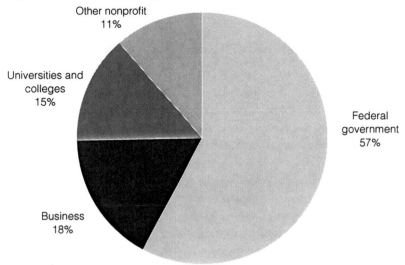

Source: National Science Foundation (2008).

the proportion is much higher when basic research is considered in isolation. Public spending accounts for 57 per cent of basic research in the US, with the private sector taking on only 18 per cent.

A core difference between the US and Europe is the degree to which public R&D spending is for 'general advancement' rather than mission-oriented. Market failure theories of R&D are more useful to understand general 'advancement of knowledge' type R&D than that which is 'mission oriented'. Mission-oriented R&D investment targets a government agency programme or goal that may be found, for example, in defence, space, agriculture, health, energy or industrial-technology programmes. While public R&D spent on general advancement usually makes up less than 50 per cent of total R&D, in 2003/2004 mission-oriented R&D made up more than 60 per cent of public R&D spending in South Korea, the US, the UK, France, Canada, Japan and Germany (Mowery 2010).

Mowery (2010) argues that trying to cut and paste lessons learned from one mission-oriented programme to another is dangerous, as each one has its own specificities (e.g. defence vs. health). To understand programme differences, he argues that the 'systems of innovation' approach is much more useful than the market failure approach. It is able to take into consideration how the dynamics of each sector and nation vary, and how each mission is defined by the specific structures, institutions and incentives used to carry it out.

State Leading in Radical (Risky) Innovation

A key reason why the concept of market failure is problematic for understanding the role of government in the innovation process is that it ignores a fundamental fact about the history of innovation. Not only has government funded the riskiest research, whether applied or basic, but it has indeed often been the source of the most radical, path-breaking types of innovation. To this extent it has actively created markets, not just fixed them, a topic examined in depth in Chapter 4. By looking at examples of the State's leading role in the development of Internet- and nanotechnology we will further develop our understanding of the link between R&D and growth, and the public–private divide.

Not all innovations lead to economy-wide growth. Economy-wide growth is generally caused by new products or processes that have an impact on a wide variety of sectors in the economy, as was the case with the rise with electricity and computers. These are what macroeconomists call general purpose technologies (GPTs). GPTs are characterized by three core qualities:

- They are pervasive in that they spread into many sectors.
- They improve over time and should keep lowering the cost to their users.
- They make it easier to spawn innovation through the invention and production of new products or processes (Helpman 1998).

Ruttan (2006) argues that large-scale and long-term government investment has been the engine behind almost every GPT in the last century. He analysed the development of six different technology complexes (the US 'mass production' system, aviation technologies, space technologies, information technology, Internet technologies and nuclear power) and concluded that government investments have been important in bringing these new technologies into being. He adds that nuclear power would most probably not have been developed at all in the absence of large government investments. In each case successful development of new technology complexes was not just a result of funding and creating the right conditions for innovation. Equally important was envisioning the opportunity space, engaging in the riskiest and most uncertain early research, and overseeing the commercialization process (Ruttan 2006). In Chapter 4 I will show that the same has been the case for the recent development of nanotechnology, which many believe is the next GPT.

Examples of the leading role played by the US government in technology development in fact abound. Lazonick (2013) presents a compelling summary of cases where the US Developmental State played a prominent role, ranging from land freely handed to private companies for the construction of railroads and the financial support of agricultural research in the nineteenth century, through the funding, support and active development of the aeronautical, space and aircraft industries in the twentieth century, to R&D grants and other types of finance for life sciences, nanotechnology and clean energy industries in the twenty-first century.

Abbate's (1999) extensive research shows how the Internet grew out of the small Defense Department network project (ARPANET) of connecting a dozen research sites in the US into a network linking millions of computers and billions of people. Leslie (2000) argues that while Silicon Valley has been an attractive and influential model for regional development, it has been also difficult to copy it, because almost every advocate of the Silicon Valley model tells a story of 'freewheeling entrepreneurs and visionary venture capitalists' and yet misses the crucial factor: the military's role in creating and sustaining it. Leslie shows that 'Silicon Valley owes its present configuration to patterns of federal spending, corporate strategies, industry–university relationships, and technological innovation shaped by the assumptions and priorities of Cold War defense policy' (Leslie 2000, 49). Notwithstanding, the Silicon Valley model still lingers in the collective imagination of policymakers as a place where VC created a revolution. The 1999 National Research Council report *Funding a Revolution: Government Support for Computing Research* is in fact an attempt to recall and acknowledge the major role the US federal government has played in launching and giving momentum to the computer revolution. We look at this further below.

Given the leading developmental role the US government plays in a vast number of sectors, it is no surprise that at a more micro level, Block and Keller (2011b) found that between 1971 and 2006, 77 out of the most important 88 innovations (rated by *R&D Magazine*'s annual awards) – or 88 per cent – have been fully dependent on federal research support, especially, but not only, in their early phases – and the *R&D Magazine*'s award *excludes* ICT innovations.

Figure 5. Classifications of new drugs

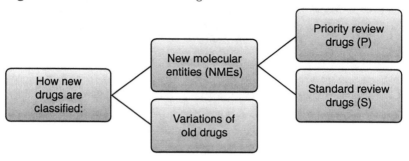

These examples are fundamental for understanding the impact of publicly funded research. It is not just about funding blue-sky research but creating visions around important new technologies. To illustrate the general point, I turn now to the specific examples of early stage government investment into the US pharmaceutical and biotechnology sectors.

Pharmaceuticals: Radical vs. 'Me Too' Drugs

The pharmaceutical industry is interesting because of the new division of innovative labour. Large pharma, small biotech, universities and government labs are all parts of the ecology of the industry. But it is especially government labs and government-backed universities that invest in the research responsible for producing the most radical new drugs – the new molecular entities with priority rating in Figure 5. The ex-editor of the *New England Journal of Medicine*, Marcia Angell (2004), has argued forcefully that while private pharmaceutical companies justify their exorbitantly high prices by saying they need to cover their high R&D costs, in fact most of the really 'innovative' new drugs, i.e. new molecular entities with priority rating, come from publicly funded laboratories. Private pharma has focused more on 'me too' drugs (slight variations of existing ones) and the development (including clinical trials) and marketing side of the business. It is of course highly ironic, given this sector's constant bemoaning of 'stifling' regulations.

Economists measure productivity by comparing the amount of input into production with the amount of output that emerges. In this sense the large pharmaceutical companies have been fairly unproductive over the last few years in the production of innovations. As Figure 6 shows, there has been an exponential rise in R&D spending by members of

Figure 6. Number of NMEs approved compared with spending by PhRMA members in the USA, 1970–2004

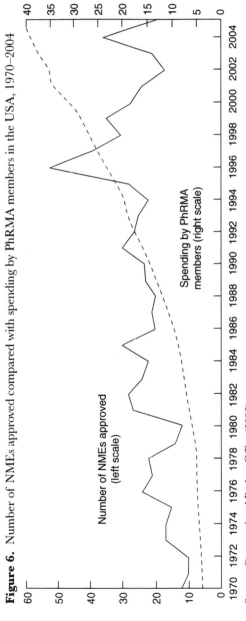

Source: Congressional Budget Office (2006).

Figure 7. Percentages of new drugs by type in the pharmaceutical industry (1993–94)

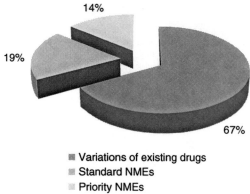

■ Variations of existing drugs
■ Standard NMEs
■ Priority NMEs

Source: Angell (2004).

the Pharmaceutical Research and Manufacturers of America (PhRMA) with no corresponding increase in the number of new drugs, commonly known as new molecular entities (NMEs). This also holds for patenting: while the number of patents has skyrocketed since the Bayh–Dole Act (1980) allowed publicly funded research to be patented, most of these patents are of little value (Demirel and Mazzucato 2012). When patents are weighted by the amount of citations they receive (the common indicator of 'important' patents), the figure is relatively flat, meaning that there are few important patents.

Of the 1,072 drugs approved by the FDA between 1993 and 2004, only 357 were NMEs rather than just variations of existing 'me too' drugs. The number of *important* 'priority' new drugs is even more worrying: only 146 of these had priority rating (NME with 'P' rating). In Figure 7 we see that only 14 per cent were seen as important new drugs.

For the sake of the argument being made in this book, what is important is that 75 per cent of the NMEs trace their research not to private companies but to publicly funded National Institutes of Health (NIH) labs in the US. While the State-funded labs have invested in the riskiest phase, the big pharmaceutical companies have preferred to invest in the less risky variations of existing drugs (a drug that simply has a different dosage than a previous version of the same drug).

All a far cry, for example, from the recent quote by UK-based GlaxoSmithKline CEO Andrew Witty: 'The pharmaceutical industry is hugely innovative... If governments work to support, not stifle innovation, the industry will deliver the next era of revolutionary medicine' (*Economist* 2010b). It is the 'revolutionary' spirit of the State labs, producing 75 per cent of the radical new drugs, that is allowing Witty and his fellow CEOs to spend most of their time focusing on how to boost their stock prices (e.g. through stock repurchase programmes). Whether this parasitic relationship is sustainable or not is discussed further in the Chapters 8 and 9.

Biotechnology: Public Leader, Private Laggard

In the UK, the Medical Research Council (MRC) receives annual 'grant-in-aid' funding from Parliament through the Department for Business, Innovation and Skills (BIS). It is government funded, though independent in its choice of which research to support. It works closely with the Department of Health and other UK research councils, industry and other stakeholders to identify and respond to the UK's health needs. It was MRC research in the 1970s that led to the development of monoclonal antibodies – which, according to the MRC, make up a third of all new drug treatments for many different major diseases such as cancer, arthritis and asthma.

A similar story can be told for the US biopharmaceutical industry. Its growth was not, as is often claimed, rooted in business finance (such as venture capital), but rather emerged and was guided by government investment and spending (Mazzucato and Dosi 2006). In fact, the immense interest of venture capital and big pharmaceutical companies in biotech was paradoxical given the industry's risky and lengthy process of recouping its investment (Pisano 2006). According to Lazonick and Tulum (2011), the answer to this puzzling paradox is two-fold. First, early investors had the availability of easy exit opportunities through speculative stock market flotations and investors willing to fund initial public offerings (IPOs). Second, significant government support and involvement helped this industry to flourish over the last several decades.

In fact, the development of the biotech industry in the US is a direct product of the key role of the government in leading the development of the knowledge base that has thus provided firm success and the overall growth of the biotech industry. As Vallas, Kleinman and Biscotti (2009, 66) eloquently summarize:

> …the knowledge economy did not spontaneously emerge from
> the bottom up, but was prompted by a top-down stealth industrial

policy; government and industry leaders simultaneously advocated government intervention to foster the development of the biotechnology industry and argued hypocritically that government should 'let the free market work'.

As this quote indicates, not only was this knowledge economy guided by government, but, strikingly, it was done as the leaders of industry were on the one hand privately demanding government intervention to facilitate the industry's development, and on the other hand publicly declaring their support for a free market. It is no wonder given this hypocrisy that so much confusion now exists among policymakers and the general public regarding the role of the government in the economy. Without question some of this confusion is explained by Block (2008), who argues that the US proceeds with 'hidden' industrial policy, but clarifies that it is hidden primarily by the fact that it is not discussed as a matter of public debate, by policymakers or by the mainstream media. Block (2008, 15) claims that 'like the purloined letter, the hidden Developmental State is in plain view. But it has been rendered invisible by the success of the market fundamentalist ideology' that typically plays out in partisan debate (as also discussed in Chapter 1). Given the efforts of international policymakers in seeking to advance their own economies and in replicating the successes of the US, it is imperative now, more than ever, that the 'real' story behind this innovation and economic growth and development be told. If the components of the Developmental State are already visible and in action, why does the logic that defies their value triumph?

Summarizing their findings of the strong role of the government in the development of the biotech industry, Vallas, Kleinman and Biscotti emphasize the significance of 'massive shifts in federal R&D that were involved', adding that, 'it is difficult to avoid the conclusion that the knowledge economy was not born but made' (2009, 71). Though pharmaceutical companies spend a lot on R&D, supplementing these private investments has been completely dependent on a 'ready supply of scientific knowledge that has been either funded or actually produced by federal agencies'.

The National Institutes of Health: Creating the Wave vs. Surfing It

State support and involvement in biotech span a wide range of forms, the most significant being that the enormous knowledge base which biopharmaceutical companies are dependent on has developed more from government investment than from business. The knowledge base has been developed from the critical investment the government has given to funding basic science. At the forefront lie the National Institutes of Health (NIH) and other government programmes which have invested in many of the key scientific achievements that the industry's success has been built on. Drawing on NIH spending data compiled in Lazonick and Tulum (2011), it is easy to see how crucial this funding was for biotech innovation. From 1978 to 2004, NIH spending on life sciences research totalled $365 billion. Every year from 1970 to 2009, with the exception of a small decline in 2006, NIH funding increased in nominal terms, in contrast to the widely fluctuating funds from venture capital and stock market investments.

Figure 8 below shows that total NIH spending between 1936 and 2011 (in 2011 dollars) was $792 billion. The budget for 2012 alone reached $30.9 billion. Thus, while business continues to lobby for tax cuts and less 'red tape', in the end they are greatly dependent on the finance of the tax receipts which they fight against. And indeed, those countries, like the UK, that are increasingly convinced that what drives business are 'low taxes and low regulation' are suffering from the flight of many companies, such as Pfizer and Sanofi.

More striking is that in the 35 years since the founding of Genentech as the first biotech company in 1976, the NIH funded the pharma-biotech sector with $624 billion (figure to 2010). As evidenced in this data, Lazonick and Tulum (2011, 9) argue that the US government, through the NIH, and by extension via the US taxpayer, 'has long been the nation's (and the world's) most important investor in knowledge creation in the medical fields'. This knowledge base was 'indispensable' and without it, venture capital and public equity funds would not have poured into the industry. They have 'surfed the wave' rather than created it.

Through a system of nearly 50,000 competitive grants, the NIH supports more than 325,000 researchers at over 3,000 universities, medical schools and other research institutions in every US state and throughout the world. These grants represent 80 per cent of the agency's budget with another 10 per cent used to directly employ 6,000 individuals in its own laboratories. The agency's 26 research centres in Maryland serve a prominent role in the biotech industry – one that is increasing as more centres and institutes continue to develop within the NIH. Beyond these 'knowledge-creating programs', traces of government support can also be seen in almost every single major biopharmaceutical product in

Figure 8. National Institutes of Health budgets, 1938–2012

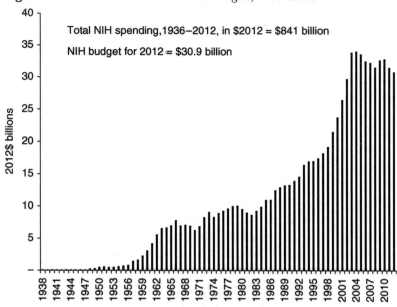

Source: Office of the Budget, National Institutes of Health (2011), 1176.

the US (Vallas, Kleinman and Biscotti 2009). Although many biotech scholars acknowledge the immense government support in the science base, overall they fail to draw the causal relationship between the successful growth of this industry, its attractiveness to investors, and the long-lasting government efforts that develop and sustain the substantial knowledge base found in the US.

So why does venture capital often get so much credit for creating the biotech revolution? The story of private and public investments in biotech is perfectly described by Paul Berg (the 1980 Nobel Prize winner in chemistry) in the quote at the beginning of this chapter. In essence, Berg was aware that the State actively paved the way for future industry development by bringing the courage, vision and funding so lacking in the private sector. Or perhaps more fairly, by investing in new technology until fear-inducing uncertainty was transformed into mere risk.

The point of this chapter was to show that the case for State investment goes beyond 'blue-sky' basic research. In fact, it applies to all the different types of 'risky' and uncertain research, since the private sector is in many ways less entrepreneurial than the public sector: it shies away from radically new products and processes, leaving the most uncertain investments to be first taken on by the State.

So while blue-sky research is necessary for innovation to occur, it is far from sufficient, and indeed the role of the State goes deeper. I continue to examine the breadth and depth of State leadership in producing the knowledge economy in Chapter 4. In Chapter 5 I review the specific case of Apple as an example of a company that has benefitted enormously from both publicly funded blue-sky research as well as State policies that facilitate commercialization.

Chapter 4

THE US ENTREPRENEURIAL STATE

...since its founding fathers, the United States has always been torn between two traditions, the activist policies of Alexander Hamilton (1755–1804) and Thomas Jefferson's (1743–1826) maxim that 'the government that governs least, governs best'. With time and usual American pragmatism, this rivalry has been resolved by putting the Jeffersonians in charge of the rhetoric and the Hamiltonians in charge of policy.

Erik Reinert (2007, 23)

Despite the perception of the US as the epitome of private sector–led wealth creation, in reality it is the State that has been engaged on a massive scale in entrepreneurial risk taking to spur innovation. In this chapter four key successful examples are given: the roles of DARPA (the US government's Defense Advance Research Project Agency), SBIR (Small Business Innovation Research), the Orphan Drug Act (the EU passed its own Orphan Drug Act in 2001, imitating the US act passed in 1983) and the National Nanotechnology Initiative. What they share is a proactive approach by the State to shape a market in order to drive innovation. The insight gained is that other than being an entrepreneurial society, a place where it is culturally natural to start and grow a business, the US is also a place where the State plays an entrepreneurial role, by making investments in radical new areas. The State has provided early stage finance where venture capital ran away, while also commissioning high-level innovative private sector activity that would not have happened without public policy goals backing a strategy and vision.

So far I have argued that while the level of technological innovation is integral to the rate of economic growth, there is no linear relationship between R&D spending, the size of companies, the number of patents and the level of innovation in an economy. What does seem to be clear, however, is that a necessary precursor for innovation to occur is to have a highly networked economy, with continuous feedback loops established between different individuals and organizations to enable knowledge to be shared and its boundaries to be pushed back.

This chapter attempts to illustrate that at the frontiers of knowledge, simply having a national system of innovation is not enough. Over time, more impressive results can be achieved when the State is a major player operating within this system. This role does not necessarily have to take place at a national level (although it can) and should not only involve long-term subsidies to certain companies ('picking winners'). Rather the State, through its various agencies and laboratories, has the potential to disseminate new ideas rapidly. It can also be nimble, using its procurement, commissioning and regulatory functions to shape markets and drive technological advance. In this way it acts as a catalyst for change, the spark that lights the fire.

The Defense Advanced Research Projects Agency (DARPA)

The role that military engagement has had for economic growth and development does not differentiate US history from other modern countries. But in the US, the experience of technological development necessary to win wars has provided strong lessons to those seeking to improve innovation policy.

The role of the State in the Defense Advanced Research Projects Agency (DARPA) model goes far beyond simply funding basic science. It is about targeting resources in specific areas and directions; it is about opening new windows of opportunities; brokering the interactions between public and private agents involved in technological development, including those between private and public venture capital; and facilitating commercialization (Block 2008; Fuchs 2010).

In contrast to the emphasis placed by market fundamentalists on Franklin D. Roosevelt's New Deal as the critical turning point in US economic history, Block (2008) argues that the Second World War was a more significant period for the development of innovation policies in the US. It was during the period following the Second World War that the Pentagon worked closely with other national security agencies like the Atomic Energy Commission and the National Aeronautics and Space Agency (NASA). The interagency collaborations led to the development of technologies such as computers, jet planes, civilian nuclear energy, lasers and biotechnology (Block 2008). The way this was done was 'pioneered' by the Advanced Research Projects Agency (ARPA), an office created by the Pentagon in 1958. This agency, also commonly referred to as the Defense Advanced Research Projects Agency (DARPA), and consequently the acronym used throughout this book, engaged in developing critical initiatives across a broad range of technologies.[1] However, it was the government support for technological advancement in the computer field that led to the establishment of a new paradigm for technology policy.

DARPA was set up to give the US technological superiority in different sectors, mainly (but not only) those related to technology, and has always been aggressively mission oriented. It has a budget of more than $3 billion per year, 240 staff, operates flexibly with few overheads, and is connected to but separated from government. It has successfully recruited high-quality programme managers who are willing to take risks because of their short-term contracts, which last anywhere between four and six years. Its structure is meant to bridge the gap between blue-sky academic work, with long time horizons, and the more incremental technological development occurring within the military.

After a Second World War victory that relied heavily on State-sponsored and -organized technological developments, the federal government was quick to implement the recommendations of Vannevar Bush's 1945 report, which called for ongoing public support for basic as well as applied scientific research. The relationship between government and science was further strengthened by the Manhattan Project (the major scientific effort led by the US, with the UK and Canada, which led to the invention and use of the atomic bomb in the Second World War), as physicists instructed policymakers on the military implications of new technology. From this point on, it became the government's business to understand which technologies provided possible applications for military purposes as well as commercial use.

According to Block (2011, 7), during this period an increased number of government workers took on a more direct role in advancing innovation, procuring additional researchers, encouraging researchers to solve specific problems, and requiring that those researchers meet specific objectives. The insight that followed was that this was something government could do for economic and civilian purposes, in addition to the traditional military function.

---

1 The literature refers to both ARPA and DARPA.

The launching of Sputnik in 1957 by the Soviets led to an eruption of panic among US policymakers, fearful that they were losing the technological battle. The creation of DARPA in 1958 was a direct result. Before the formation of DARPA the military was the sole controller of all military R&D dollars. Through the formation of DARPA a portion of military spending on R&D was now designated to 'blue-sky thinking' – ideas that went beyond the horizon in that they may not produce results for ten or twenty years. As a result of this mandate DARPA was free to focus on advancing innovative technological development with novel strategies. This opened numerous windows for scientists and engineers to propose innovative ideas and receive funding and assistance (Block 2008).

Going way beyond simply funding research, DARPA funded the formation of computer science departments, provided start-up firms with early research support, contributed to semiconductor research and support to human–computer interface research, and oversaw the early stages of the Internet. Many of these critical activities were carried out by its Information Processing Techniques Office, originally established in 1962. Such strategies contributed hugely to the development of the computer industry during the 1960s and 1970s, and many of the technologies later incorporated in the design of the personal computer were developed by DARPA-funded researchers (Abbate 1999).

Another key event during this period was the new innovation environment that emerged after a group of scientists and engineers in 1957 broke away from a firm started by William Shockley (Block 2011). The rebellious group of scientists and engineers, often referred to as the 'traitorous eight', went on to form Fairchild Semiconductor, a new firm that advanced semiconductor technology and continued 'a process of economic fission that was constantly spinning off new economic challengers' (Block and Keller 2011, 12–13). Lazonick (2009) adds that the spinoff culture ultimately began with Fairchild Semiconductor – and the firm owed nearly all of its growth to military procurement. The spinoff business model became viable and popular for technological advancement following the 1957 revolt, yet would not have been possible without State involvement and it functioning as a major early customer. A new paradigm emerged that resulted in innovative ideas moving from labs to market in far greater quantity.

Before this, government officials' leverage in generating rapid technological advancement was limited, as large defence firms still deflected the pressure and demands for innovation with the tremendous power they wielded. The leverage government officials had in advancing innovative breakthroughs was also limited by the small number of firms with such capabilities. Bonded by a shared interest in avoiding the certain risks that accompanied an uncertain technological path, the firms resisted government pressure for innovation. However, in a new environment with ambitious start-ups, the opportunity for generating real competition among firms presented itself more fully.

Programme officers at DARPA recognized the potential this new innovation environment provided and were able to take advantage of it, focusing at first on new, smaller firms to which they could provide much smaller funds than was possible with the larger defence contractors. These firms recognized the need for ambitious innovation as part of their overall future viability. With small, newer firms engaged in real competition and as the spinoff model became more institutionalized, Block (2008) notes that large firms also had to get on board with this quest for rapid innovative breakthroughs. By taking advantage of this new environment, the government was able to play a leading role in mobilizing innovation among big and small firms, and in university and government laboratories. The dynamic and flexible structure of DARPA in contrast to the more formal and bureaucratic structure of other government programmes allowed it to maximize the increased leverage it now had in generating real competition across the network. Using its funding networks, DARPA increased the flow of knowledge across competing research groups. It facilitated workshops for researchers to gather and share ideas while also learning of the paths identified as 'dead ends' by others. DARPA officers engaged in business and technological brokering by linking university researchers to entrepreneurs interested in starting a new firm; connecting start-up firms with venture capitalists; finding a larger company to commercialize the technology; or assisting in procuring a government contract to support the commercialization process.

Pursuing this brokering function, DARPA officers not only developed links among those involved in the network system, but also engaged in efforts to expand the pool of scientists and engineers working in specific areas. An example of this is the role DARPA played in the 1960s by funding the establishment of new computer science departments at various universities in the US. By increasing the number of researchers who possessed the necessary and particular expertise, DARPA was able, over an extended period of time, to accelerate technological change in this area. In the area of computer chip fabrication during the 1970s, DARPA assumed the expenses associated with getting a design into a prototype by funding a laboratory affiliated with the University of Southern

California. Anyone who possessed a superior design for a new microchip could have the chips fabricated at this laboratory, thus expanding the pool of participants designing faster and better microchips.

The personal computer emerged during this time with Apple introducing the first one in 1976. Following this, the computer industry's boom in Silicon Valley and the key role of DARPA in the massive growth of personal computing received significant attention, but has since been forgotten by those who claim Silicon Valley is an example of 'free market' capitalism. In a recent documentary, *Something Ventured, Something Gained*, for example, the role of the State is not mentioned once in the 85 minutes spent describing the development of Silicon Valley (Geller and Goldfine 2012).

Also, during the 1970s, the significant developments taking place in biotechnology illustrated to policymakers that the role of DARPA in the computer industry was not a unique or isolated case of success. The decentralized form of industrial policy that played such a crucial role in setting the context for the dramatic expansion of personal computing was also instrumental in accelerating growth and development in biotechnology.

Block (2008, 188) identifies the four key characteristics of the DARPA model:[2]

- A series of relatively small offices, often staffed with leading scientists and engineers, are given considerable budget autonomy to support promising ideas. These offices are proactive rather than reactive and work to set an agenda for researchers in the field. The goal is to create a scientific community with a presence in universities, the public sector and corporations that focuses on specific technological challenges that have to be overcome.
- Funding is provided to a mix of university-based researchers, start-up firms, established firms and industry consortia. There is no dividing line between 'basic research' and 'applied research', since the two are deeply intertwined. Moreover, the DARPA personnel are encouraged to cut off funding to groups that were not making progress and reallocate resources to other groups that have more promise.
- Since the goal is to produce usable technological advances, the agency's mandate extends to helping firms get products to the stage

---

2 Block uses this to characterize his concept of a 'developmental network state' discussed in footnote 5 on page 37.

of commercial viability. The agency can provide firms with assistance that goes well beyond research funding.
- Part of the agency's task is to use its oversight role to link ideas, resources and people in constructive ways across the different research and development sites.

The main focus is to assist firms in developing new product and process innovations. The key is that the government serves as a leader for firms to imitate, in an approach that is much more 'hands on', in that public sector officials are working directly with firms in identifying and pursuing the most promising innovative paths. In so doing, the government is able to attract top minds – exactly the kind of expertise that generates the dynamism that government is often accused of not having. As mentioned in the forward, this is clearly a self-fulfilling prophecy, because a government under constant attack will not dare be confident and dynamic.

In Chapter 6, we will see how today ARPA-E, the newest agency within the US Department of Energy, is trying to do for 'green' what DARPA did for IT.

The Small Business Innovation Research (SBIR) Programme

Contrary to conventional wisdom regarding the domination of free market ideology during the Reagan Administration, the US government in the 1980s, in fact, acted to build on the successes of DARPA's decentralized industrial policy. One of the most significant events during this period was the signing of the Small Business Innovation Development Act by Reagan in 1982, as a consortium between the Small Business Administration and different government agencies like the Department of Defense, Department of Energy and Environmental Protection Agency. The act was based on a National Science Foundation (NSF) pilot programme initiated during the Carter administration. The Small Business Innovation Research (SBIR) programme required government agencies with large research budgets to designate a fraction (originally 1.25 per cent) of their research funding to support small, independent, for-profit firms. As a result, the programme has provided support to a significant number of highly innovative start-up firms (Lerner 1999; Audretsch 2003).

In addition, the network of State and local institutions that worked in partnership with the federal programmes was expanded. An example of this is the development of organizations that were funded by state

Figure 9. Number of early stage and seed funding awards, SBIR and venture capital

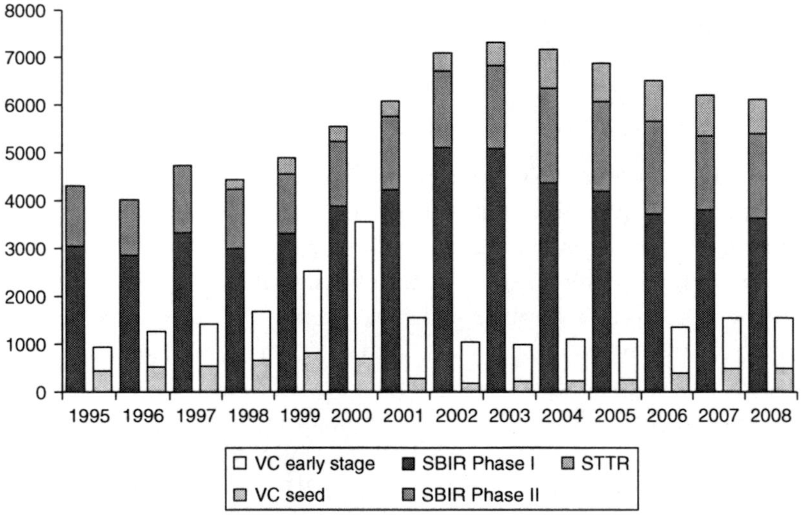

Source: Block and Keller (2012, 15).

and local governments to assist entrepreneurs in submitting successful applications to the SBIR programme to secure funds for their projects. The SBIR programme fulfils a unique role in this new innovation system, because it serves as the first place many entrepreneurs involved in technological innovation go to for funding. The programme, which provides more than $2 billion per year in direct support to high-tech firms, has fostered development of new enterprises, and has guided the commercialization of hundreds of new technologies from the laboratory to the market. Given the instrumental role of the SBIR programme and its successes, it is surprising how little attention it receives. Although the UK has, since 2001, attempted to copy its success, it has not been successful yet, as we will see in the next chapter.

Block (2011, 14) highlights the lack of visibility of the SBIR programme in an effort to illustrate what he describes as 'a discrepancy between the growing importance of these federal initiatives and the absence of public debate or discussion about them'. As indicated in the introduction of this book and again in the early stages of this chapter, this discrepancy poses an exceptional challenge; for both policymakers and the public who are engaged in economic debates as well as making efforts to address the current economic crises and while also paving the way for the future of innovation and development in the globalized world.

As can be seen in Figure 9, the role of the SBIR programme has not been diminishing, but increasing. Indeed, as venture capital has become increasingly short-termist, focused on pursuing capital gains, and seeking early exit through an IPO, the SBIR programme has had to step up its risk finance (Block and Keller 2012).

Orphan Drugs

A year after the SBIR programme was established, a further legislative spur to private sector innovation occurred, this time specific to the biotech industry. The 1983 Orphan Drug Act (ODA) made it possible for small, dedicated biotech firms to carve a sliver from the drug market. The act includes certain tax incentives, clinical as well as R&D subsidies, fast-track drug approval, along with strong intellectual and marketing rights for products developed for treating rare conditions. A rare disease is defined as any disease that affects less than 200,000 people and, given this potentially small market, it was argued that without financial incentives these potential drugs would remain 'orphans'. The impetus behind this legislation was to advance the investment of pharmaceutical companies in developing these drugs.

The protection provided by the act enables small firms to improve their technology platforms and scale up their operations, allowing them to advance to the position of becoming a major player in the biopharmaceutical industry. In fact, orphan drugs played an important role for the major biopharmaceutical firms such as Genzyme, Biogen, Amgen and Genentech to become what they are today (Lazonick and Tulum 2011). Since the introduction of the ODA, 2,364 products have been designated as orphan drugs and 370 of these drugs have gained marketing approval (FDA, n.d.).

In addition to all of the conditions outlined by the ODA, Lazonick and Tulum (2011) draw attention to the fact that multiple versions of the same drug can be designated as 'orphan'. The example of Novartis illustrates this point. In May 2001 the company received marketing approval by the FDA with market exclusivity for its 'chronic myelogenous leukemia' drug Gleevec under the ODA. In 2005 over a span of five months, Novartis applied for and was later granted orphan drug designation for five different indications for this same drug. According to the company's 2010 annual report, in 2010 Gleevec recorded global sales of $4.3 billion, thus confirming the point raised by Lazonick and Tulum (2011), that even when the market size for a drug is small, the revenues can be considerable.

When it comes to the substantial revenues that are generated from drugs designated as 'orphan' it is not only small firms that appear to be benefitting. Some of the world's largest pharmaceutical firms such as Roche, Johnson & Johnson, GlaxoSmithKline and Pfizer, among others, have applied for orphan drug designation for their products. The National Organization for Rare Disorders, a non-profit public organization largely funded by the federal government, has been encouraging large pharmaceutical firms to share their redundant proprietary knowledge with smaller biotech firms through licensing deals, in an effort to develop drugs for orphan indications. Lazonick and Tulum (2011) explain the importance of the Orphan Drug Act by calculating the share of orphan drugs as a percentage of total product revenues for major biopharmaceutical firms. The financial histories of the six leading biopharmaceutical companies reveal a dependence on orphan drugs as a significant portion of the companies' overall product revenues. In fact, 59 per cent of total product revenues and 61 per cent of the product revenues of the six leading dedicated biopharmaceutical firms come from orphan drug sales. When this calculation also includes the later-generation derivatives of drugs that have orphan status, the figure (calculated for 2008) goes up to 74 per cent of total revenues and 74 per cent of the product revenues for the six leading biopharmaceutical firms. Comparing the timing and growth of revenues for orphan and non-orphan 'blockbusters', Lazonick and Tulum (2011) show that orphan drugs are more numerous, their revenue growth began earlier, and many of them have greater 2007 sales (in dollars) than leading non-orphan drugs.

The central role that orphan drugs have played in leading the development of the biotech industry is undeniable, yet this is just one of many critical moves the US government made in supporting the biotech industry. It is also evident that Big Pharma plays a significant role in the biopharmaceutical industry, as illustrated in analyses of orphan drugs. Big Pharma and the biotech industry are significantly dependent on one another in this area, and the distinction between Big Pharma and big biopharma has become 'blurred'. However, the role of government for both these areas was crucial to their development and success. Lazonick and Tulum summarized the government's role for both during the 2000s:

> The US government still serves as an investor in knowledge creation, subsidizer of drug development, protector of drug markets, and, last but not least…purchaser of the drugs that the biopharmaceutical [BP] companies have to sell. The BP industry has become big business

because of big government, and…remains highly dependent on big government to sustain its commercial success. (2011, 18)

From this brief overview of these three examples of State-led support for innovation – DARPA, the SBIR programme and creation of a market for orphan drugs with the ODA – a general point can be drawn: the US has spent the last few decades using active interventionist policies to drive private sector innovation in pursuit of broad public policy goals. What all three interventions have in common is that they do not tie the shirt-tails of government to any one firm, yet it still 'picks winners'; there are no accusations of lame-duck industrial policy here. Instead it is a nimble government that rewards innovation and directs resources over a relatively short time horizon to the companies that show promise, whether through supply-side policies (e.g. DARPA's information and brokerage support, strategic programmes and vision building) or through demand-side policies and funding for start up interventions (the SBIR programme and orphan drugs). The government has not simply created the 'conditions for innovation', but actively funded the early radical research and created the necessary networks between State agencies and the private sector that facilitate commercial development. This is very far from current UK government policy approaches, which assume that the State can simply nudge the private sector into action.

The National Nanotechnology Initiative

The entrepreneurial role that the State can play to foster the development of new technologies, which provide the foundation for decades of economic growth, has most recently been seen in the development of nanotechnology in the US. The types of investments and strategic decisions that the State has made have gone beyond simply creating the right infrastructure, funding basic research, and setting rules and regulations (as in a simple 'systems failure' approach).

Nanotechnology is very likely to be the next general purpose technology, having a pervasive effect on many different sectors and becoming the foundation of new economic growth. However, while this is commonly accepted now, in the 1990s it was not. Motoyama, Appelbaum and Parker (2011, 109–19) describe in detail how the US government has in fact been the lead visionary in dreaming up the possibility of a nanotech revolution – by making the 'against all odds' initial investments and by explicitly forming dynamic networks that bring together different public actors (universities, national labs, government agencies) and when available, the private sector, to kick start a major new revolution which many believe will be even more important than the computer revolution. It has even been the first to 'define' what nanotechnology is. It did so through the active development of the National Nanotechnology Initiative (NNI). Motoyama, Appelbaum and Parker (2011, 111) describe how it was set up:

> The creation and subsequent development of the NNI has been neither a purely bottom-up nor top-down approach: it did not derive from a groundswell of private sector initiative, nor was it the result of strategic decisions by government officials. Rather it resulted from the vision and efforts of a small group of scientists and engineers at the National Science Foundation and the Clinton White House in the late 1990s... It seems clear that Washington selected nanotechnology as the leading front runner, initiated the policy, and invested in its development on a multi-billion dollar scale.

The government's objective was to find the 'next new thing' to replace the Internet. After receiving 'blank stares', the key players (civil servants) in Washington convinced the US government to invest in the creation of a new research agenda, to prepare a set of budget options, and to provide a clear division of labour between different government agencies. But it had first to define nanotech. The President's Committee of Advisors on Science and Technology (PCAST) did so by arguing that the private sector could not expect to lead in developing applications of nanotech that were still 10 to 20 years away from commercial market viability (Motoyama, Appelbaum and Parker 2011, 113):

> Industry generally invests only in developing cost-competitive products in the 3 to 5 year time frame. It is difficult for industry management to justify to their shareholders the large investments in long-term, fundamental research needed to make nanotechnology-based products possible. Furthermore, the highly interdisciplinary nature of the needed research is incompatible with many current corporate structures.

This quote is fascinating because of the way it highlights how the private sector is too focused on the short term (mainly, but not only, as a result of the effect the 1980s shareholder revolution has had on long-term business strategy) and that its rigid structures are not conducive to completing the R&D required. Far from being less innovative than the private sector, government has shown itself to be more flexible and dynamic in understanding the connections between different disciplines relevant to the nanotechnology revolution (that draws on physics, chemistry, materials science, biology, medicine, engineering and computer simulation). As Block and Keller (2011a) discuss, government actions for cutting-edge new technologies have often had to remain veiled behind a 'hidden' industrial policy. The public sector activists driving nanotechnology had to continuously talk about a 'bottom-up' approach so that it would not seem to be an instance of 'picking winners' or choosing national champions. Though in the end, 'while most of the policy-making process involved consultation with academics and corporate experts, it is clear that the principal impetus and direction – from background reports to budget scheme – came from the top' (Motoyama, Appelbaum and Parker 2011, 112). The approach succeeded in convincing Clinton, and then Bush, that investments in nanotechnology would have the potential to 'spawn the growth of future industrial productivity', and that 'the country that leads in discovery and implementation of nanotechnology will have great advantage in the economic and military scene for many decades to come' (Motoyama, Appelbaum and Parker 2011, 113).

In the end, the US government took action. It not only selected nanotechnology as the sector to back most forcefully ('picking it' as a winning sector), but it also proceeded to launch the NNI, review rules and regulations concerning nanotech by studying the various risks involved, and become the largest investor, even beyond what it has done for biotech and the life sciences. Although the strongest action was carried out top down by key senior-level officers in the NSF and the White House, the actual activity behind nanotech was, as in the case of the Internet and computers, heavily decentralized through various State agencies (a total of 13, led by the NSF, but also involving the NIH, the Defense Department and the SBIR programme). Across these different agencies, currently the US government spends approximately $1.8 billion annually on the NNI.

Nanotechnology today does not yet create a major economic impact because of the lack of commercialization of new technologies. Motoyama, Appelbaum and Parker (2011) claim that this is due to the excessive investments made in research relative to the lack of investments in commercialization. They call for a more active government investment in commercialization. However, this raises the question, if government has to do the research, fund major infrastructure investments and also undertake the commercialization effort, what exactly is the role of the private sector?

This chapter has highlighted the important role that government has played in leading innovation and economic growth. Far from stifling innovation and being a drag on the economic system, it has fostered innovation and dynamism in many important modern industries, with the private sector often taking a back seat. Ironically the State has often done so in the US, which in policy circles is often discussed as following a more 'market'-oriented (liberal) model than Europe. This has not been the case where innovation is concerned.

Chapter 5

THE STATE BEHIND THE iPHONE

Stay hungry, stay foolish

Steve Jobs (2005)

In his now well-known Stanford University commencement address, delivered on 12 June 2005, Steve Jobs, then CEO of Apple Computer and Pixar Animation Studios, encouraged the graduating class to be innovative by 'pursuing what you love' and 'staying foolish'. The speech has been cited worldwide as it epitomizes the culture of the 'knowledge' economy, whereby what are deemed important for innovation are not just large R&D labs but also a 'culture' of innovation and the ability of key players to change the 'rules of the game'. By emphasizing the 'foolish' part of innovation, Jobs highlights the fact that underlying the success of a company like Apple – at the heart of the Silicon Valley revolution – is not (just) the experience and technical expertise of its staff, but (also) their ability to be a bit 'crazy', take risks and give 'design' as much importance as hardcore technology. The fact that Jobs dropped out of school, took calligraphy classes and continued to dress all his life like a college student in sneakers is all symbolic of his own style of staying young and 'foolish'.

While the speech is inspiring, and Jobs has rightly been called a 'genius' for the visionary products he conceived and marketed, this story creates a myth about the origin of Apple's success. Individual genius, attention to design, a love for play, and foolishness were no doubt important characteristics. But without the massive amount of public investment behind the computer and Internet revolutions, such attributes might have led only to the invention of a new toy – not to cutting-edge revolutionary products like the iPad and iPhone which have changed the way that people work and communicate. Like the discussion of venture capital in Chapter 2, whereby venture capital has entered industries like biotechnology only after the State had done the messy groundwork, the genius and 'foolishness' of Steve Jobs led to massive profits and success, largely because Apple was able to ride the wave of massive State investments in the 'revolutionary' technologies that underpinned the iPhone and iPad: the Internet, GPS, touch-screen displays and communication technologies. Without these publicly funded technologies, there would have been no wave to foolishly surf.

This chapter is dedicated to telling the story of Apple, and in doing so, asks questions that provocatively challenge the ways in which the role of the State and Apple's success is viewed. In Chapter 8 we ask whether the US public benefited, in terms of employment and tax receipts, from these major risks taken by such an investment of US tax dollars? Or were the profits siphoned off and taxes avoided? Why is the State eagerly blamed for failed investments in ventures like the American Supersonic Transport (SST) project (when it 'picks losers'), and not praised for successful early stage investments in companies like Apple (when it 'picks winners')? And why is the State not rewarded for its direct investments in basic and applied research that lead to successful technologies that underpin revolutionary commercial products such as the iPod, the iPhone and the iPad?

The 'State' of Apple Innovation

Apple has been at the forefront of introducing the world's most popular electronic products as it continues to navigate the seemingly infinite frontiers of the digital revolution and the consumer electronics industry. The popularity and success of Apple products like the iPod, iPhone and iPad have altered the competitive landscape in mobile computing and communication technologies. In less than a decade the company's consumer electronic products have helped secure its place among the most valuable companies in the world, making record profits of $26 billion in 2011 for its owners. Apple's new iOS family of products brought great success to the company, but what remains relatively unknown to the average consumer is that the core technologies embedded in Apple's innovative products are in fact the results of decades of federal support for innovation. While the products owe their beautiful design and slick integration to the genius of Jobs and his large team, nearly every state-of-the-art technology found in the iPod, iPhone and iPad is an often overlooked and ignored achievement of the research efforts and funding support of the government and military.

Only about a decade ago Apple was best known for its innovative personal computer design and production. Established on 1 April 1976

Table 3. Apple's net sales, income and R&D figures between 1999 and 2011 (US$, millions)

Year	Net sales					Net Income	R&D	Sales/ R&D (%)
	Global	Americas	iPod	iPhone	iPad			
2011	108,249	8,315	7,453	47,057	20,358	25,922	2,429	2.24
2010	65,225	24,498	8,274	25,179	4,958	14,013	1,782	2.73
2009	36,537	16,142	8,091	6,754	n/a	5,704	1,333	3.65
2008	32,479	14,573	9,153	1,844	n/a	4,834	1,109	3.41
2007	24,006	11,596	8,305	123	n/a	3,495	782	3.26
2006	19,315	9,307	7,676	n/a	n/a	1,989	712	3.69
2005	13,931	6,590	4,540	n/a	n/a	1,335	534	3.83
2004	8,279	4,019	1,306	n/a	n/a	276	489	5.91
2003	6,207	3,181	345	n/a	n/a	69	471	7.59
2002	5,742	3,088	143	n/a	n/a	65	430	7.49
2001	5,363	2,996	n/a	n/a	n/a	(25)	430	8.02
2000	7,983	4,298	n/a	n/a	n/a	786	380	4.76
1999	6,134	3,527	n/a	n/a	n/a	601	314	5.12

Note: Apple's annual net sales, income and R&D figures were obtained from company's annual SEC 10-K filings.

in Cupertino, California by Steve Jobs, Steve Wozniak and Ronald Wayne, Apple was incorporated in 1977 by Jobs and Wozniak to sell the Apple I personal computer.[1] The company was originally named Apple Computer, Inc. and for 30 years focused on the production of personal computers. On 9 January 2007, the company announced it was removing the 'Computer' from its name, reflecting its shift in focus from personal computers to consumer electronics. This same year, Apple launched the iPhone and iPod Touch featuring its new mobile operating system, iOS, which is now used in other Apple products such as the iPad and Apple TV. Drawing on many of the technological capabilities of earlier generations of the iPod, the iPhone (and iPod Touch) featured a revolutionary multi-touch screen with a virtual keyboard as part of its new operating system.

---

1 In 1977, at the time of incorporation, Ronald Wayne sold his stake in the company to Jobs and Wozniak for $800.

Figure 10. Apple net sales by region and product (US$, billions)

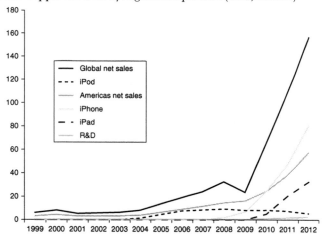

While Apple achieved notable success during its 30-year history by focusing on personal computers, the success and popularity of its new iOS products has far exceeded any of its former achievements in personal computing.[2] In the 5-year period following the launch of the iPhone and iPod Touch in 2007, Apple's global net sales increased nearly 460 per cent. As Table 3 illustrates, the new iOS product line represented nearly 70 per cent of the overall net sales of Apple in 2011.

The success and popularity of Apple's new products was quickly reflected in the company's revenues. In 2011, Apple's revenue ($76.4 billion) was so big that it surpassed the US government's operating cash balance ($73.7 billion) according to the latest figures from the US Treasury Department available at that time (BBC 2012). This surge in Apple's revenues was quickly translated into better market valuations and increased popularity of shares of Apple stock listed on the NASDAQ. As shown in Figure 11, Apple's stock price has increased from $8/share to $700/share since the iPod was first introduced by Steve Jobs on 23 October 2001. The launch of iOS products in 2007 enabled the company to secure a place among the most valuable companies in the US.[3]

---

2 When Apple first went public in 1980, its IPO generated more capital than any IPO since Ford Motor Company in 1956. This created more instant millionaires (around 300) than any other company in history (Malone 1999).

3 When Apple stocks were traded at peak levels on 10 April 2012, the surge in the stock prices pushed the company's overall market value to $600 billion. Only a few companies in the US such as GE ($600 billion in August 2000) and Microsoft ($619 billion, on 30 December 1999) have ever seen this incredible level of

Figure 11. Apple stock prices between 1990 and 2012[4]

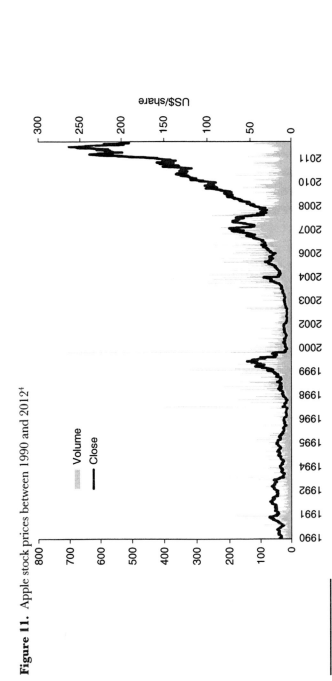

valuation (Svensson 2012). At the time of this writing, Apple's market value surpassed its long-time rival Microsoft's (nominal) record of a $619 billion valuation, as Apple stocks traded at a new peak of approximately $700/share between 18 and 19 September 2012.

4 Source: Yahoo! Finance, available online at http://finance.yahoo.com/charts?s=AAPL#symbol=aapl;range=19900102,20121231;compare=;indicator=split+volume;charttype=area;crosshair=on;ohlcvalues=0;logscale=off;source=undefined;Charts/Interactive (from 1 January 1990 to 31 December 2012).

Figure 12. Productive R&D or free lunch?

Source: Retrieved from Schmidt's article (2012) 'You Cannot Buy Innovation', Asymco, 30th January. Note: The author's calculations are based on the leading smartphone developers' 5-year average R&D figures between 2006 and 2011.

As indicated by Figure 10 and documented in company financial reports, the rampant growth in product sales following the launch of the iOS family of products paved the way for Apple's successful comeback from its wobbly conditions in the late 1980s. Interestingly, as the company continued to launch one new product after the next with increasing success, the company's financial reports reveal a steady decline in the global sales/R&D ratios, which indicate the portion of funds allocated to R&D activities in comparison to global product sales was falling over time (see Table 3). It could be argued that this is simply a testament to how unprecedented and exponential growth in product sales was relative to the annual growth of R&D expenditures. It could also be interpreted as the expected outcome of steady investment in R&D efforts. However, when viewed in the context of just how competitive the product markets are for consumer electronic products, these rather unimpressive R&D figures stand out. Long-time Apple analyst Horace Schmidt approaches this issue from a different angle by comparing Apple's R&D figures against that of the company's rivals. According to the data compiled by Schmidt (2012) and presented in Figure 12, Apple ranks in the bottom three in terms of the portion of sales allocated for supporting R&D activities among 13 of its top rivals.

Schmidt therefore inquires how Apple manages to get away with such a relatively low rate of R&D (as a percentage of sales ratios) in comparison to its competitors while still outpacing them in product sales. Many Apple experts explain this marginal R&D productivity as the company's success in implementing effective R&D programmes in a fashion that can only be seen in small technology start-ups. There is no doubt that Apple's ingenuity in engineering design, combined with Steve Job's commitment to simplicity, certainly contributed to its efficiency. But, the most crucial facts have been omitted when explaining this figure, which is that Apple concentrates its ingenuity not on *developing* new technologies and components, but on *integrating* them into an innovative architecture: its great in-house innovative product designs are, like that of many 'smart phone' producers, based on technologies that are mostly invented somewhere else, often backed by tax dollars. The following section will provide historical background on technologies that enabled the future glory of the company.

Surfing through the Waves of Technological Advancements

From its humble beginnings selling personal computer kits to its current place as the leader in the global information and communications industry, Apple has mastered designing and engineering technologies that were first developed and funded by the US government and military. Apple's capabilities are mainly related to their ability to (a) recognize emerging technologies with great potential, (b) apply complex engineering skills that successfully integrate recognized emerging technologies, and (c) maintain a clear corporate vision prioritizing design-oriented product development for ultimate user satisfaction. It is these capabilities that have enabled Apple to become a global powerhouse in the computer and electronics industry. During this period prior to launching its popular iOS platform products, Apple received enormous direct and/or indirect government support derived from three major areas:

1) Direct equity investment during the early stages of venture creation and growth.
2) Access to technologies that resulted from major government research programmes, military initiatives, public procurement contracts, or that were developed by public research institutions, all backed by state or federal dollars.

3) Creation of tax, trade or technology policies that supported US companies such as Apple that allowed them to sustain their innovation efforts during times when national and/or global challenges hindered US companies from staying ahead, or caused them to fall behind in the race for capturing world markets.

Each of these points is elaborated on in the following section, as the histories of key technological capabilities underlying Apple's success are traced.

From Apple I to the iPad: The State's very visible hand

From the very start, Jobs and Wozniak sought the support of various public and private funding sources in their effort to form and develop Apple. Each believed in the vision in their mind: that enormous value could be captured from the technologies made available mostly as a result of the prior efforts of the State. Venture capital pioneers and Silicon Valley legends such as Don Valentine, founder of Sequoia; Arthur Rock, founder of Arthur Rock & Company; Venrock, the venture capital arm of the Rockefeller Family; and Fairchild and Intel veteran Mike Markkula were among the first angel and equity investors who bought into their vision (Rao and Scaruffi 2011). In addition to the technologies that were going to help Apple revolutionize the computer industry, the company also received cash support from the government to implement its visionary business ideas in the computer industry. Prior to its IPO in 1980, Apple additionally secured $500,000 as an early stage equity investment from Continental Illinois Venture Corp. (CIVC), a Small Business Investment Company (SBIC) licensed by the Small Business Administration (a federal agency created in 1953) to invest in small firms (Slater 1983; Audretsch 1995).

As briefly discussed in Chapter 4, the emergence of personal computing was made possible by the technological breakthroughs achieved through various public–private partnerships established largely by government and military agencies (Markusen et al. 1991; Lazonick 2008; Block 2008; Breakthrough Institute 2010). When Apple was formed to sell the Apple I personal computer kit in 1976, the product's key technologies were based on public investments made in the computer industry during the 1960 and 1970s. Introduction of silicon during this period revolutionized the semiconductor industry and heralded in the start of a new age when access to affordable personal computers for wider consumer markets was made possible. These breakthroughs were the result of research carried out in various public–private partnerships at labs including those at DARPA, AT&T Bell Labs, Xerox PARC, Shockley and Fairchild, to name a few. Silicon Valley quickly became the nation's 'computer innovation hub' and the resulting climate stimulated and nurtured by the government's leading role in funding and research (both basic and applied) was harnessed by innovative entrepreneurs and private industry in what many observers have called the 'Internet California Gold Rush' or the 'Silicon Gold Rush' (Kenney 2003; Southwick 1999).

There are 12 major technologies integrated within the iPod, iPhone and iPad that stand out as features that are either 'enablers', or that differentiate these products from their rivals in the market. These include semiconductor devices such as (1) *microprocessors* or *central processing units* (CPU); (2) *dynamic random-access memory* (DRAM); as well as (3) *micro hard drive storage* or *hard drive disks* (HDD); (4) *liquid-crystal displays* (LCDs); (5) *lithium-polymer* (Li-pol) and *lithium-ion* (Li-ion) batteries; (6) *digital signal processing* (DSP), based on the advancement in *fast Fourier transform* (FFT) algorithms; (7) the *Internet*; (8) the *Hypertext Transfer Protocol* (HTTP) and *Hypertext Markup Language* (HTML); (9) and *cellular technology and networks* – all of which can be considered as the core enabler technologies for products such as the iPod, iPhone and iPad. On the other hand, (10) *global positioning systems* (GPS), (11) *click-wheel* navigation and *multi-touch screens*, (12) and *artificial intelligence with a voice-user interface program* (a.k.a. Apple's SIRI) are innovative features that have drastically impacted consumer expectations and user experiences, further enhancing the popularity and success of these products. The following sections take a closer look at the core technologies and features that Apple has managed to ingeniously integrate, initially in the iPod and later in the iPhone and iPad.

How State-funded research made possible Apple's 'invention' of the iPod

Shortly after introducing the first generation iPod in 2001, Apple began to create waves of new innovative products (e.g. the iPhone, iPad) that would eventually revolutionize the entire mobile entertainment industry. The iPod, a new portable handheld device, allowed consumers to store thousands of songs without using any cassettes or CDs. In the early 2000s, this new Apple device was gaining popularity among consumers and replacing portable devices such as Sony's Walkman and Discman in the market. This novel application of existing magnetic storage technology therefore enabled Apple to take on an iconic rival such as Sony, and eventually to rise to the top of the music and entertainment market (Adner 2012). The success of iPod in gaining a competitive market position was important in two major aspects: (1) the success was going to set the stage for Apple's comeback from years of stagnant, if not declining, growth; and, (2) the popularity of this new product would constitute precedence to a family of new innovative Apple iOS products. While this much is often known and noted, the fact that much of Apple's success lies in technologies that were developed through government support and -funded research is an often overlooked story to which I now turn.

Giant magnetoresistance (GMR), SPINTRONICS programme and hard disk drives

A rare instance of public recognition of the role played by State-backed technological research in paving the way for Apple products occurred during the 2007 Nobel Prize ceremony. European scientists Albert Fert and Peter Grünberg were awarded the 2007 Nobel Prize in Physics for their work in developing giant magnetoresistance (GMR). The GMR is a quantum mechanical effect observed in thin-film layered structures, for which the main application has been in magnetic field sensors used in hard disk drives (HDD) and other devices. In his ceremony remarks, Börje Johannson (2007), a member of the Royal Swedish Academy of Sciences, explained what the invention of GMR meant for society by attributing the existence of the iPod to this major scientific breakthrough.

Invention and commercialization of the micro hard drive is especially interesting since the technology development process from its origin to its current form illustrates the role of government not only in establishing the science base for innovation, but also in facilitating the advancement of abstract ideas into manufactured and commercially viable products (McCray 2009). What started as two separate and independent academic, State-funded and -supported research projects in physics in Germany and France culminated into one of the most successful technology breakthroughs in recent years, worthy of the Nobel Prize. Following this scientific breakthrough that Dr Fert and Dr Grünberg achieved, other researchers successfully expanded the size of data storage in conventional hard disk drives during the 1980s and 1990s, breaking new ground for future research and technological advancement (Overbye 2007).

While the major scientific breakthrough in GMR was accomplished in Europe, the US government played a critical role in the basic research as well as commercialization of this technology. Dr Peter Grünberg's laboratory was affiliated with Argonne National Laboratory (the US Department of Energy's largest R&D lab, located in Illinois) and received critical support from the Department of Energy (DoE) prior to his discovery (DoE 2007). Based on these developments in hard disk technology, companies such as IBM and Seagate moved quickly to translate the new knowledge into successful commercial products (McCray 2009). Despite the advances taking place in the hard drive industry at the time, they would experience similar competitive challenges faced by the semiconductor industry in the late 1980s, which I discuss in the following section on semiconductor devices.

In his 2009 study, McCray details how DARPA's wartime missions to create and sustain an innovation ecosystem for producing superior defence technologies was transformed during peace time by the new mission of transforming those prior investments into technologies supporting economic competitiveness. McCray (2009) documents that the Department of Defense (DoD) initiated the Technology Reinvestment Program (TRP) and allocated $800 million to upgrade the nation's existing technological capabilities following the Cold War. Through TRP, DARPA targeted dual-use technologies that would benefit the military as well as produce commercially viable technologies such as SPINTRONICS.[5] McCray (2009) especially documents the increase in scientific research efforts and publications taking place during DARPA's support for SPINTRONIC during 1990s. McCray (2009, 74) also argues that the role DARPA played in the advancement of this technology was not 'insignificant', simply because the programme was initiated during the time when Japanese competition in computer electronics was pushing computer giants such as IBM and Bell Labs to downsize spending on basic research.

Solid-state chemistry and silicon-based semiconductor devices

Since the launch of the first iPod, the first major new Apple product has evolved many times and also inspired the design of the future iPad

---

5 *SPIN TR*ansport electr*ONICS* (*SPINTRONICS*), initially called the 'Magnetic Materials and Devices' project, was a public–private consortium. It consisted of DARPA and industry leaders but was initiated (and funded) by DARPA in 1995, with the total government investment of $100 million during its existence.

and iPhone. Among the factors that have made the iPod, iPhone and iPad possible today are the small microchips that enable handheld smart devices to process large amounts of information and pass it through memory in a virtual instant. Today, central processing units (CPUs) depend on integrated circuits (ICs) that are considerably smaller in size and feature much larger memory capacity in comparison to the integrated circuits once used for processing needs and first designed by Jack Kilby and Robert Noyce in the 1950s. The invention of new silicon-based ICs led to technological developments in various fields in electronics. The rise of Personal Computers (PCs), cellular technology, the Internet and most of the electronic devices found on the market today utilize these smart, tiny devices. The journey of ICs from Bell Labs, Fairchild Semiconductor and Intel into devices such as iPhone or iPad was aided by procurement by the US Air Force and NASA. As the sole consumers of the first processing units based on this new circuit design, defence contracts helped fund the development of the infant microprocessor industry and those introducing complementary electronic equipment and devices that were simply unaffordable in regular commercial markets. Large-scale demand for microprocessors by the US Air Force was created by the Minuteman II missile programme. NASA's Apollo mission pushed the technological envelope, requiring significant improvements in the production process of microprocessors and also greater memory capacity. In turn, each of the government agencies helped to drive down the costs of integrated circuits significantly within a matter of years.[6]

Although the US was the home for early innovation in semiconductors, throughout the 1980s, Japan was developing advanced manufacturing capabilities and competitive memory products at a faster pace.[7] Given the significant role of semiconductors in defence technologies, the DoD considered the industry vital to its military capabilities and national security. Growing fears that the manufacturing equipment essential for production of these technologies, now vital to national defence, would be imported from countries like Japan spurred the DoD to act. The result was the Strategic Computing Initiative (SCI)

---

6 Lower costs became visible when the price of a microchip for the Apollo program fell from $1,000 per unit to anywhere between $20 to $30 per unit within just few years (Breakthrough 2010).

7 Roland and Shiman (2002, 153) document Japan's significant progress in the global chip market as having 0 per cent market share as opposed to the US's 100 per cent share in 1970s, to 80 per cent global market share in 1986.

which allocated over \$1 billion to support research efforts in advanced computer technologies between 1983 and 1993 (Roland and Shiman 2002). Additionally, the manufacturing of highly advanced technologies such as microprocessors had significant economic implications that required collaborative efforts between the government and industry. Recognizing the unique opportunity that semiconductor manufacturing would provide, and fearful of the consequences of lagging behind newly emerging competitors in semiconductor manufacturing such as Japan, the federal government gathered competitive domestic manufacturers and universities together to form a new partnership, the Semiconductor Manufacturing Technology (SEMATECH) consortium.

This move, to advance US-based semiconductor manufacturing technology and capability above and beyond that of the nation's competitors, was part of an overall effort to promote US economic and technological competitiveness globally. The process of organizing collaborative effort between semiconductor companies through SEMATECH was a challenge for the government. In order to make this partnership more appealing, the US government subsidized SEMATECH R&D with \$100 million annually. Over time, the members of the consortium came to recognize the benefits of the R&D partnership fostered by SEMATECH. The extensive knowledge sharing efforts that took place among members of SEMATECH helped them avoid duplicating research efforts and translated into less R&D spending. The advanced performance and affordability of microprocessors and memory chips today are to a great extent the result of years of government intervention and supervision (Irwin and Klenow 1996).

From capacitive sensing to click-wheels

As the pioneer of personal computers, Steve Jobs was on his second mission for re-revolutionizing them. His vision for Apple was to prepare the company for the post-computer era, in what he envisioned and often acknowledged in his interviews and media appearances as the new era of the consumer–computer relationship. During an interview at the 2010 D8 conference, Steve Jobs explained his vision of the future for computing by using the analogy of rapid urbanization and its effects on changing consumer views and the need for transportation (Jobs 2010). During his talk, Jobs redefined Apple's overall strategy as building a family of products around the concept of fragmented computing needs by different uses. Jobs often acknowledged his trust in the data processing technologies that had enabled Apple to come up with compact portable devices. It was these processing technologies leading to the portable iOS products that eventually replaced desktop computers. To do this, Apple had begun to work on building a periphery of portable iOS devices, with the Mac becoming the 'digital hub' that would integrate the entire product family together (Walker 2003).

Despite his strong opposition to tablet computers in the 1980s and 1990s, upon his return to Apple in the late 1990s, Jobs had decided that the time was right to focus once again on tablets. Underlying this shift in perspective was the fact that technology in semiconductor devices, batteries and displays had progressed significantly. However, a challenge still remained given the absence of sophisticated technology to successfully replace the *stylus pen*, a feature that Jobs had long despised and considered an inconvenience (Isaacson 2011, 490). The emergence of more sophisticated applications such as inertia scrolling, finger tracking and gesture-recognition systems for touch-screen-enabled displays presented Jobs and his team with the possibility of moving forward (and far beyond the stylus pen). Jobs and his team thus gathered experts together that could integrate these new technologies. The end results included replacing buttons and roll-balls on devices, developing a new navigation system, and enhancing input techniques on touch-screens.[8]

The iPod's click-wheel component that allowed users to navigate quickly through their music library was part of Apple's earlier attempts to implement touch-based features with finger scrolling. In addition to the micro hard disk drive for the storage of memory intensive digital records, the finger scrolling click-wheel feature also differentiated the iPod from the majority of other available portable music players. Although the application of finger scrolling was something novel at the time, the technology behind this feature had been around for decades. The click-wheel significantly benefitted from the *capacitive sensing* technology widely applied in the design of various other products.[9] In fact, the click-wheel feature was not the only feature of Apple products that benefitted from

---

8 During his TV interview on 30 April 2012, Tony Fadell, who was in the original iPod design team, revealed the challenges Apple was facing with finding ways to replace buttons on the new gadget. Available from: http://www.theverge.com/2012/4/30/2988484/on-the-verge-005-tony-fadell-interview (accessed 12 April 2013).

9 *Capacitive sensing* is a technology that draws on the human body's ability to act as a capacitor and store electric charge.

capacitive sensing. The iPod Touch, iPhone and iPad's *multi-touch screen* also embodies the same principles of finger(s)-operated scrolling on a glass screen.

E. A. Johnson, considered the inventor of capacitive touch-screens, published his first studies in the 1960s while working at Royal Radar Establishment (RRE), a British government agency established for R&D of defence-related technologies (Buxton 2012). One of the first notable developments of the touch-screen was at the European Organization for Nuclear Research (CERN) by Bent Stumpe and his colleague Frank Beck in 1973 (CERN 2010). Samuel Hurst's invention of resistive touch-screens was another notable breakthrough. Hurst's invention came right after leaving Oak Ridge National Laboratory (a national research laboratory in Tennessee established in 1943 and the site of the Manhattan Project and first functional nuclear reactor) for two years to teach at the University of Kentucky (Brown et al., n.d.). While at University of Kentucky, Hurst and his colleagues developed the first resistive touch-screens. Upon his return to Oak Ridge, they started a new company in 1971 to commercialize the new technology and produced the first functioning version in 1983 (Brown et al., n.d.). Earlier work on touch-screens in the 1970s and 1980s, such as that conducted by Johnson, Stumpe, Hurst and others has been carried forward in different public and private research labs, yet their work is considered foundational to today's important multi-touch applications (Buxton 2012). Among various other factors, moving from touchpads with limited functionality to multi-touch screens was a major leap forward for Apple in the smartphone race. Along with the other technological advancements they exploited, Apple has not only helped redefine the markets it competes from within but has also defined a different path for growth.

The Birth of the iPod's Siblings: The iPhone and iPad

Apple's new vision included radical redefinitions of conventional consumer products and was a great success. The introduction of the iPod generated over $22 billion in revenues for Apple. It was the company's most important global product until the iPhone was introduced in 2007. The cohesion of aesthetic design, system engineering and user experience combined with great marketing helped Apple rapidly penetrate and capture market share in different consumer electronics markets. Apple's new generation of iPods, iPhones and iPads have been built under the assumption that new consumer needs and preferences can be invented by hybridizing existing technologies developed after decades of government support. As a pioneer of the 'smartphone' revolution, Apple led the way in successfully integrating cellular communication, mobile computing and digital entertainment technologies within a single device. The iconic iPhone dramatically altered consumer expectations of what a cellular phone was and can do. With the introduction of the iPad, Apple transformed the portable computer industry that had been dominated for decades by laptops, netbooks and other devices. By offering a slimmer handheld device equipped with a large touch-screen and virtual keyboard, with solid Internet browsing and multimedia capabilities, along with broad compatibility across other Apple products and applications, the iPad virtually created a new niche and captured it at the same time. In less than a decade, Apple singlehandedly came to dominate the consumer electronics industry, a testament to Apple's ingenuity in consumer-oriented device product design and marketing, as well as their organizational capabilities in managing complex 'systems integration' (Lazonick 2011).

From click-wheels to multi-touch screens

Development of touch-screen displays recognizing multi-touch gestures was one of the most important technologies integrated into Apple's devices and for their successful introduction of pocket-sized portable devices such as the iPod. The technology allowed human–machine interaction through a new interface that allowed fingers to navigate the glass surface of LCD displays included with handheld devices. As with the *click-wheel* feature, the technology behind this ground-breaking new way to interface with electronic devices relied on earlier basic and applied research that had been supported by the State. During the 1990s, touch-screen technology was incorporated into a variety of products by numerous computer developers, including Apple, but the majority of the touch-screen technologies available during these earlier days were only capable of handling single-touch manipulation.[10] The introduction of multi-touch scrolling and gestures was developed by Wayne Westerman and John Elias at the University of Delaware (Westerman 1999).

---

10 As a world-renowned expert on touch-screen technology, Bill Buxton provides an extensive archive of electronic devices with touch-screen applications. The list of Apple products with the touchpad feature can be seen online at http://research.microsoft.com/en-us/um/people/bibuxton/buxtoncollection/ (accessed 12 April 2013).

Wayne Westerman was a doctoral candidate under the supervision of Professor John Elias studying neuromorphic systems at the (publicly funded) University of Delaware, as part of the National Science Foundation (NSF) and Central Intelligence Agency/Director of Central Intelligence (CIA/DCI) Post-Doctoral Fellowship programme (Westerman 1999). Following the completion of Westerman's PhD, he and Elias commercialized this new technology after founding the FingerWorks company. Their new product, called 'iGesture Numpad', enabled many computer users to enter input by applying 'zero-force' pressure on an electronic screen with no need of additional devices such as a keyboard or a mouse. The underlying scientific base and patent application for the new finger tracking and gesture identification system was built on the earlier studies on *capacitive sensing* and *touch-screen* technologies. FingerWorks' successful attempt to translate prior touch-screen research into a commercial product was quickly recognized by Apple, which was interested in developing a multi-touch navigation capability on a fully glass LCD display for the new generation iOS products. FingerWorks was acquired by Apple in 2005 prior to the launch of Apple's first generation iPhone in 2007, and today this new technology lies at the heart of the coveted multi-touch screen featured on Apple's iOS products. As a result, Westerman and Elias, with funding from government agencies, produced a technology that has revolutionized the multi-billion dollar mobile electronic devices industry. Apple's highly comprehensive intellectual property portfolio had benefitted, once again, from technology that was originally underwritten by the State.

Internet and HTTP/HTML

Although the iPhone appears to be a 'cool' gadget with its cutting-edge technology features and hardware components, what makes a phone 'smart' is its ability to connect phone users to the virtual world at any point in time. With the artificial intelligence application named SIRI on board, the iPhone appears to be attempting to outsmart its users. After replacing the handset-industry-standard keypads with touch-screens, SIRI is Apple's attempt to transform input entry and navigation interfaces. As Apple's 'smartphone' continues to evolve into an even smarter device, it is important to recognize and value the underlying and necessary intelligence and technological capabilities that have smart-wired, if you will, this smart device. If hardware, software, memory and the processor were to be the body, soul and brain of a computer, what does the Internet, Hypertext Transfer Protocol (HTTP) or Hypertext Markup Language (HTML) mean to any computer or smart device? Or, what would a computer or smart device be worth in the absence of Internet or without cellular communication capability? Answers to these questions can help us understand the value of the networking capabilities of smart devices. But more importantly, they can help us understand the value of support efforts that the government played in the process of inventing and developing cellular technology, the Internet and satellites.

During the Cold War era, US authorities were concerned about possible nuclear attacks and the state of communication networks following the aftermath of possible attacks. Paul Baran, a researcher at RAND – an organization with its origins in the US Air Force's project for 'Research and Development', or RAND for short – recommended a solution that envisioned a distributed network of communication stations as opposed to centralized switching facilities. With a decentralized communication system in place, the command and network system would survive during and after nuclear attacks (Research and Development 2011).[11] The technological challenges of devising such a network were overcome thanks to the various teams assembled by DARPA to work on networking stations and the transmission of information. Although DARPA approached AT&T and IBM to build such a network, both companies declined the request believing that such a network was a threat to their business; with the help of the State-owned British Post Office, DARPA successfully networked various stations from the west to east coast (Abbate 1999). From the 1970s through the 1990s, DARPA funded the necessary communication protocol (TCP/IP), operating system (UNIX) and email programs needed for the communication system, while the National Science Foundation (NSF) initiated the development of the first high-speed digital networks in the US (Kenney 2003).

Meanwhile, in the late 1980s, British scientist Tim Berners-Lee was developing the Hypertext Markup Language (HTML), uniform resource locators (URL) and uniform Hypertext Transfer Protocol

---

11 Other goals of the new network project were (a) to save computing costs, as government contractors across the US would be able to share computer resources; and (b) to advance the 'state-of-the-art' in data communications to enable transfer of information between machines over long distances. An additional goal (c) was to foster collaboration between contracted researchers in different locations.

(HTTP) (Wright 1997). Berners-Lee, with the help of another computer scientist named Robert Cailliau, implemented the first successful HTTP for the computers installed at CERN. Berners-Lee and Cailliau's 1989 manifesto describing the construction of the World Wide Web eventually became the international standard for computers all over the world to connect. Public funding has played a significant role for the Internet from its conception to its worldwide application. The Internet is now in many ways a foundational technology that has affected the course of world history by allowing users all over the globe to engage in knowledge sharing and commerce using computers and popular smart gadgets such as the iPhone, iPod or iPad.

GPS and SIRI

Another great feature that an iPod, iPhone or iPad offers is global positioning system (GPS) integration. GPS was an attempt by the DoD to digitize worldwide geographic positioning to enhance the coordination and accuracy of deployed military assets (Breakthrough Institute 2010). What initially began in the 1970s as a strictly military-use-only technology is now widely available to civilians for various uses. In fact, civilian use of GPS quickly outnumbered military utilization following the release of GPS for public applications in the mid-1990s. Yet, even today, the US Air Force has been at the forefront of developing and maintaining the system, which costs the government an average of $705 million annually.[12] An iPhone user can search for a nearby restaurant or an address, based on the NAVSTAR GPS system, which consists of a 24-satellite constellation providing global navigation and timing data for its users. This technology, as well as the infrastructure of the system, would have been impossible without the government taking the initiative and making the necessary financial commitment for such a highly complex system.

Apple's latest iPhone feature is a virtual personal assistant known as SIRI. And, like most of the other key technological features in Apple's iOS products, SIRI has its roots in federal funding and research. SIRI is an artificial intelligence program consisting of machine learning, natural language processing and a Web search algorithm (Roush 2010). In 2000, DARPA asked the Stanford Research Institute (SRI) to take

---

12 The DoD estimates that, in 2000 dollars, the development and procedure of the system cost the Air Force $5.6 billion between 1973 and 2000 (DoD 2011). The figure does not include military user equipment.

the lead on a project to develop a sort of 'virtual office assistant' to assist military personnel. SRI was put in charge of coordinating the 'Cognitive Assistant that Learns and Organizes' (CALO) project which included 20 universities all over the US collaborating to develop the necessary technology base. When the iPhone was launched in 2007, SRI recognized the opportunity for CALO as a smartphone application and then commercialized the technology by forming 'SIRI' as a venture-backed start-up in the same year. In 2010, SIRI was acquired by Apple for an amount that is undisclosed by both parties.

Changing industry standards from keypad to touchpad input and adding GPS navigation was a significant achievement when iPod was first introduced. A second game-changer for cell phone, media player and tablet computer developers was the introduction of multi-touch screens and gesture recognition. With SIRI, Apple introduced another radical idea for a device input mechanism that has been integrated within various iOS features and applications. The introduction of SIRI has launched a new round of redefining standards of human–machine interaction and creates a new means of interaction between the user and the machine. Steve Jobs often acknowledged the potential of artificial intelligence and his interest in the future of the technology. During his 2010 interview with Walt Mossberg and Kara Swisher (2010) at the California D8 conference, Jobs had shared his excitement about the recent acquisition of SIRI by Apple, and talked about the great potential the technology offered. Once again, Apple is on the verge of building the future for information and communication industry based on the radically complex ideas and technologies conceived and patiently fostered by the government.

Battery, display and other technologies

The story of the liquid-crystal display (LCD) shares great similarities with the hard disk drive, microprocessor and memory chip (among other major technologies) that emerged during the Cold War era: it is rooted in the US military's need to strengthen its technological capabilities as a matter of national security. Rising competition from the Japanese flat panel display (FPD) industry was a concern for the DoD because the US military's future demand for the technology could not be met solely by the Japanese suppliers. Given this determination, the DoD began implementing a variety of programmes geared towards strengthening the industry's competitiveness, including the formation of an industry consortium and deployment of new resources for the improvement of manufacturing capabilities and commercial products.

The major breakthrough in LCD technology came about during the 1970s, when the thin-film transistor (TFT) was being developed at the laboratory of Westinghouse under the direction of Peter Brody. The research carried out at Westinghouse was almost entirely funded by the US Army (Hart and Borrus 1992). However, when management at Westinghouse decided to shut down the research, Brody sought out possible funding opportunities elsewhere in the hopes of commercializing this technology independently. In the process of appealing for contracts to ramp up the production of TFT displays, Brody contacted a number of top computer and electronic companies including Apple and others such as Xerox, 3M, IBM, DEC and Compaq. All these major private companies refused to sign on with Brody largely because they doubted his ability to build the manufacturing capability necessary to provide the product at a competitive price compared to his Japanese counterparts (Florida and Browdy 1991, 51). In 1988, after receiving a $7.8 million contract from DARPA, Brody established Magnascreen to develop the TFT-LCD. This advancement in the LCD technology became the basis for the new generation displays for the portable electronic devices such as microcomputers, phones, etc.

Florida and Browdy argued that this pattern of the inability of private actors to build or sustain manufacturing capabilities in various high-technology fields presented a broader problem with the nation's innovation system:

> The loss of this [TFT-LCD] display technology reveals fundamental weaknesses of the U.S. high-technology system. Not only did our large corporations lack the vision and the persistence to turn this invention into a marketable product, but the venture capital financiers, who made possible such high-technology industries as semiconductors and personal computers, failed too. Neither large nor small firms were able to match a dazzling innovation with the manufacturing muscle needed for commercial production. (1991, 43)

In an attempt to retain the manufacturing of TFT-LCDs in the US, the Advanced Display Manufacturers of America Research Consortium (ADMARC) was established by the major display manufacturers with initial funding appearing from the National Institute of Standards and Technology's (NIST) Advanced Technology Program (ATP)

(Florida and Browdy 1991). The industry also received additional assistance from the US government in the form of antidumping tariffs (while at the same time touting the 'free competition' line), as well as funds and contracts provided by various military or civilian agencies that supported many start-ups in the US as part of an effort to develop manufacturing capabilities of TFT-LCDs in the 1990s (OTA 1995).

The lithium-ion battery is another example of a US-invented but Japanese-perfected and manufactured-in-volume technology. John B. Goodenough who pioneered the early research on lithium-ion battery technology received his main funding support from the Department of Energy (DoE) and National Science Foundation (NSF) in the late 1980s (Henderson 2004; OSTI 2009). Major scientific breakthroughs accomplished at the University of Texas at Austin were quickly commercialized and launched in 1991 by the Japanese electronics giant Sony. In a 2005 working paper for the National Institute of Standards and Technology (NIST), Ralph J. Brodd (2005) identified issues with the advanced battery industry innovation model that were similar to the issues within the TFT-LCD industry. Another major scientific success faded away without greater value being captured in the form of US-based high-volume manufacture. Brodd's study identifies the factors hindering the volume production of lithium-ion batteries in the US, but particularly placed emphasis on the short-termist approach of US corporations and venture capitalists. Brodd (2005, 22) argued that their short-termism was based upon achieving rapid financial returns (in comparison to their Japanese competitors' focus on maximizing market share in the long run), which often discouraged them from any interest in building the domestic manufacturing capabilities while encouraging outsourcing of manufacture as an option.

Absence of a battery technology that met the storage capacity needs of increasingly powerful electronic devices posed one of the greatest challenges that the electronics industry faced following the revolution in semiconductor devices. The invention of lithium-ion technology enabled portable devices to become much slimmer and lighter as battery capacity increased relative to size. Once again, the federal government stepped in to assist smaller battery companies through a variety of agencies and programmes that invested in the industry in an effort to develop the necessary manufacturing capabilities (Brodd 2005) – not only for electronic devices but, equally or even more importantly, for 'zero-emission' electric vehicles. The US government has been actively involved with the energy

Figure 13. Origins of popular Apple products

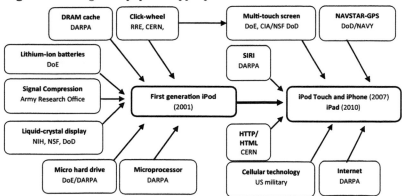

Source: Author's own drawing based on the OSTP diagram 'Impact on Basic Research on Innovation' that illustrates the benefits of basic research on innovation (2006, 8).

industry for decades as part of a broader effort to address economic and social needs, which is extensively discussed in Chapters 6 and 7.

State-of-the-art iOS products are highly complex electronic devices. Despite the fundamental differences in use, each device embodies numerous technologies that are often present in all the devices. Cellular technology is available for most of Apple's devices with the exception of its iPod media players. Cellular communication technology received enormous government support in its early days. The Breakthrough Report (2010, 5) examines the role of the US military in advancing the radiotelephony technology in the twentieth century. The Office of Science and Technology Policy (2006, 8) also documented the role of State support in the digital signal processing (DSP) technology that came about following scientific advancements in the application of the fast Fourier transform (FDT) algorithm during the 1980s. This new signal processing approach enabled real-time processing of sound (such as during a two-way phone call) as well as real-time processing of large audio or multimedia files that can improve the quality of their playback. DSP is considered be a core feature of iOS products with a media player function (Devlin 2002).

Did the US Government 'Pick' the iPod?

In a 2006 policy document where former US president George W. Bush laid out the nation's innovation strategy, the various component technologies that were featured in the first generation iPod were linked to their origins as part of the basic and applied research funded by US tax dollars (OSTP 2006). Although lacking substantial context and/or literal figures, the report does include a diagram illustrating the origins of iPod's component technologies such as its hard disk drive, Li-ion battery, LCD, DRAM cache, signal processing, etc. Figure 13 expands on the OSTP diagram by further mapping out the tech components featured in later Apple products like the iPod Touch, iPhone and iPad.

Fostering an Indigenous Sector

In addition to government efforts nurturing the science base and fostering innovation in the US, the US government has also played a critical role in protecting the intellectual 'property' of companies like Apple, and ensuring that it is protected against other trade right violations. The federal government has actively fought on behalf of companies like Apple to allow it secure access to the global consumer market, and it is a crucial partner in establishing and maintaining global competitive advantage for these companies (Prestowitz 2012). Although US-based corporations define themselves as transnational entities whose existence transcend political borders, Washington is the first place they usually turn to when conflicts in the global market arise. Accessing foreign markets protected by trade restrictions was only possible with US government acting as a backer and vanguard. For example, in the 1980s Apple had difficulties entering the Japanese market. The company called on the US government for assistance arguing that it was the government's obligation to assist the company in opening the Japanese market to US products by appealing to the Japanese government (Lyons 2012). When unfettered global competition hit home, companies such as Apple were backed by the government to ensure that intellectual property laws were carefully enforced all over the world. The added protection created for Apple by local and federal authorities continues to provide this form of subsidy, which allows the company to continue innovating.

Additionally, the US government has been providing various other types of tax and procurement support that greatly benefits American companies such as Apple. According to a Treasury Department document, companies (including Apple) overall claimed $8.3 billion in research and experiment (R&E) tax credits in 2008 (Office of Tax Policy 2011). Additionally, California provides generous R&D tax packages for which computer and electronics companies are the largest applicants (Ibele 2003).[13] Since 1996, Apple has reportedly claimed $412 million in R&D tax credits of all kinds (Duhigg and Kocieniewski 2012).

Government procurement policies have supported Apple through various critical stages, which made it possible for the company to survive in the midst of ferocious competition against its competitors. Public schools in the US have been loyal Apple customers, purchasing their computers and software each year since the 1990s.[14] Klooster (2009) argues that public schools were a critical market for Apple as it reeled from its Apple III and Lisa product flops in the late 1980s. Provisions in the (post–financial crisis) 2009 American Recovery and Reinvestment Act (ARRA) provided incentives to benefit computer and electronics companies in the US. For instance, among various other incentives, through a small change in the scope of IRS 529 plans, 'computer technology and equipment' purchases were defined as a qualified education expense, which is expected to boost up Apple's computer, tablet and software sales.[15]

In sum, 'finding what you love' and doing it while also being 'foolish' is much easier in a country in which the State plays the pivotal serious role of taking on the development of high-risk technologies, making the early, large and high-risk investments, and then sustaining them until such time that the later-stage private actors can appear to 'play around and have fun'. Thus, while 'free market' pundits continue to warn of the danger of government 'picking winners', it can be said that various US government policies laid the foundation that provided Apple with

---

13 According to a 2003 state of California legislative report assessing the results of California's research and development tax credit (RDC) programme, SMEs are the largest applicants in terms of number of claims (over 60 per cent of the applicants), while larger companies have the largest share of claims in total value (over 60 per cent of the total value of RDC claims).

14 Apple's share of the total educational computer purchases of US elementary and high schools reached 58 per cent in 1994 (Flynn 1995). Educators have also welcomed Apple's new 'textbook initiative', which is expected to reduce textbook prices significantly by increasing school use of virtual textbooks. These virtual textbooks would require iPad use and would be expected to increase Apple's iPad sales in the coming years.

15 Section 529 of the Internal Revenue Code (US tax code) includes certain tax advantages, also known as 'qualified tuition programs' or 'college savings plans'. A legislative amendment in 2011 allowed parents and students to use the funds in their college saving accounts for purchasing computers, computer equipment and accessories (including iPads). None of these purchases were considered eligible school expenses for account withdrawals before (Ebeling 2011).

the tools to become a major industry player in one of the most dynamic high-tech industries of the twenty-first century so far. Without the frequent targeted investment and intervention of the US government it is likely that most would-be 'Apples' would be losers in the global race to dominate the computing and communications age. The company's organizational success in integrating complex technologies into user-friendly and attractive devices supplemented with powerful software mediums should not be marginalized, however it is indisputable that most of Apple's best technologies exist because of the prior collective and cumulative efforts driven by the State; which were made in the face of uncertainty and often in the name of, if not national security, then economic competitiveness.

In Chapter 8, I will return to Apple, to ask what the State received back in return for the entrepreneurial, risky investments it made in both Apple the company, as well as in all the 'revolutionary' technologies that make the iPhone so 'smart'. As we will see, this is perhaps the most crucial question policymakers must ask themselves in the twenty-first century; when on the one hand we want an 'active' State with the courage to lead the next technological 'green revolution'; while on the other hand, the State has to create a revolution with constrained budgets and pressure to pursue austerity measures. Finding a solution to this 'risk–reward nexus' will be key to this dilemma.

Chapter 6

PUSHING VS. NUDGING THE GREEN INDUSTRIAL REVOLUTION

The early days at ARPA-E were pretty insane. Its first couple of employees had to put out its first solicitation, and it was inundated with 3,700 applications for its first 37 grants, which crashed the federal computer system. But they attracted an absurdly high-powered team of brainiacs: a thermodynamics expert from Intel, an MIT electrical engineering professor, a clean-tech venture capitalist who also taught at MIT. The director, Arun Majumdar, had run Berkeley's nanotechnology institute. His deputy, Eric Toone, was a Duke biochemistry professor and entrepreneur. Arun liked to say that it was a band of brothers; I like to think of it as a $400 million Manhattan Project tucked inside the $800 billion stimulus.

Michael Grunwald (in Andersen 2012)

The success of Apple helps to illustrate how the information and communication technology revolution was born as a result of State investments, and created a new high-tech global infrastructure and many of the key technologies which could drive the success of companies like Apple. In contrast, the 'green industrial revolution' being pushed by State efforts around the globe should be viewed as an attempt to transform one of the most massive infrastructures already in existence: the energy infrastructure. The massive sunk costs presented by energy infrastructure require not just support for innovative new technologies and companies, but sustained support for the markets within which those technologies compete (Hopkins and Lazonick 2012).

We cannot influence the emergence of innovative new 'green' companies, technologies, or transform energy markets without policies directed at both the demand- and supply-side, since each influences either the structure and function of markets or the investment of firms attempting to grow or transition into green technology sectors. Generally speaking, demand-side policies are environmental regulations that impact energy consumption patterns. Supply-side policies are focused on how energy is generated and distributed, and influence innovation in energy technologies and their rapid adoption. Both are critical given that demand-side policy can help set a technological direction (what is the technology for?) that also includes support for solutions (low carbon/no carbon and renewables). Examples of demand-side policies include Renewable Portfolio Standards, greenhouse gas emission reduction targets, energy-intensity targets (a measure of energy use per unit of GDP), new building standards, or even a 'carbon tax'. Each targets energy consumption patterns and establishes a demand for reduced pollution, increased clean energy, or better energy-system efficiency. Supply-side policies could include tax credits, subsidies, loans, grants or other monetary benefits for specific energy technologies, favourable energy pricing schemes (such as 'feed-in tariffs'), R&D contracts and funding for discovery and development of innovations, and so on. Such policies support the technologies that complement and provide a solution to demand-side policies.

Yet there are hundreds, if not thousands of relevant energy policies currently in play around the world, some of which have existed for decades. They occur at international, national, state and local levels. But all of the countries mentioned in this chapter have relied on both demand- and supply-side policies to supercharge the development of green industry (to very different outcomes). Many who write on the subject of energy policy forget that until wind turbines and solar PV panels (the focus of Chapter 7) can produce energy at a cost equal to or lower than those of fossil fuels they will likely continue to be marginal technologies that cannot accelerate the transition so badly needed to mitigate climate change. Understanding how businesses transform government support mechanisms into lower-cost, higher-performance products through the innovation process is typically the 'missing link' in discussions of energy policy, and this missing link can undermine not just our desire to push an energy transition – but to do it with high-road investments in innovation. State support for clean technologies must continue until they overcome the sunk-cost advantage of incumbent technologies, and these sunk costs are a century long in some cases.

That is why much of this chapter focuses on supply-side support mechanisms (although I of course also discuss crucial demand-side policies). In the current policy environment, many countries have been aggressively deploying public finance with the aim of promoting green industry – and this is the most direct support possible for business development. It is also a better 'spur' for green industrial development, given that existing demand-side policies all assume, ultimately, that a 'dynamic private sector' will readily respond to a call for reduced pollution or more renewable energy. Not only that, but, demand-side policies do not necessarily include provisions that force targets to be met with 'domestic resources' or local economic development.[1] Demand-side policies are critical, and their importance is real – especially in signalling future market potential – but they too often become pleas for change and like supply-side policies, are vulnerable to changing political administrations. To be successful they must address the uncertainty and cost behind the innovations that are required to meet the targets.[2]

Supply-side policies are important for putting money 'where the mouth is', by financing firms directly or indirectly through the subsidy of long-term market growth, in the hope that it will accelerate the formation of innovative companies that can deliver a green industrial revolution. Given the success of these policies, and in addition, the success and spread of renewable energy sources like wind and solar power, the opportunity for 'smart grids' to digitize energy supply networks is both created and stabilized. I say created, because the intermittent nature of renewable power will have to be more closely managed. I say stabilized, because the need ('demand') for smart grid technology will be greatest in the countries that go farthest towards integrating renewable energy into their grids. Success in transforming our energy system is as full of collective and complementary industrial changes, in other words, but getting serious about renewable energy is a necessary and critical step towards bringing energy technology into the twenty-first century.

As such, this chapter examines the prospects of a new technological revolution based on innovations that tackle climate change. I begin with a

---

1 US states, for example, often have the ability to 'trade' renewable energy credits (RECs), or securitized environmental benefits. The RECs permit states to meet their renewable targets through the purchase of RECs rather than by actual energy infrastructure change. While it is good to meet targets, there is no guarantee that doing so will be achieved with state-based supply chains or companies, leaving many of the economic benefits of 'going green' on the table.

2 Martinot (2013, 9) shows that renewable development targets are a useful proxy for tracking which countries are most aggressively pursuing a renewable energy/low-carbon agenda: '120 countries have various types of policy tragets for long-term shares of renewable energy, including a binding 20% target for the European Union' while countries like 'Denmark (100%) and Germany (60%)' and China are moving even further towards a green transistion for no later than '2030 or 2050'.

brief discussion of the factors driving interest in developing a green economy. The second section introduces the different approaches that countries are taking to build a 'green' economy, with the double aim of recovering from the current economic recession and mitigating environmental problems. Some countries, like China and Germany, are making a big push into clean technology sectors with coherent policy frameworks that include demand and supply measures coordinated by an overarching 'green' vision. Other countries, like the US, the UK and other European laggards are deploying patchy strategies that lack a clear direction and fail to offer long-term incentives, resulting in a start–stop approach to green initiatives that produce dubious outcomes at best.

The ambivalent US approach is examined in detail in the third section, which shows how contradictory governmental initiatives prevent the full deployment of a clean technology sector, constraining investment and stalling broad deployment of new energy technologies. The US approach is important because it represents a paradigmatic case, where historic financial commitment by the public sector is challenged by ambiguous governmental initiatives: on the one hand, it is trying to 'nudge' the development of green technologies by stimulating venture capitalists (VC) to take a leading role; on the other hand, the US is also attempting to 'push' by funding coordinated public R&D and deployment initiatives. Meanwhile, current efforts to support manufacturing growth have transformed into a classic argument against 'picking winners' instead of an examination of how the State can more actively finance necessary supply chain development. The US has taken a 'fund everything' approach, hoping that a breakthrough disruptive energy innovation, that might also be 'green', will sooner or later emerge in labs, and that VCs will appear to finance the leading start-ups and make these innovative technologies commercially viable and eventually widely diffused. This has not been the case, because the development of many clean technologies requires long-term financial commitments of a kind that VCs are not willing or able to undertake. The fourth section concludes by analysing the different national approaches discussed in the second and third sections.

Funding a Green Industrial Revolution

First, what is a 'green industrial revolution'? There are many ways to conceptualize a green industrial revolution, but the basic premise is that the current global industrial system must be radically transformed into one that is environmentally sustainable. Sustainability will require an energy transition that places non-polluting clean energy technologies at the fore. It moves us away from dependence on finite fossil and nuclear fuels and favours 'infinite' sources of fuel – the 'renewable' fuels that originate from the sun. Building a sustainable industrial system also requires technologies for recyclable materials, advanced waste management, better agricultural practices, stronger energy efficiency measures across sectors, and water desalinization infrastructures (to address resource and water scarcity, for instance). Without question, any green industrial revolution must transform existing economic sectors and create new ones. It is a direction that continues without a clear stopping point but with a growing public benefit in the form of avoided planetary destruction. This is a point that is complementary to the work of Perez (2002, 2012) where it is argued that 'green' is not a revolution but the full 'deployment' of the IT revolution throughout all sectors in the economy – transforming areas such as product obsolescence, by making 'maintenance' a high-tech area rather than a marginal low-tech one.

Closely associated with the need for a green industrial revolution is the problem of climate change. Climate change is a global environmental crisis that impacts all of us and which is a direct result of current centres of major economic activity. Climate change is driven by the emission of greenhouse gases (GHGs), and the majority of these gases are a by-product of the dominant energy production technologies (fuelled especially by coal, increasingly natural gas, but also oil) that power modern economies. As such, energy generation is a sector where innovation and change are critically needed if the worst impacts of climate change are to be avoided. The range of choices available to policymakers is broad, given that greenhouse gas emissions can be managed or avoided with technology, mandate, or through complex economic regulations that incentivize or discourage decision making at the firm or individual level.

Given that fossil fuel technologies and infrastructures are embedded in modern societies, creating 'carbon lock-in' (see Unruh 2000), this chapter takes clean energy as a paradigmatic example of technology that needs to be widely deployed in order for the green industrial revolution to succeed. Solar and wind power, which emit no pollutants during their operation, are two exemplary clean energy technologies with established histories that are carefully examined in the next chapter. Wind and solar power are technologies that also provide expanded opportunities for the innovative IT sector. IT benefits from the added 'direction' provided by clean energy initiatives. As characteristically 'intermittent' and 'diffuse' sources of energy, wind and solar power have benefitted from what Madrigal (2011, 263) describes as 'throwing software at the problem': increasing the productivity and reliability of wind and solar projects with advanced computer modelling, management of power production and remote monitoring. Investments in a 'smart grid' are meant to digitize modern energy systems to optimize the flexibility, performance and efficiency of clean technologies while providing advanced management options to grid operators and end users. Such flexibility and control is not unlike the sort that emerged with digitized communication networks. The ICT revolution that created digitized communications not only created new commercial opportunities (such as through the medium of the Internet), but has provided an invaluable platform for the generation, collection, access and dissemination of knowledge of all forms. Given time and broad deployment, the smart grid could change the way we think about energy, create new commercial opportunities and improve the economics of renewable energy by establishing new tools for optimal energy supply management and demand response.

To begin the green industrial revolution and to tackle climate change we are again in need of an active State that takes on the high uncertainty of its early stages, which the business sector fears. Yet, despite the buzz surrounding 'clean technology' as the 'new economic frontier', and the 'green revolution' as the imminent third 'industrial revolution', there is in reality little that is truly new about many clean technologies. For example, wind and solar power have histories reaching back well over 100 years (and further still if considering non-electrical exploitation of the power sources). While the industrial revolution is often told as a story of steam and fossil fuels (Barca 2011), we have relied in the past on what would today be considered biomass, wind and hydro power.[3] Despite our past experience and current knowledge of 'clean' energy technologies, government support seeking to make clean energy a dominant part of the energy mix has historically either been non-existent, or tended to wax and wane. The lack of focus and commitment to a clean technology future is what is preventing a more rapid transformation of the fossil energy infrastructure into a clean energy infrastructure.

---

3 Some examples include water wheels, windmills, the sail, and wood burning for heat or steam. Animal power is another relevant source of energy used by humans in the past, aiding agricultural production and providing a primary mode of transportation.

But there are some rays of hope. In this early part of the twenty-first century, governments around the world have once again taken the lead in pumping up research and development (R&D) of many clean technologies like wind and solar power, and efforts are being made to establish modernized energy grids. They also subsidize and support the growth of leading manufacturers that compete for domestic and global market leadership. Finally, governments deploy both policy and finance to encourage stable development of competitive markets for renewable energy. As has been the case in the development of other industries such as biotech and IT, private businesses have entered the game only after successful government initiatives absorb most of the uncertainty and not a little risk of developing new energy technologies in the first place.

The 'green' industry is still in its early stages: it is characterized by both market and technological uncertainty. It will not develop 'naturally' through market forces, in part because of embedded energy infrastructure but also because of a failure of markets to value sustainability or to punish waste and pollution. In the face of such uncertainty, the business sector will not enter until the riskiest and most capital-intensive investments have been made, or until there are coherent and systematic policy signals in place. As in the early stage of IT, biotech and nanotech industries, there is little indication that the business sector alone would enter the new 'green' sector and drive it forward in absence of strong and active government policy. Thus, while 'nudging' might incentivize a few entrepreneurs to act, most business actors will need stronger signals to justify their engagement in clean technology innovation. Only long-term policy decisions can reduce the uncertainty of transforming core business from legacy into clean technologies. In fact, no other high-tech industry has been created or transformed with a 'nudge'. Most likely, a strong 'push' is needed.

National Approaches to Green Economic Development

There are differences in how countries are reacting to the challenge of developing a green economy. This section shows how some countries are using the post-crisis stimulus spending as a way to direct government investments into global clean technology industries, with two goals: (a) to provide economic growth, while (b) mitigating climate change. While some countries lead, others are lagging behind. As investments in innovation are cumulative and the results are 'path dependent' (innovation today is dependent on innovation yesterday), it

Figure 14. Global new investment in renewable energy (US$, billions)

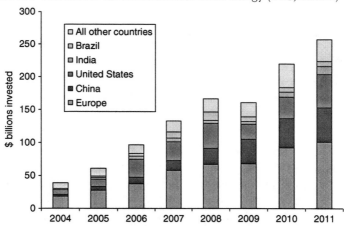

Source: Frankfurt School of Finance and Management (2012).

is likely that the leaders emerging from this race will remain leaders for years to come. In other words, those acting first will enjoy a first-mover advantage.

Yet, failure of some governments to provide the 'vision' and to really 'push' clean technology is having an impact on the amount of investment occurring. Countries that pursue a 'patchy' policy towards clean technology will not stimulate enough investment to alter their 'carbon footprints', nor should they expect to host the clean technology leaders of the future. An example of a country going for a 'big push' is China; Germany is also a first mover among European countries. The US has shown contradictory trends, with the State making early and substantive investments in green technologies. By proceeding without a clear vision and goal in mind, however, and without a long-term commitment to several key technologies, the US has failed to significantly alter its energy mix. The UK is also lagging behind.[4]

In the US, the 2009 American Recovery and Reinvestment Act stimulus packages devoted 11.5 per cent of their budget to clean technology investments, lower than China (34.3 per cent), France (21 per cent) or South Korea (80.5 per cent), but higher than the UK (6.9 per cent). In July 2010 the South Korean government announced

---

4 Other EU countries that seem to be moving ahead are Finland, France, Denmark and Norway, while Ireland and Spain seem lagging behind in promoting green economic development.

Figure 15. Government energy R&D spend as % GDP in 13 countries, 2007

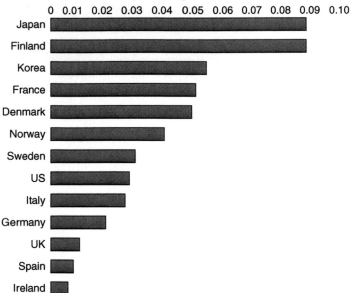

Source: UK Committee on Climate Change (2010, 22).

that it would double its spending on green research to the equivalent of $2.9 billion by 2013 (almost 2 per cent of its annual GDP), which means that between 2009 and 2013 it will have spent £59 billion on this type of research in total. Figure 14 shows that Europe, the US and China have dominated global new investment in renewable energy between 2004 and 2011. In Europe, investments are led by Germany. How the ensuing eurozone crisis will affect investments over the next five years is unknown, but the recent trend has been of increasing overall investments.

Figure 15 further shows that, within Europe, government investments in energy R&D differ greatly, with the UK, Spain and Ireland spending less than the US and many other Asian and European countries. The problem is that the business sector is not filling the gap. In the UK, the overall investment of £12.6 billion in 2009/10 is, according to the Public Interest Research Centre (2011, 5), 'under 1% of UK Gross Domestic Product; half of what South Korea currently invests in green technologies annually; and less than what the UK presently spends on furniture in a year'.

Other than R&D expenditures, State investment banks are taking a leading role in clean technology development in some emerging countries. In China, investments by the China Development Bank (CDB) are a key source of its success in solar power. The CDB extended $47 billion after 2010 to approximately 15 leading Chinese solar PV manufacturers to finance their current and future expansion needs; though firms had drawn on approximately $866 million in 2011 (Bakewell 2011). The rapid scaling of solar PV manufacturing firms made possible by public finance has quickly established Chinese solar technology manufacturers as major international players. As such, they are able to slash the cost of solar PV panels so quickly that some are arguing that this access to credit is the reason behind bankruptcies of solar companies based in the United States and Europe (in the case of US-based Solyndra, reviewed below, this was exacerbated by the exit of the original venture capital).

The Brazilian Development Bank (BNDES) approved over $4.23 billion in clean technology financing in 2011 (Fried, Shukla and Sawyer 2012, 5). In biotechnology, BNDES has been focusing on financing firms past the 'Death Valley' stage. Death Valley is the phase of the innovation process that occurs between having a proof of concept and full testing and approval (see Figure 2). Many firms 'die' during this period due to a lack of committed business finance, making public finance a crucial alternative. The commitment of BNDES to clean technology is a promising sign.

The next sections briefly look at the contrasting approaches taken by China, the UK and the United States in attempting to drive clean technology and renewable energy development. The US example will be further explored in the next section.

China's 'green' 5-year plan

Facing backlash in European and US markets (through trade war and tariffs backed by government and initiated by competing firms) against the success of its nascent solar industry in lowering prices, China opted to revise its *domestic* solar power development goal to 20 GWs by 2015 – at a time when just 3 GWs exists in the country currently (Patton 2012). If they complete this development on schedule, they will very likely become the second-largest market for solar power in the world, developing as much solar energy in three years as Germany has in a decade. Complementing these targets are regional feed-in tariffs that fix the price of energy produced by wind and solar projects on more favourable terms (Landberg 2012). Other incentives for Chinese energy developers ensure that today's technologies can recover their costs in seven years, and generate returns for decades, while manufacturers continue to improve technologies (C. Liu 2011). China's goal of 100 GWs of wind power by 2015, and 1,000 GWs by 2050 is a second aggressive goal promoting economic development and reduced carbon emissions (Y. Liu 2012). It is equivalent to a 'moonshot' in comparison to other countries – as 1,000 GWs of wind power would approximately equal the *entire* electric capacity of the US or European electric grids today, which are among the largest on Earth. So far, China's targets have only been revised upwards, suggesting that ample opportunity for domestic industry will persist into China's foreseeable future.

China's visionary and ambitious 12th 5-year plan (2011–15) aims to invest $1.5 trillion (or 5 per cent of GDP) across multiple industries: energy-saving and environmentally friendly technologies, biotechnology, new generation ITs, advanced manufacturing, new materials, alternative fuels and electric cars. Overarching these investments are intentions to adopt a 'circular' approach to economic development that places sustainability first, a directive which defines pollution- and waste-control as forms of competitive advantage (see Mathews et al. 2011). Accompanying investment in industrial development are energy-intensity reduction targets, emission controls, and renewable development goals (a combination of supply-side and demand-side policies). Martinot and Junfeng (2007, 11) highlighted goals for a 30 per cent reduction in China's energy intensity between 1995 and 2004, and an additional goal to reduce intensity by a further 20 per cent by 2010. China will continue to make policy that reduces its energy pollution, since it is the world's leading emitter of CO_2 (Hopkins and Lazonick 2012).[5] According to Climate Works, the 12th 5-year plan 'marks the first time China has formally incorporated mitigating climate change into its core economic strategy' (2011, 2–4), though China pursued pollution and emission reductions also during the 11th 5-year plan.

Recognizing that the competitive advantage of the future depends on effective resource management as well as reduced waste and pollution, China's 'green development' strategy is re-framing the notion of how 'optimal' economic development unfolds with aggressive demand- and supply-side measures. China's 'win–win' plans make 'profit' and

---

5 China also signed the Kyoto Protocol in 1998, and ratified it in 2002. The US is the one country that has signed (in 1998) but never ratified the protocol.

'environment' complementary pursuits rather than trade-offs (as they are often treated in many Western economies). As a result, China maintains globe-dominating shares of solar hot water heating, wind power, and is poised not only to continue as a major manufacturer of solar PV panels, but also become a major market for them.

In sum, China now prioritizes clean technologies as part of a strategic vision and long-term commitment to economic growth. While already providing billions of dollars for new renewable energy project finance, China is in fact just *beginning* its serious investment in solar and wind technology (Lim and Rabinovitch 2010).

UK's start–stop approach to green initiatives

The weak approach to green investment being taken by the UK fits within the broader pattern set by the EU countries in responding to the current economic challenges. An Ernst & Young report (2011, 2) described a record global investment of $243 billion in 2010 into 'cleantech' (including private and public investment such as feed-in tariffs for solar projects), but they comment that the 'market is in flux' (meaning: signals are unclear) in the face of challenging financial conditions, with big variations in investment across geographies and technologies.[6]

Despite the UK prime minister's pledge in 2010 to lead 'the greenest government ever' (Randerson 2010), the UK has in reality *cut* spending for established programmes, scaling back investment in green technologies. In 2010/11, £85 million was cut from the Department of Energy and Climate Change budget, including £34 million from the renewable support programmes. Furthermore, a cut of 40 per cent has been applied to the 2011 budget of the Carbon Trust and a 50 per cent reduction to the Energy Saving Trust. When combined with a reluctance to guarantee sources of finance for green technology development over the long term – including failing to guarantee grants for electric cars beyond one year and pledging to review the feed-in tariff (FIT) structure in 2012 – the UK has not created an optimum environment for green investment (an April 2011 revision had already halved the feed-in tariff for commercial installations above 50KW in order to fund the promised support for small residential installations). Nor has the effect of previous initiatives been proven: the April 2009 UK budget tried to

---

6 The report shows that China receives the most investment, followed by the US, with countries in Europe struggling to balance financial commitments to developing clean technologies against managing national deficits.

accelerate emissions reduction in power generation by requiring carbon capture and storage (CCS) to be fitted to all new coal-fired stations (and retrofitted to all existing stations by 2014); yet according to the House of Commons Energy and Climate Change Committee, this could result in a renewed expansion of gas-fired generation rather than substantial investment in CCS technology. This example shows how 'misguided' policy fails to encourage innovation, in this case, in CCS technologies. The case is even more problematic, as it favours gas-fired power plants thus deepening fossil fuel dependence in the UK's electricity matrix.

The fact that business only invests when there are clear signals about future returns means that those countries that fiddle too much with such signals discourage investment or miss out on it entirely. Both Vestas (of Denmark) and General Electric (GE, of the US) have alluded to the lack of clear policy signals in the UK as their reasons for cancelling plans for onshore and offshore wind manufacturing and development.[7] Sarah Merrick of Vestas (Bakewell 2012) commented that 'it's very difficult to see that there's much visibility in terms of what's likely [to] happen beyond the end of the [renewable obligation]' making it 'very difficult for investors to make those [sic] long-term decisions'. Investors cannot make long-term business decisions based on short-term government policies.

The main initiative of the UK coalition government was to establish a green investment bank to provide Seedcorn funding for green technologies. It is based on the notion that the green revolution can be led by the business sector. All that is required is a nudge or incentives provided by the State. This is wrong (no other tech revolution has occurred this way), and the current levels of funding being discussed are too insignificant to make an impact. The green investment bank initiative does not learn from lessons of previous technological revolutions: *active* State-led investments position a country to 'be first', and reap increasing future returns. While China makes available 47 times more money than the solar companies can use, Britain is fiddling with 'play money'.

The UK government often presents 'green' investments as a trade-off to growth, with the argument that during an economic downturn, policymakers must focus on clear investment strategies and not risky ones. Yet the slow green development taking place worldwide is precisely what could make it an excellent catalyst for economic growth. Given that innovation is

---

7 Unclear signals include the repeated changes in feed-in tariff policies which have undermined solar industry's confidence and growth and the decision to set up a Green Investment Bank, with limited capital and no borrowing powers until 2015.

about having the right networks in the economy and then commissioning specific technologies, an argument against direct government subsidies and grants could be made, regardless of their purpose. A lack of government support, in this sense, would not be troublesome if innovative forces were coming from elsewhere, like from the private sector. But they're not.

Countries like the UK are at risk of falling behind in green technologies, after having been seen as a country that was catching up in the last decade. In the future, if current patterns persist, the UK will most likely become an importer of green technology rather than leading producer.

United States: An ambiguous approach to green technologies

A clue to what is required to accelerate the green 'revolution' is found in the US, where government-funded initiatives are busy building on their understanding of what has worked in previous technological revolutions. But while the US has been good at connecting and leveraging academia, industry and entrepreneurship in its own push into clean technologies (historically with the Department of Energy and more recently with the Advanced Research Projects Agency – Energy, or ARPA-E), its performance has been uneven. As one of the 'first' countries to seriously push into wind and solar power in the 1980s (and the first crystalline silicon solar cells were invented in the US in the 1950s), the US failed to sustain support and watched as Europe, Japan and now China take the lead. Worse, the US failed to alter its energy mix significantly, setting up its position for decades as a world-leading CO_2 emitter. With world-class innovative capability, the world's largest economy and a massive energy grid, the US is ideally positioned to kick off a clean technology revolution, yet it has not. In the context of the 2012 election season, clean energy development was again facing extreme uncertainty, and the very real possibility of losing government support at a critical juncture.[8] Jeffrey Immelt, CEO of GE, bluntly describes the current structure of the US energy industry and its lack of an energy policy as 'stupid', estimating that other nations already have a 10-year lead on the green economy (Glader 2010).

---

8 One hot-button issue for the wind industry was, for example, the expiration of the production tax credit. Re-extended through 2013, it will again face expiration at the end of that year. Despite having been created in 1992, the frequent threat of expiration of the production tax credit has contributed to its propagation of boom and bust cycles of development, rather than allowing it to act as a signal of long-term commitment to wind power.

Pros and cons of the US model

Nudging with venture capital

A key reason for uneven US performance has been its heavy reliance on venture capital to 'nudge' the development of green technologies. The United States is the VC capital of the clean technology world, with $7 billion invested in 2011 versus $9 billion globally. The 2012 Jumpstart Our Businesses Act (JOBS Act) has attempted to provide VCs with even less investment risk, by relaxing financial disclosure requirements for 'smaller' firms (those with less than $1 billion in annual revenue). It also legalizes 'crowd funding', meaning that VCs can recruit a wider range of investors (and individuals) when taking firms public. How this can generate actual job growth – when it seems tailored to ensure that VC investors can reap massive returns on small firms touting government technologies – is difficult to know. On the one hand, less transparency and 'information' about young companies increases the risk investors of all other kinds face. On the other hand, it could improve VC commitments to small firms given that risk is spread across a greater population of investors. If the struggles of current clean technology firms are evident, however, the long-term growth of the firm and hence job growth is much more sensitive to long-term government support than it is to IPO returns (the usual target of VC). Moreover – as in the case of solar energy, for instance – VCs have shown themselves to be 'impatient capitalists': They are not interested in sustaining the risks and costs of technological development over a long-term period. VCs also have limits to the financial resources they can allocate to fully finance the growth of clean technology companies.

Since some clean technologies are still in very early stages, when 'Knightian uncertainty' is highest, VC funding is focused on some of the safer bets rather than on the radical innovation that is required to allow the sector to transform society so as to meet the double objective of promoting economic growth and mitigating climate change. Ghosh and Nanda (2010, 9) argue that it is virtually only public sector money that is currently funding the riskiest and the most capital-intensive projects in clean technology – the ones in the upper right hand corner in Figure 16. VC funding is concentrating mainly in areas shown in the bottom left of the figure. This is highly problematic since it indicates that VCs do not seek out clean technology sectors that are both innovative and capital intensive. These sectors are those which could support development of advanced clean technologies. Unless the government eases capital

Figure 16. Subsectors of venture capital within clean energy

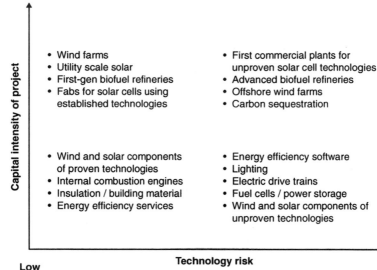

Source: Ghosh and Nanda (2010, 9).

constraints or makes its own investments, these important areas will continue to experience underinvestment and underdevelopment.

Clean technology companies, like those in biotech, can face a number of challenges while attempting to transition from R&D results to commercial production. Also, the amount of capital required to reach economies of scale is typically higher than in the IT sectors (which is where VC wealth originated in the first place). Indeed, the more recent trend has been that VCs were attracted to clean technology as a result of government support, and nearly all their funding poured into *established* technologies, some of which were already benefitting from decades of development (Bullis 2011).[9]

The success of companies like First Solar (see the next chapter) in the US, for example, was built over several decades, during which VCs entered at a relatively late stage and exited soon after the initial public offering (IPO) of stock was completed. Much of the risk of investing

---

9 More incremental innovations that deal with energy efficiency appear to be given priority over the cutting-edge biofuels or advanced solar technologies. In the case of wind turbines, VCs have tended to ignore the technology altogether, suggesting that VCs do not always identify or become interested in technologies which, as of 2012, have become important energy sector leaders and a first choice for many nations interested in new renewable energy development.

in First Solar was actively underwritten by the US government, which supported development and commercialization of their innovative thin-film solar technology, going so far as to aid in developing the manufacturing process.

In addition, federal and state incentives provide billions to support the establishment and growth of a domestic solar PV market, ensuring that companies like First Solar have an opportunity to capture market share and reap economies of scale. The combination of public support and First Solar's current position as a dominant thin-film producer and solar PV cost leader makes its success nearly assured, and it is hard to imagine how such a company could fail, provided that public investment continued.

The impatience of VCs: How Solyndra got burned by its investors[10]

The example of Solyndra illustrates how the sudden exit of VC can also ruin the prospects of companies developing innovative technologies that had also been supported by taxpayers. Solyndra was a one-time darling among clean-tech companies and first to obtain a loan guarantee as part of the US ARRA's $37 billion loan guarantee programme. The programme was administered by the Department of Energy (DoE) under the executive director of the Loan Programs Office Jonathan Silver, who had joined the DoE in 2009 and was himself a former VC and hedge fund manager. Solyndra, a manufacturer of high-tech copper indium gallium (di)selenide (CIGS) solar panels, received $527 million from the programme and invested in a new, more automated factory that would boost output and economies of scale. Solyndra had hoped that its CIGS solar PV technology would provide a significant cost advantage following an explosion in the price of raw silicon around 2008, the primary ingredient in market-dominating crystalline silicon (C-Si) solar panels.

Shifts in global solar markets prevented Solyndra from capitalizing on its investments. Before Solyndra could exploit the economies of scale provided by its increased manufacturing capacity, the cost of raw silicon collapsed. The cost of competing C-Si solar PV technology also fell even more drastically than predicted as a result of Chinese development

---

10 This section is based on William Lazonick and Matt Hopkins, 'There Went the Sun: Renewable Energy Needs Patient Capital', Huffingtonpost.com (2011). Available online at http://www.huffingtonpost.com/william-lazonick/there-went-the-sun-renewa_b_978572.html (accessed 12 April 2013).

and investment in the technology. Despite the government's support and $1.1 billion obtained from its business investors, Solyndra declared bankruptcy in the fall of 2011. All of the stakeholders involved were betting on the company's success, not failure, and yet, for the critics, Solyndra has become a contemporary symbol of the government's inability to invest competently in risky technology and to 'pick winners'.

Solyndra's key business backers were venture capitalists (VC), and, like all VCs, they eagerly awaited an initial public offering (IPO), merger or acquisition to provide an 'exit' from their investments. Any of these 'exits' allows them to monetize the shares of stock they receive in exchange for investing in a given firm. The best-case scenario is obtaining massive financial returns reaped through capital gains created by the sale of stock as opposed to a return on investment created by cash flow from operations. But a successful 'exit' is not always possible in uncertain markets, as Solyndra proved. When Solyndra's key investors abandoned their $1.1 billion investment, 1,000 jobs were lost, and a $535 million government-guaranteed loan was wasted. Rather than staying the course, in other words, Solyndra's investors jumped ship.[11]

The irony is that government support often makes companies like Solyndra more attractive to investors, who seek the State's 'patient capital' and respond to its signals. The conclusion that might follow is that the government should focus exclusively on commissioning the development of the riskiest technologies, or, as some argue (Kho 2011), that VC 'isn't for factories' (even with a government loan guarantee). But this is not happening either. For one, the US now faces backlash from republicans against the loan guarantee programme, indicating that they believe the government should do nothing to promote commercialization of clean technologies.[12]

---

11 Solyndra is not the only company to go belly up when the business community ran out of patience or tolerance for risk. Intel spun off Spectrawatt, its solar panels division, in 2008, and seeded the company with $50 million. Spectrawatt then benefitted from $32 million in state and federal funding to facilitate their growth in New York. Spectrawatt expected to begin manufacturing C-Si and multi-C-Si solar PV cells in 2010 (Anderson 2011). The company was derailed by a batch of defective components, the rise of serious Chinese competition and a refusal of its business investors to provide an additional $40 million to continue operations (Chu 2011).

12 The issues raised by the impatient capital financing clean technology firms in the US economy are not insurmountable, but the cynical response of conservative policymakers has been H.R. 6213, or the 'No More Solyndras Act', sponsored by Representative Fred Upton (Michigan) and 21 other House Republicans.

Now bankrupt, Bathon (2012) clarifies that Solyndra will only be able to repay all its stakeholders if it wins a $1.5 billion lawsuit launched against the Chinese solar companies that it blames for its failure. Solyndra alleges that the Chinese deliberately priced solar panels at levels that did damage to itself and its competitors, and also that Chinese companies benefit unfairly from government support. The glaring hypocrisy of the suit would not seem offensive were it an opportunity to compare, for the public, the failure of US solar policy in supporting manufacturing to the success of China's policies. Rather than engage with the intricacies of policy and industry dynamics, most industry commentators have preferred to focus on the US's efforts to protect its solar PV firms by raising a trade war against the Chinese.

Even after selling off its major assets, including its $300 million headquarters and manufacturing facility (constructed in 2010), only about $71 million was left to distribute to the company's stakeholders – including taxpayers (see Wood 2012). Laid-off workers will receive $3.5 million and the government will receive about $27 million on its defaulted loan. Meanwhile, Solyndra's parent company, 360 Degree Solar Holdings (set up by Solyndra's VC backers and the DoE during a February 2011 debt restructuring) is positioned to cash in on as much as $341 million in future tax credits should it find other profitable investments. Taxpayers stand to subsidize equity investors, in other words, long after the company shuts its doors.

Impatient capital can destroy firms promising to deliver government-financed technology to the masses, but critics often focus on the government as the source of failure rather than examining the behaviour of the smart, profit-hungry business community in producing that failure by jumping ship, restricting their total commitments, or demanding financial returns over all other considerations. If VCs aren't interested in capital-intensive industries, or in building factories, what exactly are they offering in terms of economic development? Their role should be seen for what it is: limited. More importantly, the difficulties faced by the

---

The act passed Congress in September 2012, by a vote of 245–161, but has not yet gone further. The act seeks to end the DoE guaranteed loan programme, which would end future support of this type for clean technologies. This act also ignores the business community's failure to commit resources to clean technology over the last several decades. The Republican-led 'investigation' of Solyndra has been used as justification for an attack on clean technology investments more generally, even as the loan programme provides support for nuclear power plants, auto manufacturers, renewable energy projects and so on.

growing clean technology industry should highlight the need for better policy support – not less, given that existing financing models favour investors and not the public interest.

Pushing with DoE and ARPA-E

The inability of VCs to provide the needed long-term support for the development of radical innovations has been counterbalanced with government programmes for many decades. The US DoE was formed in 1978 to unite several government agencies and 17 national laboratories together, formalizing energy innovation as a regular government pursuit in response to frequent global energy crises. Through this broad network, the DoE has historically funded a number of initiatives supporting clean technologies, on both the demand-side and supply-side, with its multi-billion dollar annual budgets.[13] This includes $3.4 billion and $1.2 billion in R&D funding for solar or wind energy between 1992 and 2012 (in $2011). While a case can be made showing that the US has historically funded fossil and nuclear energy to a much greater degree, for our purposes it is more important to recognize that the impact of the DoE can be found in the histories of most major wind and solar companies of the United States. Collaboration with industry is frequent in the US, and the range of support offered by the DoE includes grant and contract funding, loan financing, R&D and leverage over a vast knowledge base by funding university research and public–private collaborations all over the country.

The DoE's support for clean energy research expanded considerably during the first Obama administration. With the passage of the ARRA,

---

13 Briefly, it should be noted that there are a number of other federal agencies that impact energy innovation in the United States. One is the Department of Defense (DoD), which will spend $10 billion on renewable energy annually by 2030, according to recent estimates (see Korosec 2011). As with many other federal agencies, the DoD is beholden to increasingly strict energy efficiency requirements, and will allocate funding across a variety of clean technology sectors such as solar, wind and water power, biofuels and energy storage. A $2 billion DoD solar PV project is already underway at Fort Irwin, California (Proebstel and Wheelock 2011). The Defense Logistics Agency of the DoD and DARPA allocated $100 million of the agency's $3 billion budget to a variety of clean energy military applications (see Levine 2009). As a top energy consumer of the government, spending approximately $4 billion annually on energy needs, and with several times the combined square footage of Walmart, the DoD's influence over the development and penetration of many clean technologies will have a long-term impact on their success (see serdp.org).

the DoE allocated over $13 billion dollars to develop clean energy technologies and to modernize energy infrastructure, while reducing waste and facilitating a transition to greater sustainability. In 2009 the DoE awarded $377 million in funding for 46 new multi-million dollar Energy Frontier Research Centers (EFRCs) located at universities, national laboratories, non-profit organizations and private firms throughout the US. Spanning a period of five years, the DoE has committed $777 million in total to this initiative. The scale of funding signals that the DoE is committed to moving inventions through to technological maturity and into the stage of production and broad deployment. Hundreds of millions of dollars are being allocated to firms (through matching funds and loan programmes) by the DoE to support the development of productive facilities for solar panels, batteries for electric cars, and biofuel projects, along with programmes focusing specifically on advancing the deployment of solar PV on homes and businesses. These recent initiatives represent an enormous expansion of government spending to shape innovation in the civilian economy.

ARPA-E – Disruption by design

The Advanced Research Projects Agency – Energy (ARPA-E) was established by the America Competes Act of 2007 and first funded by the 2009 ARRA. Modelled specifically after the DoD's Defense Advanced Research Projects Agency (DARPA) model, ARPA-E's directive was 'to focus on "out of the box" transformational research that industry by itself cannot or will not support due to its high risk but where success would provide dramatic benefits for the nation' (Advanced Research Projects Agency – Energy, 'About', n.d.). As mentioned earlier, DARPA is today a multi-billion dollar programme that has been described as a path-breaking force of innovation for over fifty years, conducting key research that provided the basis for the Internet, for Microsoft Windows, Stealth Fighters and GPS, using what Erica Fuchs describes as a system based on bottom-up governance (Fuchs 2009, 65; see also Chapter 5 on Apple's iOS product family).

One radical idea behind DARPA is that it both expects and tolerates failure. Fuchs (2009) attributes DARPA's success to its organizational attributes. Programme managers – characteristically world-class researchers – are provided full autonomy and freedom of exploration necessary to undertake the risks of developing a technological direction and solution. DARPA researcher activities take place outside of regular government, academic, or industry research activities, providing a level of freedom and autonomy. DARPA is not about government 'picking winners and losers', it is about the government taking the lead in R&D which is not taken on by the risk-adverse business sector or by agencies like the DoE, which are under greater pressure to produce results. DARPA's activities are typically conducted to meet national security needs, however, which are not questioned in the same manner as the ARPA-E, which describes its mission as investing in high-risk energy technologies that are 'too early' for private sector investment. As such, the need for the agency as well as conflict over what is 'too early' will likely continue to be a subject of debate. It is also interesting to consider the degree to which the fact that DARPA operates under the banner of 'national security' rather than 'economic performance', contributes to the covering up of the State as a key economic actor. Maybe a 'solution' to ARPA-E is to operate under the banner of 'energy security'.

Like DARPA, ARPA-E doesn't create its own research agenda; instead, it invites researchers from academia and industry to explore high-risk ideas, setting an agenda through collaboration and collective knowledge of the state-of-the-art and realm of possibilities. Project funding draws from government and business sources, indicating that its R&D agenda attracts funding from multiple stakeholders (Hourihan and Stepp 2011). The expectation is that the opportunity to conduct high-risk and path-breaking research 'will attract many of the US's best and brightest minds – those of experienced scientists and engineers, and especially, those of students and young researchers, including persons in the entrepreneurial world'. ARPA-E's website claims that its organization is meant to be 'flat, nimble, and sparse, capable of sustaining for long periods of time those projects whose promise remains real, while phasing out programs that do not prove to be as promising as anticipated'. With a focus on network expansion, the agency was also established to develop a 'new tool to bridge the gap between basic energy research and development/industrial innovation'. In 2012 it will spend $270 million on high-profile energy projects. However, this is down from $400 million received in 2010 and a far cry from the billion dollar allocations given to DARPA (Malakoff 2012).

ARPA-E's current project list includes producing working prototypes of potentially disruptive energy technology, or technology which enables 'transformation' of energy infrastructure (Advanced Research Projects Agency – Energy, 'Mission Statement', n.d.). Scientists are free to explore energy innovation without the expectation that all ideas will work or produce immediate commercial value. In essence, it fills the research gap created by business interests too risk-adverse to invest in the energy technologies of tomorrow given the uncertainties of today.

While active investments, of the 'DARPA' type, are more conducive to growth than 'hands-off' policies, the problem is choosing the 'direction' of the investments, as these can be determined by agendas set by existing industry or academia. The risk is having a bias towards a suboptimal trajectory ('path dependence'), rather than a radically new trajectory based on genuine risk-loving, disruptive technologies and a 'mad' science attitude. Providing research and product development for the military is also different from providing it for energy markets. Energy markets are dominated by some of the largest and most powerful companies on the planet, which are generally not driven to innovate, mainly because energy commodities (gas and electricity) have no real product differentiation despite originating from different technologies. Price is therefore the deciding factor in most cases. The companies that have developed and which control existing energy technologies have massive sunk costs which increase the risk innovation poses. Finally, the energy industry has tended to develop by favouring the stability and reliability of the energy system over the rapid adoption of new technology (Chazan 2013).

New energy technologies alter the means by which energy is produced, and the cost of the energy that they produce is typically greater than legacy technologies when other factors (such as environmental impact) are not factored or incurred by the energy producers. Military researchers are given a clear 'mission' to fulfil, where cost is of little or no concern, since the government is not 'price sensitive' and can act as the leader in innovation procurement. In the energy field, conflict will continue to centre on what each nation envisions as its strategy for meeting future energy needs, coupled to competing economic and social objectives such as maximizing export potential or prioritizing zero-carbon emission.

The US has had a 'fund everything' approach hoping that sooner or later innovative and economically viable energy technologies will emerge. The problem with using climate change as a primary justification for investing in energy technologies is that it is not the only relevant environmental issue faced today. It is also an issue that can be partially 'solved' with the aid of non-renewable technologies like nuclear power or carbon sequestration. Is that really what we want? Deployment of resources meant to facilitate the innovative process must occur alongside the courage to set a technological direction and follow it. Leaving direction setting to 'the market' only ensures that the energy transition will be put off until fossil prices reach economy-wrecking highs.

Pushing – Not Stalling – Green Development

The history of US government investment in innovation, from the Internet to nanotech, shows that it has been critical for the government to have a hand in both basic and applied research. National Institute of Health (NIH) labs, responsible for 75 per cent of the most radical new drugs, performs applied research. In both the cases of basic and applied research, what the government does is what the private sector is not willing to do. State funding makes things happen. The $10 billion pumped into the NIH by the ARRA is, according to Michael Grunwald, 'driving some exciting breakthroughs in cancer research, Alzheimer's, genomics, and much more' (Andersen 2012). So the assumption that one can leave applied research to the business sector, and that this will spur innovation, is one with little evidence to support it (and may even deprive some countries of important breakthroughs). The question is really *what* applied research will be done, and *who* will do it.

'Nudging' economies is not conducive to igniting a real 'green revolution'. Those nations that cling to the bogus idea that government investment has some sort of a natural balancing point with the business sector will miss their opportunity to seize on a historic energy transition, or be forced to import it from elsewhere. In reality, government and business activities frequently overlap. Clean technology businesses, like most businesses, are apt to call for subsidy and government-led R&D in their respective sectors. I noted earlier that venture capitalists and 'entrepreneurs' respond to government support in choosing technologies to invest in, but are rarely focused on the long term.

Getting to the much-needed green revolution presents a serious problem: given the risk aversion of businesses, governments need to sustain funding for the search for radical ideas that push a green industrial revolution along. Governments have a leading role to play in supporting the development of clean technologies past their prototypical stages through to their commercial viability. Reaching technological 'maturity' requires more support directed to prepare, organize and stabilize a healthy 'market', where investment is reasonably low risk and profits can be made. Many of the tools to do this are already deployed around the world, but where strategy, tools and taxes are abundant, political will is often the critical scarce resource. Without the full courage and commitment of the richest economies, which are also some of the heaviest polluters, retracting support for critical technologies during difficult economic times is likely to be a recipe for disaster.

Real courage exists in those countries that use the resources of government to give a serious 'push' to clean technologies, by committing to goals and funding levels that attempt seemingly impossible tasks. Courage is China's attempt to build a US and European electric grid–sized market for wind turbines by 2050 and to increase its solar PV market by 700 per cent in just three years. Courage is also development banks stepping in where commercial banks doubt, promoting development, growth of the firm and a return on investment to taxpayers that is easier to trace. It is important that tax money is traceable in its promotion of technologies and generation of returns. Success makes support for another round of risky investments more likely, and creates better visibility for the positive role that government can play in fostering innovation.

If some European countries have demonstrated the value of long-term policy support for R&D and market deployment, the United States has in contrast demonstrated how maintenance of a state of uncertainty can lead to missed opportunities (see next chapter for examples of solar and wind power technologies). The US got here by failing to adopt a long-term national energy plan that places renewables at the forefront, while also refusing to reduce or abandon support for other, more mature energy technologies, leaving the task of direction setting with its states. Wind companies like Vestas and GE have not been shy about pointing out how changes in policy, such as the expiration of key subsidies for renewable energy in the US or a 'lack of vision' in the UK, will alter their investment decisions to the detriment of the host countries. Plans for new manufacturing plants and development activities are cancelled, or shifted to other countries where the outlook is more promising. State leadership in such 'swing' countries ultimately restricts resources available to clean technologies until the next energy crisis visits and the federal government springs into action.

Here the US (and others) might learn from the examples of other countries, which have established development banks that can provide more control over development activities and later-stage firm growth. Focused to a large extent on financing renewable energy projects, some development banks also use their leverage to provide opportunities for manufacturers that invest in the development of domestic supply chains. The returns from these loans provide a more visible benefit to taxpayers, and promote job growth with greater certainty, primarily because development banks can cater to the interests of the public.

The Importance of Patient Capital: Public Finance and State Development Banks

Advanced clean technologies (like all radical technologies) have many hurdles to clear. Some hurdles may relate to technical development (such as improving or inventing production techniques), others are due to market conditions or competition. In the case of renewable energy sources like wind or solar power, broad social acceptance or the need to provide energy at a price lower than possible by other firms and technologies are also major hurdles (Hopkins and Lazonick 2012). The residential, commercial and utility energy markets that they compete within are subject to unstable or inadequate government support. Given these challenges, the financial risk of supporting a firm until such time that it can mass produce, capture market share and reach economies of scale, driving down unit costs is too great for most VC funds (see Hopkins and Lazonick 2012, 7). VCs are also unwilling to participate in technological development that does not lead to a successful IPO, merger or acquisition. It is from these 'exit' opportunities that they derive their profits. While a high degree of speculation is behind all VC investment decisions, they are unlikely to invest at all without a strong push from government in the form of a targeted technological development. Indeed, in the absence of an appropriate investment model, VC will struggle to provide the 'patient capital' required for the full development of radical innovations.

In the innovation game, it is crucial that finance be 'patient', and be able to accept the fact that innovation is highly uncertain and takes a long time (Mazzucato 2010). Patient capital can come in different forms. German feed-in tariff (FIT) policy is a good form of public 'patient capital' supporting the long-term growth of renewable energy markets. By contrast, the availability but also frequent uncertainty surrounding tax credits in the US and the UK are a form of 'impatient capital' – which indeed has not helped industry take-off. The most visible patient capital made available to renewable technology manufacturers and developers has been delivered through State-funded investment or 'development banks'. According to the Global Wind Energy Council (GWEC):

> The main factor that distinguishes development banks from private sector lending institutions is the ability of development banks to take more risk associated with political, economic and locational aspects. Further, since they are not required to pay dividends to

private stakeholders, the development banks take higher risks than commercial banks to meet various national or international 'public good' objectives. Additionally, long-term finance from the private sector for more than a ten year maturity period is not available. (Fried, Shukla and Sawyer 2012, 6)

The role and scope of development banks is more diverse than simply financing projects. Development banks can set conditions for access to their capital, in an effort to maximize economic or social value to their home country. Most development banks deliberately seek to invest in areas that have high social value, and are willing to make risky loans that the commercial sector would shy away from. Additionally, while these banks support consumption of renewable energy, they can also support manufacturing. Development banks are flexible financiers, and can provide significant capital to renewable energy projects, which can represent as great an investment risk as the capital seeking to produce new technologies.[14]

As we have observed in the United States, VCs typically provide the finance meant to bridge the company's transition into commercialized production, yet they often cannot provide the capital needed or are unwilling to do so should an expected IPO, merger or acquisition be delayed or prevented by market uncertainty. Commercial banks likewise may perceive small clean technology firms or renewable energy projects as too risky and cannot be expected to fill the investment gap. Indeed, this is because commercial and institutional investors do not 'see' technology – they see the returns (or lack thereof) being provided by managed risk portfolios over a period of time. Development banks can therefore provide opportunities by financing the growth of strategic firms such as those in the green industry and in the markets they supply.

Public finance (such as provided by State development banks) is therefore superior to VC or commercial banking in fostering innovation, because it is committed and 'patient', allowing time for companies to overcome the significant uncertainty engendered by innovation. State investment banks, especially but not only in emerging countries like China and Brazil, are revealing themselves to be crucial actors not only

---

14 Approximately $40 billion has been provided by development banks between 2007 and 2010 in support of a variety of renewable energy projects. Wind, solar and biomass technologies have been the largest benefactors of development bank funding in recent years, with GWEC pointing out that wind projects commanded over 50 per cent of development bank finance in 2010.

for 'countercyclical' lending – crucial especially in recessions – but also in the provision of support to highly uncertain and capital-intensive innovation in clean technology. Moreover, the returns earned by public investment banks allow for a virtuous cycle that rewards the use of taxpayers' money in a direct way, while creating other indirect benefits (e.g. public goods).

To be sure, as shown in previous chapters, business and the State have been historical partners in the process of economic and technological development. Yet without governments that are willing to bear key part of the risk, uncertainty and costs of disruptive technological development, businesses would not likely carry it out on their own.[15] The financial and technological risks of developing modern renewable energy have been too high for VC to support, owing to the size and duration of technical risks beyond the traditional proof of concept. Even if proof of concept is achieved, it may not be feasible to produce at the scale required for profitable production. A key problem is that VCs are looking for returns that are not realistic with capital-intensive technologies, which are still very 'uncertain' both in terms of their production and distribution (demand). The speculative returns possible in the ICT revolution are not a 'norm' to be replicated in all other high-tech industries.

Historically, different types of government policies have played important roles in the origins of many green technologies. To illustrate this point the next chapter looks at the history of two renewable energy technologies: wind turbines and solar photovoltaic (PV) modules.

---

15 This is why the American Energy Innovation Council (AEIC) began calling in 2010 for the US to triple expenditures on clean technology to $16 billion annually, with an additional $1 billion given to the Advanced Research Projects Agency – Energy (ARPA-E). This would alleviate the 'bare cupboard' from which some of the richest companies on the planet could choose a technology to take to the market. Their claim that the cupboard is bare is dubious, as many clean technologies exist that don't need billions in additional development to be part of today's energy solutions. But the implication is clear: business investment will follow if the government takes the lead. See Lazonick (2011b; 2012, 38).

Chapter 7

WIND AND SOLAR POWER: GOVERNMENT SUCCESS STORIES AND TECHNOLOGY IN CRISIS

We are like any international company: we deal with government. With the Chinese government, German government, U.S. government, with many international governments. And of course we get support from government in the form of research and development grants and government subsidies to grow. I think almost every US solar company obtained a grant from US government as well, and German companies get subsidies from the German government. Because this is a very young industry which requires government support. But the industry is on the verge of becoming independent from government subsidy. We believe that by 2015, 50% of countries will reach grid parity – meaning no subsidy from the government.

Shi Zhengrong, CEO,
Suntech Power (2012)

While Chapter 6 looked at how different countries are making the investment in the R&D, manufacturing and diffusion of a 'green industrial revolution'; sowing the seeds of change to such a major economic and social shift is not without its challenges. In this chapter, I attempt to delve deeper into the interaction of policy and economic development by providing historical examples of how (in)effective innovation policies can be, and how the State plays an important role in promoting radically new technologies – not merely by inventing new tax credits, but by getting and staying involved in every aspect of the wind and solar power business. As a result, we see that the State is playing a role in the invention of technology, its development, its successful manufacture and its deployment. I will look at the recent history of wind technologies, following the energy crisis of the 1970s. I then present a brief history of pioneering solar energy companies. Both sections show that behind many wind and solar firms, and their core technologies, was the active visible hand of the State, which, as shown in previous chapters, also contributed to the emergence of the Internet, biotech, nanotech and other radical technology sectors. It was particular State agencies that provided the initial push and the early stage high-risk funding, and that created an institutional environment that could establish these important technologies. These sections emphasize that the US approach (with historical origins) resulted in many benefits of State investment being seized by countries other than the US, such as Germany, Denmark and China.

Were it not for the commitments of governments around the world to R&D and the diffusion of technologies like wind turbines and solar PV panels, the energy transformation taking off in the last decade would not have occurred. The 'push' has required major regulatory shifts, financial commitments and long-term support for emerging companies. It is not always clear how to connect the dots between dominant firms and their technologies and the efforts of governments around the world, but it is clear that *no* leading clean technology firm emerged from a pure 'market genesis', that is, as if the State played no role at all. This is a reality I explore in the second part of this chapter.

Yet the clean technology revolution appears to be at a crossroads, if not in crisis. Based on lessons from history, in the concluding section I return to the myths discussed in Chapter 2, and use them to debunk some 'clean technology myths', showing that contrary to common sense perception: (a) R&D is not enough; (b) VC is not so risk loving; and (c) small is not necessarily beautiful. In order for the crossroads to be decided and a green direction to be taken, government policies must overcome the naïve perspective pushed by these myths and distorting ideologies.

Wind and Solar Power: Growth Powered by Crisis

The apparent willingness of the State to accept the risk of clean technology development has had a positive impact. In the last few decades wind turbines and solar photovoltaic (PV) panels have been two of the most rapidly deployed renewable energy technologies on the planet, spawning growing industries that are emerging in many regions of the world. In 2008 $194 billion was directed at emerging clean technologies in an effort to provide badly needed economic

Figure 17. The global market for solar and wind power (US$, billions), 2000–2011

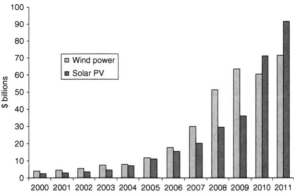

Source: Pernick et al. (2012).

stimulus to counteract the global economic crisis (NSB 2012, 62). An unofficial global 'agreement' was thus reached out of the economic crisis, and that agreement was that the time for clean technologies had come (again). A green energy revolution seemed to be within the realm of possibilities.

Yet it is easy to overstate the progress being made in some clean technology sectors. While wind markets contracted in 2010, in large part as a result of the unfolding financial crisis in the United States (now the second largest wind power market in the world behind China), solar markets nearly doubled in size between 2009 and 2010, surpassing wind power for the first time in history. Figure 17 shows that the growth of these markets has been rapid. Together, wind and solar power represented a $164 billion global market in 2011, compared to just $7 billion in 2000.

Wide-scale deployment of solar PV panels and wind turbines are two technological solutions for meeting future energy needs and mitigating climate change. Like the technologies behind Apple's iPod, iPhone and iPad (see Chapter 5), the 'ecosystem' of innovation in clean technology is one in which the public sector has taken the leading role. Wind and solar power technologies have been the fruit of major government investments that catalysed their historical development around the world.

While the US and China possess the largest quantity of wind capacity deployed worldwide, Denmark produced the leading manufacturer of wind turbines decades ago: Vestas. In the US leading manufacturers also emerged during the 1980s, but each was lost through acquisition or bankruptcy.[1] Germany's solar resources are inferior to those of the United States, yet it remains the world leader of deployed solar PV power. China has emerged as the world's major solar PV manufacturing region, successfully out-competing US, Japanese and European rivals that led in prior decades.

What must be explained is how a country like the US can become a leading market, but fail to produce a leading manufacturer, and conversely, how a country like China can produce a leading manufacturer in the absence (until recently) of a domestic market. What distinguishes these nations has nothing to do with their 'comparative advantages' as producers of wind turbines or solar PV panels, and it has nothing to do with a natural abundance of wind or sun. Historically, the development of wind and solar power has reflected differences in government policies meant to *foster* these power sources. For some countries, this is a process that has unfolded over many decades. For others, it is a process of 'catching-up' – but no matter the case, it is the tools deployed by government that have supported and attempted to drive outcomes. The international histories of wind power technology development and of leading wind and solar companies provide examples of the extent to which those industries have benefitted directly (and indirectly) from different kinds of public funding and support.

From the First 'Wind Rush' to the Rise of China's Wind Power Sector

The first 'Wind Rush' (1980–85) had as a backdrop the energy crises of the 1970s. A number of countries actively invested in utility-scale wind turbines as a solution to mitigating fossil-dependence in electricity generation. In the 1970s, Denmark, Germany and the United States started massive wind energy R&D projects. The goal was typically to build 1 MW and larger machines, creating designs that could be commercialized and exploited by existing large firms typically

---

1 Several factors contributed to the decline of US companies. Falling fossil fuel prices in the 1990s did not help renewable energy companies to survive. Power purchase contracts negotiated in the 1980s with favourable pricing terms also matured, exposing many developers to major revenue reductions for the electricity they sold. In the case of Kenetech, warranty losses incurred from their newest turbine model were substantial, and other firms were vulnerable to the uncertainty emerging from the decision to liberalize energy generation markets.

involved in aerospace technology or agricultural machinery (Soppe 2009; Heymann 1998; Nielsen 2010). The US outspent Germany and Denmark on wind energy R&D, and despite enlisting the National Aeronautics and Space Agency (NASA) to lead the programme, failed to produce a viable commercial design. Germany's attempt met a similar fate. Only Denmark is credited with succeeding in transforming government-funded R&D into a commercial success story, giving it a valuable advantage during the wind industry's formative years.

Heymann (1999, 661) credits the success of Danish industry less with the technological push of State-supported R&D collaboration, arguing that Danish craftsman ultimately produced reliable designs that scaled over time. Kamp (2002, 205) and Nielsen (2010, 176) draw the point of divergence between nations to the decision of the Danes to pursue and develop technology based upon a prior wind turbine design called the Gedser, which was a robust and reliable three-bladed horizontal-axis machine. Developed by Johannes Juul, testing of the Gedser had been financed in its early days by the Danish ratepayer-owned SEAS utility and the Association of Danish Utility Companies (Heymann 1998, 117; Kamp 2002, 130). Later, the government of Denmark and the US provided millions to test the Gedser design as part of efforts to develop wind turbines for modern energy grids (Kamp 2002, 133). Despite the example of the Gedser, the US and Germany pursued lighter-weight, aerodynamically efficient, but often unreliable designs based on prototypes originally conceived around the Second World War in Germany and the US.

Denmark's push into wind turbines included State-sponsored prototype development which brought large manufacturers in to develop experience with the technology and create a functional supply chain. Companies like Bonus and Vestas were able to purchase patents generated by the Danish research programme and smaller-scale wind turbine pioneers, giving them control over collective knowledge and learning taking place. They then applied their experience producing farm equipment and superior capital to produce robust machines on a larger scale and eventually seek vertical integration (Kamp 2002; Heymann 1998). Denmark's R&D activities overlapped with investment tax credits that were phased out over a decade. The tax credits helped launch a domestic market for wind energy, while California state and federal incentives created export opportunities for Danish producers.

'Big government' R&D in the US and Germany was largely dubbed a 'failure' precisely because reliable wind turbine designs that could be successfully commercialized were not produced immediately as an outcome of their programmes. Obviously, if governments are willing to take the big risks that business will not take, they are bound to fail sometimes and succeed others. But if they do not do it, they will not succeed at all. However, that particular failure led to a renewed emphasis in the US, under the Reagan administration, of government as characteristically unable to 'pick winners', an ideology often used by conservative economists and policymakers to limit or reject government intervention into the clean technology industry.[2]

Unlike the US (which drastically slashed funding for the wind programme), Germany did not give up on publicly funded R&D measures despite their 'failures', but expanded on them by publicly funding industrial and academic R&D, as well as funding a demonstration programme that allowed for controlled testing of German designs (Soppe 2009, 11). In reviewing this history, Soppe (2009, 12) adds that Germany also promoted several different development paths, by funding development of turbines of different sizes (as opposed to biasing funds in favour of huge machines, like the US did initially). Denmark's programme was less expensive and more successful, attributable in part to the entry of heavy-farm manufacturers like Vestas, which understood rugged design vis-à-vis aerospace emphasis on light weight and maximum efficiency.

Whether we judge it a success or failure, the actions of these governments signified that wind energy was again in demand, and while the US struggled to maintain a dominant manufacturing presence, it succeeded in establishing a dominant market – 'pushing' not merely 'nudging' one into existence – into which private firms could enter

---

2 Such a view ignores various facts: (1) the fact that many large, private companies which had competency working with high-technologies were partners in that failure. These companies included such giants as Lockheed Martin, General Electric, MAN, Westinghouse and Growian. Each acted as a contractor under the US or German programmes; (2) the role that impatient finance, such as with venture capital in solar power, plays in speeding up the process of technological development or contribution to its failure. Indeed, wind turbine technology was not well understood, and rapidly scaling turbine designs in an attempt to maximize productivity of the technology would have to occur at a pace slower than envisioned at the time. In effect, the government and business community underestimated the challenge at hand, though critics tend to focus on the failure of government and not of finance; and that (3) failure is hard to judge unless we have proper metrics to be able to understand the spillover effects that investments have, even when there is no final product. These international projects did establish networks of learning between utilities, government R&D, the business community and universities.

with confidence. Once again the '*lion-esque*' State leads the way for the 'domesticated' animals – the private companies – to act.

Ironically, favourable conditions for wind energy created by the US government and the state of California were not just opportunities for US-born companies. They also attracted Vestas of Denmark, which became the turbine supplier of choice for the Zond Corporation, a California-based wind energy developer. With few proven wind turbine models available to choose from, Zond became a wind turbine importer, ordering over 1,000 turbines from Vestas, almost single-handedly financing the early growth of that company's wind business. In like fashion, when the tax programme ended in California at the end of 1985, Zond refused to pay for its last shipments of wind turbines (which had been delayed in shipping), contributing to Vestas' bankruptcy. To survive, Vestas abandoned its farm machinery business and quickly re-emerged as an exclusive producer of wind turbines, becoming a world leader. Without the government support of the United States and the state of California at the time, and the leniency of the Danish government allowing Vestas to restructure, Vestas would likely not have become a leading world producer.

Of the handful of new companies emerging in the US to capitalize on the call to bring wind energy to America, it was US Windpower (later renamed Kenetech) that would become an early leader and technological ancestor to General Electric's (GE) wind turbine division – one of the largest in the world. Kenetech's strategic choices were influenced by government investments made in wind energy. Originally founded in Massachusetts, Kenetech moved to California in response to the ample policy support provided. It had derived components of its business plan, knowledge of wind technology and its working prototype technology from the University of Massachusetts–Amherst, a public university with an active wind power programme partly funded by the DoE. Kenetech was also one of the first wind companies to utilize computers to electronically control and regulate their turbines, optimizing the performance and reliability of designs which were otherwise less robust than their Danish counterparts.[3] Kenetech remains one of the few US-based wind turbine manufacturers to have grown from a seed stage to an initial public offering (IPO), but which, in 1996, ended in bankruptcy due to major warranty losses incurred following the release of a state-of-the-art, variable-speed

---

3 Moreover, as discussed in Chapter 5, the Apple II, which ran Kenetech's first projects, would also not have been possible without government investments.

wind turbine. According to Ruegg and Thomas (2009, 37–8) GE has the largest number of patent families linking back to DoE-funded research, but Kenetech was one of a very small number of a companies with more than five. Ruegg and Thomas draw 'extensive links' between DoE research and leading wind power companies, suggesting that DoE research 'has been particularly influential on technology developed by General Electric and Vestas, the two leading global manufacturers of utility-scale turbines' (2009, 41–2).

Unlike Vestas, Kenetech did not enjoy lenience from the US government or from its investors, and about 1,000 people lost their jobs when the company folded. Zond Corporation purchased Kenetech's variable-speed wind turbine technology and developed wind turbines with the assistance of the DoE. Zond was later (partially) acquired by Enron (in 1997), and when Enron collapsed in scandal, General Electric (GE) purchased Zond's technologies to quickly become one of the world's largest wind turbine suppliers. From that point forward, the powerful combination of government subsidies for wind power markets granted at the federal and state levels, along with the resources, stability and technology of a big corporation, made GE 'America's champion' wind producer (Hopkins 2012). To date, though threatened worldwide by Chinese competition, GE dominates the US market for wind turbines, and the technologies developed by the contribution of both State and business support (such as through Kenetech and Zond) create an important but also easily forgotten story of technological development. The US wind industry tells a story of how innovation and positive economic growth occurs as a result of State support for business.

The basic science of wind power was advanced by the DoE through national labs and universities over the years, which drove down the cost of wind power and boosted reliability in a number of ways. Knowledge of aerodynamics was of particular importance, given that wind turbine operating environments are unlike those of planes or helicopters. Advanced computer modelling boosted the reliability and efficiency of turbine designs, and frequent industry collaborations yielded newer models with better capacity factors (a rough proxy of efficiency). Advanced mapping of wind resources also provided wind power developers with accurate siting information that could aid in their project design. After spending $1.2 billion, the cost of wind energy fell from approximately 30–50 cents/kWh in the 1970s to as little as 3 cents/kWh in the 2000s (aided by State-funded R&D for airfoil design and other turbine components), while the efficiency of turbines more than tripled, their operating availability reached nearly 100 per cent, and expected life spans reached 30 years.

The importance of government support is seen most starkly through the consequences of its withdrawal: when the United States government abandoned subsidies for wind power development in the mid-1980s, and slashed the DoE's R&D budget in a backlash against attempts to promote energy innovation, the domestic market stagnated and momentum for the industry shifted to Europe, or, more accurately, to Germany. Germany's federal Ministry for Research and Technology launched a programme to develop 100 MWs of wind power in 1989. Combined with a feed-in tariff (FIT) programme, which provided above-market prices for wind power and a 70 per cent tax credit to small producers, Germany began its reign as the hottest market for wind power development in the world (Lauber, Volkmar and Mez 2006, 106). Combined with greenhouse gas (GHG) reduction targets, and the intention of meeting renewable energy development goals with domestic manufacturing, Germany also set aside national and state funding of approximately $2.2 billion to support continued wind energy R&D. Germany's long-term approach to wind energy development gained momentum in the 1990s and continues today, enabling the emergence of leading manufacturers while providing stable annual growth in deployed wind capacity. The 20-year investment horizons provided by government incentives are twice as long as those in the US, reducing market uncertainty and boosting investor confidence.

China was a relative latecomer to wind power technology, despite having pushed investment in renewable energy in the 1980s as a technical solution for rural electric infrastructure development (Mia et al. 2010, 440). China's partially State-owned Goldwind, a major wind turbine manufacturer, was established in 1998, and initially licensed German technology from Jacobs (a company later purchased by REpower) and Vensys Energiesysteme GmbH (Lewis 2007, 15). Goldwind turbines benefitted from aggressive Chinese domestic content rules, which were enacted in 2003 to require 70 per cent local content in all wind turbines sold in China (Martinot 2010). This effectively shut the door on foreign firms in the country; while China's dominant wind manufacturers strengthened their domestic supply chain and presence.

Chinese wind power developers also received 25-year fixed price contracts that were set through a 'concession' programme (competitive bidding). Wind projects had access to low-cost financing, and after

2005, China began to publicly fund R&D and projects with grants or favourable loan terms. China has also prioritized reducing its overall energy intensity (the relationship between energy consumption and GDP), and established goals for renewable energy development. At this time, China is seeking 1,000 GWs of wind power development by 2050. The effect has been clear, which is that China rapidly surpassed the United States as the world's biggest wind energy market in 2010. Met predominantly with the output of domestic wind turbine manufacturers, China has also eroded the global market shares of other companies around the world.

Solar Power Companies and the Origin of Their Technologies

Many of the same policy shifts driving the California wind market of the 1980s provided the catalyst for a global market for solar PV panels to emerge. Bell Labs had invented the first crystalline-silicon (C-Si) solar PV cell back in 1954 while it was still a part of the AT&T regulated monopoly. The first major opportunities for solar PV technology were created by the DoD and NASA, which purchased solar cells made by US-based Hoffman Electronics to power space satellites.[4] While the space race made the government a spare-no-expense and cost-be-damned customer for early solar manufacturers, the transition of solar PV technology to Earth was facilitated in part by the cost and performance advantage it had in markets for remote power applications, leading to diverse applications such as signal lighting on offshore oil rigs, corrosion protection for oil drilling, remote communication towers and road signs (Perlin 1999). In most cases, however, the existence of such lighting was a result of regulation, and the choice of solar PV/battery power for oil rigs was based in part by the EPA making it illegal for oil companies to dispose of spent batteries in the ocean in 1978 (Perlin 1999, 62).

There are several modern governmental initiatives helping to establish leading solar PV firms and markets around the world. Many examples of innovative emerging firms can be found in the US, where First Solar, Solyndra, Sunpower and Evergreen each developed state-of-the-art C-Si or thin-film solar technologies.

---

4 Hoffman had acquired the original Bell Labs patent through acquisition of National Fabricated Products in 1956.

First Solar emerged out of the search for commercialized cadmium telluride (CdTe) thin-film solar PV panels and became a major US-based CdTe thin-film producer. First Solar dominates the US market for thin-film solar PV panels, and has produced record-setting technology and low-cost manufacturing, which have enabled the company to generate over \$2 billion in revenue each year since 2009. First Solar's patents have 'extensive links' to prior DoE research (Ruegg and Thomas 2011, 4–11), and early development of First Solar's leading CdTe technology was a result of founder Harold MacMaster working in collaboration with the University of Toledo's State-funded solar research facilities, scientists and the National Renewable Energy Laboratory (NREL). First Solar's partnership with the NREL reaches back to 1991, when the company was still known as Solar Cells. The collaboration resulted in the development of high-rate vapour transport deposition, a superior means of manufacturing glass CdTe thin-film panels, which First Solar began to produce in 2003 (NREL 2012). This innovation amounted to major cost reductions of CdTe panels over time, as the process was perfected. Even now, First Solar remains one of the larger solar PV manufacturers on the planet.

Described in greater detail in the previous chapter, Solyndra had been founded by Chris Gronet, a Silicon Valley scientist with experience in the semiconductor industry. Building on national research conducted on copper indium gallium (di)selenide (CIGS) solar PV, Gronet and his employees developed innovative technology with state and federal support behind them. Able to deposit CIGS onto tubular glass gave Solyndra's solar PV panels a unique look – while also enabling them to capture direct and reflected light without add-on tracking systems. Additionally, Gronet's panels had a trick interlocking system that made them easy to install – reducing their cost relative to other technologies.

SunPower is a leading manufacturer of high performance C-Si solar PV panels with world-record-setting technology. This is also owed in part to prior investments of the State. SunPower's success ties back to DoE research patents, in this case related to solar PV shingles, module frames and shingle systems (Ruegg and Thomas 2011). Established in 1985 by Dr Richard Swanson, SunPower had early R&D support from the DoE and the Electric Power Research Institute (EPRI) while developing technology at Stanford University.

Evergreen Solar was a spinoff of the now defunct Mobil Solar, started when a group of scientists 'defected' from the company to develop a rival vision of string-ribbon wafer technology. Evergreen grew with the aid of the government, attracting $60 million in Massachusetts state subsidies, the highest ever offered to a single company by the State. Promising to create manufacturing jobs for Massachusetts, Evergreen was easily lured to China which offered favourable loan terms from its public-owned banks to subsidize a new plant. In obtaining this financing, Evergreen agreed to share its innovative technology with its partner Jiawei Solar (Sato 2011). Despite accumulating nearly a half-billion in losses over its history, Evergreen completed a $42 million IPO in 2000, and enriched its executives with $36 million in compensation and stock sales (and this value is based on the limited data available). In other words, public support helped deliver value to VCs and top executives, but failed to create promised economic benefits for the US, while possibly transferring innovative technology to China. The state of Massachusetts tried to sue Evergreen to recover some of their money (Haley, Usha and Schuler 2011, 36), an indication that policymakers are not always as passive a steward of taxpayer dollars as assumed, and rightly want to capture the benefits of the industries they underwrite with taxpayer dollars.

Suntech of China was a global market share leader in C-Si solar PV manufacturing in 2011.[5] Suntech has benefitted from the import of PV manufacturing equipment from bankrupt US companies (and the acquisition of Japan's MSK corporation), the abundant and willing public finance of national and local Chinese banks, and booming European markets for solar PV. Founder Zhengrong Shi received his PhD and established many important relationships at the University of New South Wales, Australia, which hosts world-leading solar researchers such as Professor Martin Green, with whom Shi would develop technology before incorporating some into his firm's products. Shi studied solar PV and spent 13 years in Australia, working for Pacific Solar, which was a joint-venture between the University of New South Wales and an Australian utility company, before returning to China (Flannery 2006). Shi had been lured by the city of Wuxi, which offered him $6 million to set up solar PV manufacturing there in 2000 (Crouch 2008). Suntech's Pluto C-Si technology is a derivative of record-setting PERL C-Si technology developed at the University of New South Wales, and the company has actively sought to incorporate aspects of this foreign technology into its commercial products. As such, its products

---

5 Details on Suntech are based on a forthcoming piece of work by Matt Hopkins and Yin Li, 'The Rise of the Chinese Solar Photovoltaic Industry and its Impact on Competition and Innovation'. This piece of work is for an upcoming book on Chinese innovation tentatively titled *Is China Becoming an Innovation Nation?*

are quickly approaching the high performance of rivals like US-based SunPower.

Suntech, like most Chinese solar PV manufacturers, depended on the presence of large export markets to grow. It generates a substantial share of its revenues from European markets for solar PV, which are driven by strong feed-in tariffs (FIT) and other supportive government policies that spend billions encouraging domestic development of solar PV. It has also benefitted from policy support in China, however, which granted the company a preferential 15 per cent tax rate, millions in grants, and a $7 billion line of credit from the Chinese Development Bank (which followed millions in committed local government finance), which had otherwise made $47 billion in favourable loan terms available to Chinese solar companies in 2010 (Pentland 2011).

It has been this large amount of committed public finance and other public investments that made the difference to Chinese solar PV manufacturers, who have the resources needed to grow as well as the commitment of its government to help them when weather shifts in global markets as it begins building a stronger domestic market for solar PV power. Already a leader in solar hot water heating, China is showing early signs that a domestic market will take off, thanks to rapid policy response and trade tensions emerging from tensions surrounding China's rapid rise in global solar PV markets (Choudhury 2012).

Solar Bankruptcies: Where There's a Will There's a Way

But at the time of this writing, Wuxi Suntech (a wholly owned subsidiary of Suntech Power Holdings) has declared bankruptcy. Just days after defaulting on a $541 million bond payment to investors in March of 2013, investors sued, and the fallout is raising serious questions about the future of China's young solar industry. Once hailed as the 'Sun King' by *Forbes* in 2006, a holder of 15 patents in solar technology, with a genuine rags-to-riches life story, Shi's legacy as the world's first solar billionaire and one of the wealthiest persons in the world at one point is rapidly deteriorating as accusations of mismanagement accompany attempts to oust him from the executive offices and board of the company he once founded (Flannery 2006; Ma 2013). Now expected to be taken over by State-owned Wuxi-Guolian, the company has divided its assets into the subsidiary Wuxi Suntech, with foreign investors being routed through Suntech Power, making them 'structurally subordinate' to the public banks that have been pumping up the firm with patient capital (Bradshaw 2013).

Forcing Suntech into insolvency means that Shi, who holds a 70 per cent interest in Suntech Power (and 30 per cent of its shares overall), and the rest of its major shareholders are likely to lose an estimated $1.28 billion invested in Suntech's stocks and bonds, while the company's nationalization attempts to protect the interest of thousands of workers, the public banks backing the firm, and the State. Public banks, for their part, hold the majority of the company's estimated $2.2 billion in debt.

The outcome of China's Suntech bankruptcy stands in stark contrast with that of US-based Solyndra. Facing bankruptcy, Solyndra underwent emergency reorganization and received a last-minute $75 million capital injection from its private investors prior to its bankruptcy (the government had insisted that the funds come from private backers). The DoE's loan programme executive director Jonathan Silver (a former venture capitalist) worked for 'taxpayer safety' while CEO Brian Harrison (formerly of Intel and who had replaced Chris Gronet in 2010) worked to gut a 'bloated' R&D department and complete an advanced, fully automated new factory with DoE funds on a cost-cutting mission, and as a result both sales and costs were initially moving in the right directions (Grunwald 2012, 414–15). As noted in greater detail above, the capital injection came with the not-insignificant caveat that private investors would be first in line to reclaim losses should the company fold. Yet all parties involved also knew that the company 'would be more valuable in bankruptcy if it had a completed plant' (Grunwald 2012, 415). Even without additional funding from the US government, then, the attempt to rescue Solyndra is badly botched politics (and economics) at its finest even if it could be described as a heroic and gutsy fourth-quarter play.

It is interesting to push the comparison between Suntech and Solyndra further. Solyndra was overwhelmingly funded by private interests, while Suntech was funded by public interests. Both companies have failed, yet the outcome expected of each was the 'same' – that each would create jobs and massive profits and compete for wealth with other countries, the main measures of success we care about. Yet, competition occurred within a global context – that is, a global industry which finds its policy support, like its firms, functioning in different places all around the world, presumably to maximum performance. Yet Solyndra's production and Suntech's production were each, in a manner of speaking, competing for that next German customer. Both firms from the US and China committed the same mistakes. They scaled too rapidly, and did not have the market for their own domestic energy grids – each country possessing gigantic 1 TW domestic market capable of providing a near-limitless opportunity for firms that, ironically, die for a lack of customers that can absorb their output. With such amazing infrastructure already in place, would anyone else think it was absurd if GM, Ford and Chrysler went bankrupt for a lack of roads?

Yet Solyndra has disappeared from the world, while Suntech as yet survives. Suntech's fate is not to be decided by its investors, however – who naturally prefer to have funds returned over all other considerations. Solyndra's failure highlights the 'parasitic' innovation system that the US has created for itself – where financial interests are always and everywhere the judge, jury and executioner of all innovative investment dilemmas. Perhaps, done differently, and with an eye to the value of economic development beyond short-term financial performance, Solyndra would have grown to hundreds of thousands of employees, with billions in revenue like GE. Suntech's fate, on the other hand, will be decided by the State, which has made the larger investments in the firm, and which proceeds into bankruptcy with a much broader perspective of Suntech's position in the Chinese economy and its future. Suntech was preserved by the State during the downturn, and its 20,000 jobs have already become critical to the Jiangsu province, which may experience a painful structural adjustment should the firm be liquidated, shuttered and forgotten (imagine firms like Google with its 54,000 employees, or Facebook with its 4,600, suddenly shuttering). Solyndra was too 'small to survive' (versus too big to fail) to warrant a 'bail-out', yet the government had, as it always has, the ability to 'rewrite the rules' and could have weighed the cost of letting Solyndra fail against letting it succeed. It might have even, as with Suntech, considered firing the executives responsible for its financial decline. One way to calculate such a cost would be to ask what 1,000 jobs are worth to the future revenues of the government, or better yet what those revenues are worth when the company becomes a major employer like Facebook, Google or GE.

We'll continue to spend our time imagining success until we recognize that innovation unfolds as part of a global process, not an individual or even organizational process (though that is critical to grasp). Clean technology is already teaching us that changing the world requires coordination and the investment of multiple States, otherwise R&D, support for manufacturing, and support for market creation and function remain dead ends while the Earth literally suffocates on the industries we built a century ago.

One of the biggest challenges for the future, in both cleantech and whatever tech follows it, will be to make sure that in building collaborative ecosystems, we do not only socialize the risks but also the rewards. It is only in this way that the innovation cycle will be sustainable over time, both economically and politically. Politically it is important for taxpayers to understand how they benefit from the massive State investments that build the foundation for future private profits. As jobs are increasingly global, rather than resisting this with nationalistic dogma, there are concrete ways for returns from State investments to be captured so that the citizens who funded technological development can be sure to share in the gains. It is to this theme that I turn to in the next chapter.

Competition, Innovation and Market Size (Who's Complaining?)

I argued above that the state of California was a partial reason for the growth and (early) success of Vestas – the current world-leading wind turbine manufacturer. In similar fashion, the growth of US and Chinese firms have depended, to an extent, on the resource commitment and leadership of Germany's policies. Germany's distributed solar power generation approach made it the world leader in solar PV development however. By revising its feed-in tariffs (FIT) policy in 2000 to provide better pricing for solar PV (and to set unique pricing for other renewable technologies according to their expected performance), Germany made solar PV competitive with traditional power sources and even wind energy. At the same time, Germany also established a '100,000 roofs' programme to encourage residential and commercial investment in the technology. The action kicked the solar PV industry into high gear, and Germany grew its solar PV capacity from just 62 MWs in 2000 to over 24,000 MWs by 2011. This is similar to completing 24 nuclear power plants in about 10 years – a remarkable feat that would never occur given ordinary nuclear power plant construction times (and public opposition to them).

Also similar to the California phenomenon described above, Germany's forward-thinking policies have been both a blessing and a curse. On the one hand, Germany's growing market enabled the rapid growth of dominant domestic manufacturers to emerge (such as Q-Cells). But it also provided growth opportunities for competing firms from the US, China and elsewhere, which relied on Germany to absorb their expanding production capacity. At the same time, these and other countries have not followed suit in establishing equally strong domestic markets for solar PV despite observing the German example. The excess capacity created in part by the 'start and stop' of solar PV policies in places like Spain is currently crippling solar companies around the world. Q-Cells, once a German champion, is now property of Korea's Hanwha Group (Reuters 2011).

Meanwhile, the rise of China as a regional centre for major solar PV manufacturers has had a serious fallout on the industry as a whole, prompting a 'trade war' in the United States and Europe, manifest in the form of tariffs levied against Chinese solar PV producers.[6] But while US and European companies find themselves unable to compete, the US government, for example, has reacted with calls to end support for clean technology development when struggles point out, if anything, that more is needed. The trade war only serves to strengthen the myth that industrial development occurs through invisible market forces that cannot be created or controlled by government to socially beneficial outcomes. With the government acting as 'referee' in the trade dispute, China's public support for clean technology industry development is framed as 'cheating', rather than effective. At the same time, multiple countries are attempting to capture the global market for clean technology with similar policies that include direct and indirect support for firms, or, in other words, if China is cheating, they are as well. Plummeting solar PV prices are supposed to be a good thing – they will eventually position solar PV to compete favourably with fossil fuels. But in this case, falling prices (and shrinking profit margins) frustrate many and ignore the shortcomings of industrial policy in countries like the US, which we could describe as lacking an adequate supply of patient capital conducive to innovative firm formation and growth, as well as a long-term vision for energy transition (Hopkins and Lazonick 2012). What is separating China from its international peers is its courage to commit to renewable energy and innovation in the short *and* long run.

Some argue that there is a risk that the rapid growth of Chinese wind and solar companies potentially stifle innovation (W. Liu 2011). The charge is that Chinese companies reduce costs and grab market share with older technologies, setting a technological direction which prevents newer technologies from penetrating world markets. If this is proven to be the case, then governments should heed the signal that more needs to be done to ensure that critical energy innovations can establish

---

6 At the time of writing, Europe was still undecided on tariffs.

themselves in markets that are becoming crowded with competing technologies. These complaints seem to ignore that there are advantages to C-Si technology – such as the presence of abundant raw materials for their manufacture. Other approaches rely on rare earths and such a supply is limited. Furthermore, these complaints ignore the reality that US innovations produced by companies like Innovalight (now owned by DuPont) or 1366 Technologies can be incorporated into Chinese panels (and are).[7] In any case, at some point convergence towards a dominant design is needed before mass diffusion of solar power can be achieved.

Conclusion: Clean Technology in Crisis

There is nothing 'accidental' about clean technology development or the formation of markets for renewable energy. There are no 'genius' firms or entrepreneurs acting independently of their society or simply in reaction to the fear of climate change or a privileged knowledge of future profits. Rather, clean technology firms are leveraging technologies and cashing in on the prior investments of an active public sector, and responding to clear market signals proclaimed by progressive government policies about the desired change, and to the availability of support for clean technology industrial growth. The hope is that innovation will produce economic wealth, employment opportunities and a solution for climate change.

While the performance of countries has varied tremendously over the decades, it is obvious that Germany has provided a glimpse of the value of long-term support, China has demonstrated that a rapid scale-up of manufacturing and deployment is possible, and the United States has shown the value of R&D but also the folly of permitting uncertainty, shifting political priorities and speculative finance to set the clean technology development agenda. Governments leading the charge into clean technology do not have to allow themselves to be cheated when investments go sour. Nor should they expect that taxpayers will happily bear the full risks of investing in these technologies and establishing markets without a clear future reward to be gained.

The challenge moving forward is to create, maintain and fund a long-term policy framework which sustains momentum in the clean energy sector building up over the last decade. Without such

7 As noted in Chapter 6, 1366 Technologies developed radically low-cost multi-crystalline silicon manufacturing equipment – with the aid of the US's new ARPA-E programme, which had contributed $4 million to development.

long-term commitments, it is likely that clean technology will become a missed opportunity for many nations. Such a framework would include demand-side policies to promote increased consumption of solar and wind energy, as well as supply-side policies that promote manufacture of the technologies with 'patient' capital.

The challenges of developing clean technologies go far beyond establishing risky public sector energy innovation hubs, such as ARPA-E seeks to become. Governments must reduce the risk of commercializing energy innovations while establishing and managing the risks of competing in diversified and global energy markets. When difficulty has arisen in the past, such as when wind or solar markets faltered following retraction of US support for renewables in the late 1980s, the tendency has been to focus on how government investment is flawed, while the role of business in contributing to that failure is ignored, or written off as part of the 'natural' behaviour of competitive markets. Worse, some interpret difficulties as proof that a technology 'can't compete' or will never compete with incumbent technology and should be shelved rather than exploited. This would go against the historical record, which suggests that all energy technologies have needed and benefitted from lengthy development periods and long-term government support. What matters more is that the effort continues as if the future of the planet depended on it – because it does. Addressing the challenge thus requires overcoming a worldview based on myths, referred to in Chapter 2 above.

Myth 1: It's all about R&D

R&D contributing to clean technologies like wind and solar power has occurred on a global scale for decades, as a result of significant public investments and learning, and the leveraging of a broad community which has been inclusive of educational and business knowledge networks. The technology works as a result, and improvements in cost and efficiency have proceeded despite the unequal commitments of governments and businesses over time. The cost of energy they produce has also fallen over the long term, while fossil fuel prices continue to be volatile and rise over time.

Some firms may conduct important R&D for decades and remain money losers without a clear commercial prospect in the pipeline. As shown by the history of First Solar, the government's role in pushing innovations out of the lab and into markets does not end with R&D but can include a role in overcoming commercialization barriers, such as a lack of production capabilities. Likewise, First Solar's VCs needed to endure challenges and an investment horizon which stretched their commitment.

As many argue, the challenges faced by clean technologies are therefore seldom technical; they are *political* (and social) and include a need for greater commitments of patient capital by governments and businesses around the world. R&D works, but it is not enough. Nurturing risky new industries requires support, subsidy and long-term commitments to manufacturing and markets as well. Governments must also confront the reality that for most developed nations, the deployment of clean technologies is occurring within a well-developed infrastructure. The clean slate approach is not possible, meaning that investment is intended to manage a transition to clean technology, one that threatens fossil and other energy industries that have the benefit of a longer development period and significant sunk costs. Finally, not all in the business community are shy about calling for an active government role in clean technology. Yet the time is overdue to begin discussing what the real role of business is in technological development beyond funding R&D. The failure of clean technology companies is also a business failure, not merely a policy failure, and it delays the exploitation of important new energy technologies. Worse, it may hand those technologies to other nations with similar objectives.

Myth 2: Small is beautiful

While many large conglomerates like GE, Exxon, GM or British Petroleum have had a role in clean technology development in the past, many look to smaller start-ups for evidence of the coming 'revolution' in the energy sector. Yet these small firms tend also to be young, and incubate for long periods before taking off commercially.

As argued by Hopkins (2012) and summarized above, GE 'inherited' the prior investments of the State and innovative firms in its rise as a major wind turbine manufacturer. GE also announced in 2011 (but has since delayed) a $600 million investment in Colorado in thin-film solar PV, using CdTe technology similar to First Solar's. As with their entry into the wind power business, their entry into solar PV will have strong ties to the prior investments of the State. Yet GE's own resources are vastly superior to those of small start-ups, which include billion dollar R&D budgets, billions in annual profit available to reinvest in core technologies, complementary assets such as a vast global network, and, as with the wind industry, significant rapport and reputation that reduce its 'risk' to investors. The investments of GE might ensure a more enduring solar industry presence for the US in the future, in similar fashion as its entry to wind power became in 2002. For renewable energy scale matters, and larger firms can more easily supply enormous energy grids spanning the continents. Perhaps most importantly, large firms like GE more easily win the confidence of investors and utilities, given their extensive operating history, financial resources, experience with electricity infrastructure and vast social networks. It is not so coincidental that wind projects picked up to a feverish pace following GE's entry to the wind energy business.

Yet we should not underestimate the role of small firms nor assume that only big firms have the right resources at their disposal. Small firms that grow into big firms, such as Amazon, Google or Apple, are active promoters of their own business models, often to the frustration of 'legacy' industries which one could argue would never have taken the same technologies so far, so fast. The willingness to disrupt existing market models is needed in order to manifest a real green industrial revolution, and it is possible that start-ups, lacking the disadvantage of sunk costs, are the right actors for the job.[8]

Myth 3: Venture capital is risk loving

The United States is the VC capital of the clean technology world, allocating billions to the sector each year – far more than the rest of the world combined. VC financiers are 'impatient capitalists', however – they are driven primarily to generate financial returns for themselves over all other considerations. Many are not interested in sustaining the risks of technological development over a long-term period, preferring instead to cut their losses and resume a search for high returns elsewhere. VCs want to finance technologies with low capital requirements that are

---

8 It should be subject to a debate whether public support for energy innovation is meant, in the long term, to be 'handed off' to large firms that could have made their own investments. Subsidies should be preventing innovative newcomers from going 'bust'. If the point of government R&D is to promote innovation, then it is wasteful to not examine how the competitiveness of would-be manufacturers could be improved. Also, while many oil companies have contributed to solar PV innovations in the past, for example, it is unclear how they would be willing to shift to that technology and abandon the technologies which provide their major sources of revenue. In fact, as solar PV markets have become more competitive, past leaders like BP Solar pulled out rather than staying the course.

close to market penetration. VCs also lack the resources to fully finance the growth of clean technology companies, which are capital intensive and competing within very complex markets. The billions they pour into companies across clean technology sectors is little, for example, compared to the hundreds of billions of State funding committed to financing renewable energy projects.

The success of companies like First Solar was built over several decades, during which VCs entered at a relatively late stage and exited soon after the IPO was completed. Much of the risk of investing in First Solar was taken on by the US government, which actively promoted their solar technology through to commercialization. Subsidies supporting a domestic market and a market in Europe, coupled to First Solar's position as a dominant thin-film producer make it hard to imagine how such a company could fail. Yet the value extraction provided, and even promoted, by equity-driven investment and compensation methods ensures that VCs, executives and top managers of firms can reap massive gains from stock performance, whether short lived or not. This perverse incentive not only redistributes the investment in innovation away from its other core stakeholders (governments, schools, workers), but it risks undermining firm performance. Rather than make the risky investment in future innovation, those in positions of strategic control squander resources in a search for financial returns.

At the same time many US firms have gone bust, less for lack of innovative technology and more for lacking access to additional capital to continue operations following uncertainty in markets or a sudden reversal of fortune. This encouraged Evergreen to 'follow the finance' out of the US and into China. Spectrawatt and Solyndra were undone by a lack of available capital as well. Despite common global market conditions, China's companies benefit from a system of public finance that will not quit before they do. When VCs do not take the risks, then is up to the State to fill in the vacuum.

Building a green innovation ecosystem (symbiotic not parasitic)

Innovation cannot be pushed without the efforts of many, and it cannot proceed without a long-term vision that sets the direction and clarifies objectives. When government policies fail, public dollars can be wasted and promising technologies may fail to meet their potential, because politicians or taxpayers refuse to commit more resources.

When businesses fail, thousands of jobs can disappear, investors lose confidence and the reputations of the technologies are scarred. Uncertainty and stagnation can prevail, while the potential for promising new solutions vanishes. With government and business activities so intimately linked, it is often impossible to point blame accurately. At the root of it, there is only collective failure.

What should be clear is that the green energy revolution that has been experienced so far is a result of a complex long-term multi-decade-long technological development and diffusion process that unfolded on a global scale. The process has benefitted from major government investments that encouraged the establishment of new firms and supported their growth by creating market opportunities. The variety of policies was meant to produce technological development, market efficiency, scale and efficient regulation. Overarching this process is a broad call to accelerate economic growth through innovation in clean technologies that mitigate climate change and promote energy diversity. The long-term vision is to transform our current productive system into a sustainable green industrial system. That is a mission set on producing long-lasting benefits to the public while delivering on a promise of superior economic performance.

Key to the future of the green revolution taking off will be the building of innovation ecosystems that result in *symbiotic* public–private partnerships rather than parasitic ones. That is, will increased investments by the State in the ecosystem cause the private sector to invest less, and focus its retained earnings on areas like boosting its stock prices rather than on human capital formation and R&D?

The next chapter goes back to the case study of Apple computers, to ask whether the active State investments in innovation – which have benefitted specific companies like Apple (at both the company level as well as the key underlying technologies used) – have created results for the State which can be justified by the taxpayer funds that were invested. Larger tax receipts? More jobs? Or greater future investments by Apple in innovation? Only by asking these questions can we make sure that the entrepreneurial State does not become a naïve one.

Chapter 8

RISKS AND REWARDS: FROM ROTTEN APPLES TO SYMBIOTIC ECOSYSTEMS

Years ago when I lived in California we used to say that California was twenty years ahead of the rest of the nation. I fear we may have been right.
Norman R. Augustine, former chairman and CEO
of Lockheed Martin Corporation (NAS 2010, 79)

This book has highlighted the active role that the State has played in generating innovation-led growth. As has been argued, this has entailed very risky investments – speculation for Schumpeterian 'creative destruction'. However, while in finance it is commonly argued that there is a relationship between risk and return, in the innovation game this has not been the case. Risk taking has been a collective endeavour while the returns have been much less collectively distributed. Often, the only return that the State gets for its risky investments are the indirect benefits of higher tax receipts that result from the growth that is generated by those investments. But given the presence of different types of tax loopholes and the fact that tax receipts often do not accurately reflect the source of earnings (e.g. income vs. capital gains), taxes have proved a difficult way for the State to get back its return for innovation investments. And indeed, even if taxes derived from State-backed innovations were collected properly, it is not clear whether the amount would be enough to fund the innovation investments that characterized Silicon Valley, which will always imply colossal failures for every big hit, like the Internet – that is simply the nature of the truly uncertain innovation process.

There is indeed lots of talk of partnership between the government and private sector, yet while the efforts are collective, the returns remain private. Is it right that the National Science Foundation did not reap any financial return from funding the grant that produced the algorithm that led to Google's search engine (Block 2011, 23)? Can an innovation system based on government support be sustainable without a system of rewards? The lack of knowledge in the public domain about the central entrepreneurial role that government plays in the growth of economies worldwide, beyond Keynesian demand management and 'creating the conditions' for growth, is currently putting the successful model in major danger.

In theory, the socialized generation and privatized commercialization of biopharmaceutical – and other – technologies could be followed by a withdrawal of the State if private companies used their profits to reinvest in research and further product development. The State's role would then be limited to that of initially underwriting radical new discoveries, until they are generating profits that can fund ongoing discovery. But private sector behaviour suggests that public institutions cannot pass the R&D baton in this way. It also suggests that the State's role cannot be limited to that of planting seeds that can be subsequently relied on to grow freely – if it is interested in creating economic growth and technological change it must be willing to support technologies until they can be mass produced and broadly deployed. And of course the broader role of the State in areas as diverse as 'security', contract enforcement and reduction of inequality means that the 'backseat' is not – regardless of the innovation game – a choice to be considered.

Many of the problems being faced today by the Obama administration are due to the fact that US taxpayers are virtually unaware of how their taxes foster innovation and economic growth in the US; they do not realize that corporations are making money from innovation that has been supported by their taxes. Meanwhile, these taxpayer-propped corporations are neither returning a significant portion of the profits back to the government nor investing in new innovation (Mazzucato 2010). The story US taxpayers are told is that economic growth and innovation are outcomes of individual 'genius', Silicon Valley 'entrepreneurs', venture capitalists or 'small businesses', provided regulations are lax (or nonexistent) and taxes low – especially compared to the 'Big State' behind much of Europe. These tales are also being told in the UK where it is argued that the only way for the country to achieve growth is for it to be privately led and for the State to go back to its minimal role of ensuring the rule of law.

To make growth 'fairer' and more 'inclusive' – and for the gains to be more equitably shared – economists, policymakers and the general public must have a better understanding of which stakeholders truly take part in the fundamental risk sharing necessary to catalyse innovation-led growth. As has been argued, risk taking and speculation are absolutely necessary for new innovation to occur. The real Knightian uncertainty that innovation entails, as well as the inevitable sunk costs and capital intensity that it requires, is in fact the reason that the private sector, including venture capital, often shies away from it. It is also the reason why the State is the stakeholder that so often takes the lead, not only to fix markets but to create them.

To consider this question more fully, I first go back to Apple, and witness the severity of the risk–reward problem. It might feel like I am 'picking' on Apple – but there is no company like Apple that most epitomizes the 'image' of why the market is the engine of capitalism in the popular imagination (versus the heavy State discussed in the Introduction and in Chapter 1). While in Chapter 5 we have tried to balance that image by discussing the very active role that the State has had in Apple's success, in this chapter I argue that keeping that story untold has allowed Apple to avoid 'paying back' a share of its profits to the same State that funded much of its success. Later, in Chapter 9, I examine the question more closely through an explicit call for a new approach – a 'framework' – to understand the relationship between risks and rewards, and thus the relationship between innovation and in/equality. It will be argued that industrial and innovation policy must include redistributive tools in order to justify the 'entrepreneurial' investments required by the State – tools able to cover the inevitable losses (as failures are part of the trial and error process), but also to replenish the innovation fund which is necessary for the next round of innovation.

Back to Apple: What Did the US Government Get Back for Its Investments?

In this digital age, innovation is key to 'smart' growth. But 'inclusive' growth (EC 2010) requires also thinking about the distribution of returns. Risk is inherent within the innovation process and often, when a technology is successfully transformed into a commercial product or service such as the iPhone, for instance, the risk bearer is rewarded with huge returns. This is also because innovation is so highly 'cumulative' – innovation today builds on innovation yesterday. Thus, depending when a particular actor in the 'ecosystem' enters the innovation chain, he/she is able to capture not only his/her contribution, but potentially the entire area (the integral) under the cumulative innovation curve (Lazonick and

Mazzucato 2013). In many ways, this explains the success of venture capitalists who in different sectors, such as IT and biotechnology, entered decades *after* the State invested in the most risky and capital-intensive technologies (see the eloquent quote by Berg which opens this book), and yet made a 'killing' far out of proportion to their contribution. And it can be argued that the killing has been justified by the wrong 'story' of where the success of the technologies came from. Hence the need for the Apple story to be told from start to finish.

What is uniquely apparent in the case of Apple, however, is that the company's executives and shareholders are not the sole (nor largest) bearers of the risk that was part of developing innovative products such as the iPod, iPhone and iPad. Rather – as told in detail in Chapter 5 – the success of these technologies is overwhelmingly due to the foresight of the US government in envisioning radical innovation in the electronics and communication fields going back to the 1960s and 1970s. It was not Apple executives nor its shareholders who rose to the challenges associated with the risks involved in basic science and technology investment. When no one else stepped up to the plate to take on the challenge, it was the US government, mainly the military, that dared to risk striking out and in the end, hit the home runs. Apple incrementally incorporated in each new generation of iPods, iPhones and iPads technologies that the State sowed, cultivated and ripened. These investments were made in part to address national security concerns, and only later did it become a question of enabling the exploitation of (past) technological development for commercial applications, and by extension, job creation and economic competitiveness. And the point is that Apple understood this game: creatively pioneering the field of consumer electronic dreams by stepping up to the plate and playing off the positive externalities left behind by the government's heavy hitters. But, today, it is companies like Apple who continue to ride the wave of success, keeping track on only one side of the scoreboard and rigging the end result to their advantage.

Apple's job-creation myth: Not all jobs are created equally

Apple is not only a 'new economy' company in the sense of the type of technology and knowledge that it makes intense use of, but also in terms of its strategy with the labour market. In this respect, it is useful to first consider the difference between the New Economy Business Model (NEBM) and the Old Economy Business Model (OEBM), emphasized by Lazonick (2009). The latter dominated the US corporate environment from the immediate post–Second World War era until the 1980s, and was characterized by stable employment opportunities in hierarchical corporations, generous and equitable earnings, subsidized medical coverage and substantial defined-benefit pension schemes upon retirement (Lazonick 2009, 2). In the OEBM, employment stability was highly valued and thus interfirm mobility was low. In contrast, the NEBM, widely adopted by high-tech firms developing IT, represents no or low commitment on the part of corporations to offer stable employment, skill formation and predictable and rewarding careers. On the other hand, employees not only do not expect to develop a life-long career in a single enterprise, but highly value the benefits of interfirm mobility. 'The NEBM represents dramatically diminished organizational commitment on both sides of the employment relation as compared with its Old Economy predecessor' (Lazonick 2009, 4). Globalization of the workforce is thus a consequence not only of the development of information and communication technologies, but also of the NEBM, whereby companies are footloose to seek the best combination of low-wage/high-skill employees amongst countries and locations.

Apple is often in the spotlight due to its tremendous success in product sales and corporate financial wellbeing. In August 2012, Apple's market value climbed past $623 billion, surpassing the nominal record set by Microsoft during the heyday of technology stocks in 1999. However, such popularity and success has come with a price and now Apple's success is under great scrutiny. Recent public debates involving Apple have raised issues regarding corporate tax revenues, declining manufacturing and job creation in the US, and critiques of its overseas manufacturing and production activities. Apple claims that it has directly or indirectly created 304,000 jobs over the course of its history. If one takes this figure and then adds the estimated 210,000 jobs that are focused on developing mobile applications for the Apple Store, the aggregate total is estimated at 514,000 jobs that are either created or enabled/supported by Apple (Apple 2012). Apple bases its claims on a report developed by the Analysis Group, a private consulting firm Apple hired to study its impact in the job market.[1] The attention to these numbers stems largely from the ongoing debate regarding whether or not technology companies have been contributing to overall job creation within the

---

1 The full report is not available publically. However Apple shared some of the report's findings online on their website. Available online at http://www.apple. com/about/job-creation/ (accessed 12 April 2013).

domestic manufacturing sector. Apple directly employs individuals in 47,000 jobs out of the total 304,000 that the company claims; over 27,000 jobs are employed within the 246 Apple Stores located in 44 US states. The company does not reveal exactly what portion of the 304,000 figure includes manufacturing jobs specifically (or those jobs created by overseas manufacturers such as Foxconn). Instead, it appears that this figure includes a highly diverse group of occupations within the Apple 'universe' – anyone from FedEx employees to healthcare personnel are counted as Apple employees (Vascellaro 2012).

Apple's public claim of being a strong job creator in the US has rarely been scrutinized adequately by the media, which instead contributes to the public frenzy about Apple's alluring new products. While predictions (and often rumours) about the future of Apple and its products tend to dominate the public (media) discussions on the company, during one of these media frenzies, journalist David Segal, in his *New York Times* article of 23 June 2012, discussed the company's great expansion in the retail segment of its business and the prospect of those new jobs. Apple's demand in the labour market has shown a greater increase in the retail and other services segments of its business as Apple set up more stores, data and call centres around the country. Even with online retailers such as Amazon threatening to disrupt the retail industry, forcing companies to close stores or to focus on online sales, Apple has been eager to increase its stores and focus on complete consumer satisfaction via person-to-person sales in order to boost sales. Segal (2012) documents the wage disparity between the broad employment base in the retail arm of the business and Apple's top executives. In doing so, he also discusses the lack of career prospects and upward mobility these positions at Apple tend to provide for employees. Although the company's image appeals to specific demographics for employment, pay-wise the company's remuneration policy is only slightly better than Walmart, since the company fails to offer sales commissions or a stock option plan for the majority of store employees (Segal 2012). While diffusion is key to the success of any innovation, the contribution of retail employees is not rewarded accordingly.

Labour disputes at Taiwanese contract manufacturing company Foxconn's production facilities in China, where fancy Apple products are assembled, are also rarely scrutinized. Isaac Shapiro (2012) at the Economic Policy Institute, however, compared Apple's executive pay with the average pay received by employees at the Chinese factories manufacturing Apple products. His data reveal sharp differences: in 2011, the top 9 Apple executives received a total of $440.8 million;

and, in 2012, the compensation package for these Apple executives was $411.5 million. To put this in greater perspective, the average employee at Foxconn earns $4,622 annually, meaning the top 9 executives earned the same amount of money as 95,000 workers did in 2011 and 89,000 workers did in 2012. Borrowing the method that Shapiro used, one could factor that the top 9 Apple executives are expected to earn the same amount of money as roughly 17,600 of the company's US retail employees did in 2011 (64 per cent of the total) and 15,000 (55 per cent of the total) in 2012 (Shapiro 2012).[2]

When Apple's CEO, Tim Cook, announced in February 2012 that the company has more cash ($98 billion) than it currently needs to sustain its operations, many analysts and shareholders expected Apple to return a portion of its record-high cash to its shareholders (Liedtke 2012). The top executives were intrigued by the question of what to do with the excess sitting cash, since the company had not been distributing dividends or repurchasing its own stocks during Steve Jobs' tenure. As many have predicted, Apple has recently announced a 3-year dividend and share repurchase plan that would divert slightly less than half of the company's current cash stock ($45 billion) to its shareholders (Dowling 2012). To date, no additional benefit package has been designed to benefit the company's employee base; the implication is that only Apple's shareholders are allowed to benefit financially from the company's recent and current success, even though many at the base directly contribute to it.[3]

Apple's love–hate relationship with US tax policies

The US government has a vested interest in the success of US corporations globally. Generating innovative products is reflected

---

2 Shapiro estimates a $25,000 annual earning for retail employees in 2012 and Lazonick estimates $26,000 for non-professional employees in 2011. To be consistent with Shapiro's China comparison, $441 billion in 2011 and $411.5 billion in 2012 compensation figures for top 9 Apple executives as well as the $26,000 annual earning figure for Apple's US retail employee have been used in the calculations.

3 A series of changes were implemented in 2012 to boost Apple's retail profit margins (new formula to calculate staff levels, cut in shift hours). Although the changes also included a pay rise for its retail employees, Apple also began laying off numerous recently hired retail personnel to offset the additional costs of the pay rise. Apple later recognized that these changes were a 'mistake' and reversed some of them. See Fiegerman (2012) and Haslam (2012).

in the corporations' overall success in generating financial returns so the domestic economy can expect to benefit as tax revenues increase. While it is evident that the success of products like the iPhone and iPad has provided handsome rewards for Apple, it is difficult to determine whether the US government has managed to recuperate its investment.

Experts argue that the current US tax system was designed for an industrial age where the nature of the production model and process required some degree of stickiness or embeddedness to the physical location of businesses. In today's terms, capital moves much faster, much farther, and is even virtual. In his 1999 book *Capital Moves*, Jefferson Cowie (1999) retraced the travel route of RCA, one of the most successful US companies at the beginning of the twentieth century, in its global search for locations that could lower factory costs. Among today's most successful corporations, this motivation to lower manufacturing and production costs still exists – and is in fact widespread amongst firms adopting the New Economy Business Model, referred to earlier. However, with the advent of transnational/multinational corporations, and an increasingly globalized economy, the jobs are not simply shuffled domestically from say, Camden, New Jersey through to Bloomington, Indiana and to Memphis, Tennessee. In today's world, companies like Apple have a much larger, global canvas to work with in driving down costs.

The absence of regulatory institutions to govern globalization makes it easy for companies such as Apple to turn trade into a complex web of affairs. The journey of popular Apple products such as the iPod, iPhone and iPad, begins in the corporate R&D base that is housed mainly in California (where product design and architecture is created, developed and tested), with other locations spread amongst various technology clusters in the US. As explained in Chapter 5, Apple's products have been designed and engineered utilizing the innovative technologies that have been developed largely through federal funding and research. Once a product is designed and engineered, they are ready to be launched in consumer markets. But they first need to be produced – and this doesn't happen in California, but where manufacturing labour is cheap. So, for example, you may have a customer walk into a store and place an order for an iPhone. This newly purchased product consists of components that are mostly manufactured in places such as South Korea, Japan and Taiwan, and the whole device is then assembled in China. Kraemer and colleagues (2011) estimate that, of the total value that is created per device, Apple recoups 58.5 per cent in profit. By further deducting the share of other non-Apple US profits (approximately 2.4 per cent) from the total value, then 30 per cent of the value is captured in non-US markets. The estimates for iPad and iPod value distributions are slightly higher. Almost 53 per cent of the iPad and 49 per cent of the iPod's value has been reportedly captured in non-US markets (Linden et al. 2009; Kraemer et al. 2011).

How much of value captured in the US is really converted into taxes? In recent times, Apple's record-breaking product sales with relatively high profit margins as well as the company's significant cash stock have come to dominate the public media discourse equally with the popularity of its products. In April 2012, several journalists from the *New York Times* published a series of articles on Apple. In these articles, controversial information regarding Apple's tax strategies and employment practices emerged. In the third part of the series, 'How Apple sidesteps billions in taxes', the corporate scheme that enables the company to significantly minimize its tax liabilities was carefully outlined. According to Charles Duhigg and David Kocieniewski (2012), Apple has used common practices which have resulted in a much lower tax bill for the US government. Furthermore, according to a *New York Times* investigation, Apple formed a subsidiary in Reno, Nevada, where there is no corporate income or capital gains tax in order to avoid state taxes. Creatively naming the company Braeburn Capital, Apple used the subsidiary to channel a portion of its US profit, instead of including that money in the profit total reported in California, where its headquarters are located. Since 2006, Apple reportedly earned $2.5 billion in interest and dividends, and to avoid capital gains tax in California, the interest and dividend earnings have been reported in Nevada. The state of California's infamously large level of debt would be significantly reduced if Apple had fully and accurately reported its US revenues in the state where a major portion of its value (architecture, design, sales, marketing etc.) was created and achieved. These facts simply reinforce that the tax system is not one that can be relied on for recouping investments in risky innovation, in this case by the state of California.[4]

The corporate tax-shuffling scheme outlined above is not used by Apple for just domestic tax purposes. In fact, Duhigg and Kocienicwski (2012) note that Apple adopts a similar approach in the global sphere by setting up

---

4 In fact, hundreds of millions of dollars' worth of special tax packages have been approved by the local authorities for Apple to set up data operations in locations such as Reno, NV, Austin, TX, Maiden, NC and Prineville, OR. For more information about this issue, please see Sande (2012), Lee (2012) and Blodget (2011).

various subsidiaries in corporate tax havens such as Luxembourg, Ireland, the Netherlands and the British Virgin Islands in order to shuffle profits around and benefit from low-tax advantages. US tax code allows American companies to assign their product or service intellectual property (IP) rights to their foreign subsidiaries, which also allows companies to reduce their tax liabilities at a significant rate. In the case of Apple, as Duhigg and Kocieniewski explain, the company's Irish subsidiaries reportedly own the IP rights of many products and receive royalty payments from Apple's product sales. Ownership of those Irish subsidiaries is also shared with another Apple subsidiary (Baldwin Holdings Unlimited) in another tax haven location, the British Virgin Islands.

It is difficult to calculate the exact figures regarding how much Apple has managed to save through this global tax-shuffling scheme. Sullivan (2012, 777) argues that if Apple were to report half of its profit in the US as opposed to only 30 per cent, the company's tax liability in 2011 would have been $2.4 billion higher than it actually was. According to Sullivan, if Apple had actually reported 70 per cent of its profits in the US, the difference would have been $4.8 billion. Sullivan justifies his argument and calculations with the following:

> There will never be a precise answer as to where profits are created. But if the corporate tax is a tax on income, it is reasonable to place products where value is created. In Apple's case, can there be any doubt that most of its value is created inside the United States? (2012, 777)

Both Sullivan (2012) and Duhigg and Kocieniewski (2012) highlight the fact that such global tax-shuffling schemes are certainly not unique to Apple. Rather, other technology companies like Google, Oracle and Amazon also benefit from enacting similar global tax schemes.[5] In an article from Bloomberg, a similar strategy utilized by Google helps

---

5 A recent report (McIntyre et al. 2011) reveals that some 30 major US companies pay almost no tax in the US whatsoever. GE is a top tax dodger – paying no taxes at all in 2009 and 2010. In fact, some companies finish their year with a net credit. The report claims that GE has about a thousand employees organizing their exploitation of tax benefits and shelters. Such 'net credits' distort the motives under which business may be operating. In an updated press release, the Citizens for Tax Justice found that GE's effective tax rate between 2002 and 2011 was just 1.8 per cent, a far cry from the official US corporate tax rate of 35.1 per cent (Citizens for Tax Justice 2012).

the company benefit from the tax breaks afforded by the same global locations as used by Apple (Drucker 2010). Interestingly, in addition to the taxes that companies like Apple, Google, Amazon and Microsoft already manage to avoid, these companies are also pressuring legislators for a 'repatriation tax holiday' for their stockpile of cash parked in tax-free locations. Such a holiday has been estimated to reach $79 billion over the decade and there is no assurance that the repatriated profit would be utilized for further development of existing capabilities (Duhigg and Kocieniewski 2012). The pledge for a 'repatriation tax holiday' is even more appalling in light of Apple's and other major corporations' share repurchase programmes (Lazonick 2011). Given the pervasive attention paid to 'maximizing shareholder value' over all other concerns, nothing therefore guarantees that the repatriated cash will not end up in executives' and shareholders' pockets.

While public policies on innovation should not just focus on areas like R&D tax credits, but rather on creating the market and technological opportunities that will increase private investment (neither Bill Gates nor Steve Jobs were sitting around thinking of the savings they could find from tax credits), it is also true that once such investments are made, business can make large savings (higher profits) with different types of tax credits and reductions. The fact that some of the businesses that have benefitted most from large public investments are the same that have lobbied for tax reductions that have significantly reduced the public purse should open eyes and lead to policy changes – the subject of Chapter 9.

It is important to emphasize that Steve Jobs' success in leading Apple was due to his focus on the long run through the messy world of innovation and design – and that it is no coincidence that under his leadership Apple did not enact short-term practices like stock-repurchase or dividend programmes, which use up money that could be employed on research and design. His steadfast focus on architectural innovations that *disrupt* the markets in which they compete are the reason that he managed and deserved to capture a significant share of the rewards – and recognition – that followed. However, Apple is a 'collective' organization as well, and the company's success is dependent on the full participation of its talented workforce to succeed. Ignoring how such innovation depended greatly on State-funded radical components, and denying the State its reward (via taxes, and as argued in Chapter 9, in more direct ways as well) will not help future shiny apples to emerge.

The paradox of miracles in the digital economy: Why does corporate success result in regional economic misery?

The 2008 recession helped reveal the stark decline in US competitiveness, which laid dormant for various reasons until the financial crisis hit. The high debt level of the state of California is just symptomatic of a larger epidemic facing the US. Even before the crisis hit hard, the National Academy of Sciences (NAS) was requested by a bipartisan group of US senators and members of Congress to assemble a team of experts whose purpose was to identify the reasons for the decline in US competitiveness. The committee was put in charge of providing policy recommendations that would help the US re-emerge as the global leader in science and technology. In 2005, the NAS committee provided its recommendations in a 500-page document titled 'Rising above the Gathering Storm', declaring that State interventions were the necessary and key solution for repositioning the nation as a leader of innovative capabilities. In 2010, the NAS policy recommendations were again revisited and a follow-up report concluded that immediate action was needed in order to stop the current trends and minimize the repercussions of continued US competitive decline.

Augustine's statement that opens this chapter draws attention to the overwhelming innovative climate that existed in California – a climate from which companies, like Apple, have significantly benefitted over the years. The innovation and creativity that this environment spurred was in large part due to the direct investment and procurement by the US government and military in the fields of communication and information technology. The ultimate purpose of putting tax dollars to use for the development of new technologies is to take on the risk that normally accompanies the pursuit of innovative complex products and systems required to achieve collective goals. It is this hefty risk that tends to serve as a disincentive for the business sector to invest on its own. In theory, the effects of successful innovation, which leads to a superior outcome, should be seen and experienced within the wider economy. As superior outcomes lead to new products and/or services that, in turn, improve the quality of lives, create new employment opportunities for the able workforce, significantly increase the nation's foreign export and competitiveness, and then lead to significant increase in tax revenues, it is often believed that investments in innovation would eventually be reinvested in the nation's tangible and intangible assets.

Through this upward cycle of multiplying State investments in the science and technology base, the national economy would pave the way for future sustainable prosperity. And yet, the irony of these successes is that as companies such as Apple, Google, GE, Cisco etc. are flourishing financially, their home economy is struggling to find its way out of debilitating economic issues like the growing trade deficit against Asian economies, declining manufacturing activities, increasing unemployment, widening budget deficits, inequality, deteriorating infrastructure etc. The current economic turmoil cannot be explained solely by the banking crisis, the credit crunch or the collapse of the mortgage market. The problems faced today are structurally complex and run much deeper. It is important to assess the effects of innovation, whether they have resulted in an increase in the number of new jobs that pay liveable wages or better, an increase in tax revenues, and/or an increase in the export of high-value goods and services. Decades of government investment in the science and technology base have made the US a successful innovator, but have paradoxically failed to secure high levels of employment, to increase tax revenues, and to promote export of goods and services. Apple is the prime example of how and why the national economy experiences such paradox.

There are interesting policy questions to be raised in response to the growing interest and research regarding Apple and other tech companies' innovative products and success. As argued in Lazonick (2009) the Old Economy Business Model was key in creating the golden age of the mass-production/Fordist technological revolution, with the capital, labour and the State all sharing its potential and benefits. This was an era in which 'job stability' and real-income growth was deemed more important than insecurity and 'start-up' millionaires. It is important to remember that while innovation is a key source of long-run growth, promoting innovation is not the same thing as promoting 'equitable' growth. Equitable growth is delivered, to a greater extent, by working conditions and good salaries within business organizations.

The big question for us here is: will the New Economy Business Model transform itself so as to distribute the benefits of the ICT revolution? Despite all the success that these new technologies have brought to Apple, how does Apple decide to distribute the wealth created within the company? Will the company continue providing more secure jobs with adequate job training, living wages, potential for upward mobility, and benefits necessary to sustain a real work–life balance? Or, perhaps, will the company utilize its record-breaking cash stock to reward a privileged minority consisting of executives, shareholders and investors? Its decisions have real impacts not only on the performance of the economy, but on the quality of life it delivers to its thousands of employees.

Where Are Today's Bell Labs?

The innovation ecosystem, which has evolved as a result of decades of support and interventions by the US government, has handsomely rewarded the new economy businesses. In many ways, it has been a 'field of dreams' for business enterprises like Apple. And while the policy literature by definition recognizes the role of the State, it has failed to make the direct connection between the State's policy activity and results regarding firm development, strategic decision making and innovation. The State, even by those that believe in public policy, is described as a facilitator not a dynamic engine. And as a result, US corporations have often lost sight of what has made today's success possible.

A recent MIT multidisciplinary study[6] has looked at the strengths and weaknesses of the US innovation system and the causes of relative decline of manufacturing in America. The study has strived to understand why the development of promising innovations are stalling or simply moving abroad before reaching commercial scale. One of the reasons unveiled by the study is the fact that large R&D centres – like Bell Labs, Xerox PARC and Alcoa Research Lab – have become a thing of the past in big corporations; they have mostly disappeared. Long-term basic and applied research is not part of the strategy of 'Big Business' anymore, as corporate R&D now focuses on short-term needs. The study argues that 'large holes in the [US] industrial ecosystem have appeared':

> In the thirties, a corporation like DuPont not only invested for a decade in the fundamental research that led to nylon, but once the lab had a promising product, DuPont had the capital and the plants to bring it into production. Today, when innovation is

---

6 The Production in the Innovation Economy (PIE) project draws on several disciplines (economics, engineering, political science, management, biology and others) to shed light on how the United States' strengths in innovation can be scaled up into new productive capabilities in an era of increased global competition. On 22 February 2013, PIE researchers released a preview of the project's findings, which will appear in two books to be published in Fall 2013: *Making in America: From Innovation to Market* and *Production in the Innovation Economy*. The findings and quotes from the following paragraphs are therefore from this preview: PIE Commission, *A Preview of the MIT Production in the Innovation Economy Report* (Cambridge, MA: MIT Press, 2013).

more likely to emerge in small spin-offs or out of university or government labs, where do the scale-up resources come from? How available is the funding needed at each of the critical stages of scale-up: prototyping, pilot production, demonstration and test, early-manufacturing, full-scale commercialization? When scale-up is funded mainly through merger and acquisition of the adolescent start-ups and when the acquiring firms are foreign, how does the American economy benefit? (PIE Commission 2013, 26)

The study argues that corporations are reluctant to provide the public good that spilled over to society from these labs because they cannot capture the full rent from R&D. Yet, as discussed in Chapter 3, this is the usual explanation for why the government must fund areas like basic research, which are hard to appropriate. What is not clear however is why and how this has changed over time. The wedge between private and social returns (arising from the spillovers of R&D) was just as true in the era of Bell Labs as they are today. And what is missing most today is the private component of R&D working in real partnership with the public component, creating what I call later a less symbiotic ecosystem. It is thus less important to talk about partnerships and ecosystems and more important to talk about the 'type of' ecosystems that we want to have, symbiotic or parasitic, and what sort of policies can get the private sector to 'step up to the game', rather than step out by focusing only on short-term profit-raising areas, expecting the government to carry out the high-risk investments. Is it right that in an era when the NIH budget for the R in R&D is rising every year, hitting close to $30.9 billion in 2012, large pharmaceutical companies are closing down their R&D units in the name of 'open innovation'? Is this reaction one which will improve the innovation ecosystem?

Future competitiveness – consequently the socioeconomic prosperity – of nations and regions is highly dependent on their ability to maintain their most valued asset: the innovation ecosystem that they are part of. Given, however, that the innovation game can also be rigged, it is crucial to understand not only how to build an effective innovation 'ecosystem', but also and perhaps especially, how to transform that ecosystem so that it is symbiotic rather than 'parasitic', so that public–private partnerships increase the stake, commitment and return of all players investing in the innovation game.

Chapter 9

SOCIALIZATION OF RISK AND PRIVATIZATION OF REWARDS: CAN THE ENTREPRENEURIAL STATE EAT ITS CAKE TOO?

A new pharmaceutical that brings in more than $1 billion per year in revenue is a drug marketed by Genzyme. It is a drug for a rare disease that was initially developed by scientists at the National Institutes of Health. The firm set the price for a year's dosage at upward of $350,000. While legislation gives the government the right to sell such government-developed drugs at 'reasonable' prices, policymakers have not exercised this right. The result is an extreme instance where the costs of developing this drug were socialized, while the profits were privatized. Moreover, some of the taxpayers who financed the development of the drug cannot obtain it for their family members because they cannot afford it.

Vallas, Kleinman and Biscotti
(2009, 24)

The Skewed Reality of Risk and Reward

In finance, it is commonly accepted that there is a relationship between risk and return. After the financial crisis, many have rightly noted that finance has increasingly privatized the rewards of their activities while socializing the risk (Alessandri and Haldane 2009). This dysfunctional dynamic has also been happening in the innovation game. Risk taking has been an increasingly collective endeavour – with the State playing a leading role in the 'open innovation' system – while the returns have been much less collectively distributed.

Many people correctly highlighted the financial crisis and subsequent bailouts as proof that we were operating an economy that socialized risk and privatized rewards of economies in a manner that enriched elites at the expense of everyone else. The bailouts highlighted the financial sector as a potentially parasitic drain on the economy that we are forced to accept. In the financial sector, banks have sliced risk so finely, traded it, and cashed it in so many times that their share of profits far outstrips those of the 'real economy'. Financial firms have grown to such incomprehensible sizes and embedded themselves so deeply into the global economy that they could be described as 'too big to fail'; many fear that regardless of their recklessness, their essential survival ensures that the next time their hubris peaks they will get bailed out by the State (bankrupting the State in the process). Fairly or not, they are positioned to win on the upside, and also on the downside. The fact that interest rates are counted in GDP as a 'service' rendered for the sector's intermediation of risk should be revisited now that we know who assumes the real risk. Interest in this sense is purely rent, usury.

What we have seen in the course of this book is that a similar dysfunction occurs in the world of manufacturing – even in the best of manufacturing. So while the financial crisis has correctly made many policymakers want to nurture the 'real economy' through industrial strategy, policies must be careful not to add fuel to the fire. Instead of throwing money at 'life sciences' or IT, we must first correct some of the dysfunctions in these sectors. In pharmaceuticals, while the State undertakes the riskiest research, it is Big Pharma that cashes in the major rewards. Even as clean technologies like wind and solar power struggle to gain a foothold in world energy systems, the executives and shareholders (even of the losing firms!) find themselves able to reap millions in returns underwritten in part by the State (Hopkins and Lazonick 2012). And in 'new economy' sectors, companies like Apple reap the benefits from State-funded technologies, as well as State-funded risk finance, and then pay hardly any tax which could be used to fund future 'smart' technologies. Where is the future in such a system of socialized risk and privatized rewards?

The conversation that is needed in rebalancing the economy is thus not only about the size and balance of activities in the financial sector. It is not enough for countries to push innovation or plead for manufacturing revival. What is needed is a functional risk–reward dynamic that replaces the dysfunctional 'socialized risk' and 'privatized rewards' characterizing the current economic crisis and evidenced in modern industry as well as finance. The right balance of risk and rewards can nurture – rather than undermine – future innovation and reflect its collective nature through a broader diffusion of the benefit.

As argued in previous chapters, the fact is that not enough attention is given to the question of who the real risk takers are within the innovation process. The 'bumpy' uneven distribution of risk discussed in Chapter 1 has allowed some agents (like VCs) in the innovation ecosystem to describe themselves as the lead risk takers, and in so doing lobby for large shares of the rewards (Lazonick and Mazzucato 2013). Interestingly, while some well-known venture capitalists recognize the leading role of the State (Janeway 2012), they are less ready to give away some of the returns they have been able to capture from such investments, and even less willing to allow the State to increase capital gains and corporate income taxes, for which reduction the VC industry itself has been one of the chief lobbyists (Lazonick 2009, 73). Venture capitalists, having convinced policymakers (and much of the mainstream media) that they are the 'entrepreneurial' force in the 'knowledge economy', benefit from major tax breaks and low rates placed upon capital gains (from which they derive the majority of their economic returns).

The idea of an entrepreneurial State suggests that one of the core missing links between growth and inequality (or to use the words of the EC 2020 strategy, between 'smart' and 'inclusive' growth) lies in a wider identification and understanding of the agents that contribute to the risk taking required for that growth to occur. Bank bonuses, for example, should not logically be criticized using arguments against the greed and the underlying inequality that they produce (even though these generate powerful emotions). Rather they should be argued against by attacking the underlying logical foundation on which they stand – which is that such compensation is a reflection of risks taken in the process of economic development.

The received wisdom is that bankers take on very high risks, and when those risks reap a high return, they should in fact be rewarded – 'they deserve it'. A similar logic is used to justify the exorbitantly high returns that powerful shareholders have earned in the last decades, which has been another prime source of increasing inequality. The logic here is that shareholders are the biggest risk takers since they only earn the returns that are left over once all the other economic actors are paid (the 'residual' if it exists, once workers and managers are paid their salaries, loans and other expenses are paid off, and so on). Hence when there is a large residual, shareholders are the proper claimant – they could in fact have earned nothing since there is no guarantee that there will be a residual (Jensen 1986; for a critique see Lazonick 2012). Or so goes the theory.

Shareholder-value ideology is based on this notion of shareholders as the 'residual claimants' and thus the lead risk takers with no guaranteed rate of return (Jensen 1986). This argument has been used to justify shareholders' massive returns (Lazonick 2007; Lazonick and Mazzucato 2013). Yet this framework assumes that other agents in the system (taxpayers, workers) *do* have a guaranteed rate of return, amongst other things ignoring the fact that some of the riskiest investments by government have no guarantee at all: for every successful investment that leads to a new technology like the Internet, there are a host of failed investments – precisely because innovation is so uncertain. But reducing the ability of the State to either collect tax, or to receive its fair share from the returns, hurts its future ability to take such risk – a matter to which I turn to in the next section.

Most importantly, identification of who bears risk cannot be achieved by simply asserting that shareholders are the only contributors to the economy who do not have a guaranteed return – a central, and fallacious, assumption of financial economics based on agency theory. Indeed insofar as public shareholders simply buy and sell shares, and are willing to do so because of the ease with which they can liquidate these portfolio investments, they may make little if any contribution to the innovation process and bear little if any risk of its success or failure. In contrast, governments may invest capital and workers may invest labour (time and effort) into the innovation process without any guarantee of a return commensurate with their investments – and without guarantee that they will be 'bailed out' (or not laid off) in case of failures. For the sake of innovation, we need social institutions that enable these risk bearers to reap the returns from the innovation process, if and when it is successful.

A better understanding of risk gives credit to the role of the public sector in innovative activities. Doing so makes it immediately logical for there to be a more collective distribution of the rewards, given that the presence of innovation is a result of a long-term cumulative, collective and uncertain process (and not just well-timed speculative finance). Central to this understanding is the need to better identify how the division of 'innovative labour' maps into a division of rewards. The innovation literature has provided many interesting insights on the former, for example the changing dynamic between large firms, small firms, government research and individuals in the innovation process.

But there is very little understanding on how rewards are divided. And, as has been argued, governments and workers also make investments in the innovation process (if not greater investments) without guaranteed returns – Apple's case is clear in this respect.

The critical point is the relation between those who bear risk in contributing their labour and capital to the innovation process and those who appropriate rewards from the innovation process. As a general set of propositions of the risk–reward nexus, when the appropriation of rewards outstrips the bearing of risk in the innovation process, the result is inequity; when the extent of inequity disrupts investment in the innovation process, the result is instability; and when the extent of instability increases the uncertainty of the innovation process, the result is a slowdown or even decline in economic growth. A major challenge is to put in place institutions to regulate the risk–reward nexus so that it supports equitable and stable economic growth.

To achieve this it is essential to understand innovation as a collective process, involving an extensive division of labour that can include many different stakeholders. As a foundation for the innovation process, the State typically makes investments in physical and human infrastructure that individual employees and business enterprises would be unable to fund on their own, both because of the high amount of fixed costs that investment in innovation requires and also because of the degree of uncertainty that such investment entails. The State also subsidizes the investments that enable individual employees and business enterprises to participate in the innovation process. Academic researchers often interact with industry experts in the knowledge-generation process. Within industry, there are research consortia that may include companies that are otherwise in competition with one another. There are also user–producer interactions in product development within the value chain. Within the firm's hierarchical and functional division of labour, there is the integration of organizational learning into process routines that leverage the skills and efforts of large numbers of people.

A New Framework

What are the mechanisms that can help ensure that growth is not only 'smart' but also 'inclusive' (e.g. the goal of the EC's 2020 strategy)? What explains the reasons why innovation and inequality have gone hand in hand? While the classical economists (such as David Ricardo or Karl Marx) studied innovation and distribution together through, for example, the analysis of the effect of mechanization on the wage/profit ratio, for years studies of innovation and distribution have been separated. Today, they have been brought back together mainly by the de-skilling perspective and its realization that innovation has a tendency of allowing those with high skills to prosper, and those with low skills to get left behind (Acemoglu 2002). Yet skills and technology in this perspective remain exogenous, their existence taken as givens. Neither can the framework explain where innovation and better job skills come from. Given those issues, it is very hard to accept that the main source of inequality – between the top 1 per cent of income earners and the bottom 99 per cent – is the super 'high skills' of the 1 per cent relative to everyone else (Atkinson et al. 2011). Explaining such a massive wage gap requires a new framework.

In Lazonick and Mazzucato (2013), we build a *risk–reward nexus* framework to study the relationship between innovation and inequality – which is nested in a theory of innovation. We ask: What types of economic actors (workers, taxpayers, shareholders) make contributions of effort and money to the innovation process for the sake of future, inherently uncertain, returns? Are these the same types of economic actors who are able to appropriate returns from the innovation process if and when they appear? That is, who takes the risks and who gets the rewards? We argue that it is the collective, cumulative and uncertain characteristics of the innovation process that make this disconnect between risks and rewards possible.

We argue that when, across these different types of collective actors (in the 'ecosystem'), the distribution of financial rewards from the innovation process reflects the distribution of contributions to the innovation process, innovation tends to reduce inequality. When, however, some actors are able to reap shares of financial rewards from the innovation process that are disproportionate to their contributions to the process, innovation increases inequality. The latter outcome occurs when certain actors are able to position themselves at the point – along the cumulative innovation curve – where the innovative enterprise generates financial returns; that is, close to the final product market or, in some cases, close to a financial market such as the stock market. These favoured actors then propound ideological arguments, typically with intellectual roots in the efficiency propositions of neoclassical economics (and the related theory of 'shareholder value'), that justify the disproportionate shares of the gains from innovation that they have been able to appropriate. These ideological arguments invariably favour financial contributions to the innovation process over both worker contributions and taxpayer contributions. Ultimately, precisely because innovation is a collective and cumulative process, the imbalance in the risk–reward nexus not only results in greater inequality but also undermines the innovation process itself.

Finding a way to realign risk taking with rewards is thus crucial not only for decreasing inequality but also for fostering more innovation.

Direct or Indirect Returns

Given the commonly accepted relationship between risk and return in finance theory, if the State is so important to funding high-risk investments in innovation, it should follow that the State should earn back a direct return on its risky investments, Such returns can be used to fund the next round of innovations, but also help cover the inevitable losses that arise when investing in high-risk areas. So rather than worrying too much about the State's in/ability to 'pick winners', more thought should be dedicated to how to reward the wins when they happen so that the returns can cover the losses from the inevitable failures, as well as funding new future wins. Put provocatively, had the State earned back just 1 per cent from the investments it made in the Internet, there would be much more today to invest in green tech.

Many argue that it is inappropriate to consider direct returns to the State because the State already earns a return from its investments, *indirectly* via the taxation system. Such an argument assumes, however, that the taxation system already draws revenue 'fair and square' from multiple sources and by extension, that tax expenditures reflect the best possible configuration of support for economic growth. The reality is, however, that the tax system was not conceived to support innovation systems, which are disproportionately driven by actors who are willing to invest decades before returns appear on the horizon. Not only that, but the argument ignores the fact that tax avoidance and tax evasion are common and realistically will not disappear (in the UK, recent research suggests that the total 'tax gap', i.e. tax income not collected, which includes tax evasions, tax avoidance and late payments, is £120 billion, nearly the same size of the national deficit which stands at £126 billion).[1]

Given that modern businesses are often global organizations doing business within multiple governments responding to the needs of

---

1 http://www.taxresearch.org.uk/Documents/FAQ1TaxGap.pdf (accessed 1 March 2013).

multiple Developmental States, it is all but impossible to judge whether the State's support for innovation in one region is adequately returned to it by the businesses active there. The movement of capital (business) means that the particular region doing the most to fund the innovation might *not* be positioned to reap the economic benefits later in terms of, for example, local job creation and taxes. Assuming that the taxation system accurately captures the proper share of revenue that arises from State investments is both problematic and naïve.

Apple is a paradigmatic example here. As shown in Chapter 5, Apple received its early stage funding from the US government's SBIR programme, and all the technologies which make the iPhone 'smart' are also State funded (with links to US programmes): the Internet, wireless networks, GPS, microelectronics, touch-screen displays and the latest voice-activated SIRI personal assistant. Yet, as discussed in Chapter 8, Apple has commonly used practices that have resulted in a much lower tax bill for the US government. It has also elected to scatter its own R&D and manufacturing activities around the globe, leaving little to the US but low-paid retail positions within a network of retail stores. Given the company's global footprint, the US tax system is not one that can reliably or accurately recoup State investments that helped forge 'winners' like Apple by supporting a series of risky innovations.

But the problem is even more evident in the pharmaceutical industry. As discussed earlier, three-quarters of the new molecular biopharmaceutical entities owe their creation to publicly funded laboratories. Yet in the past ten years, the top ten companies in this industry have made more in profits than the rest of the Fortune 500 companies combined. The industry also enjoys great tax advantages: its R&D costs are deductible, and so are many of its massive marketing expenses, some of which are counted as R&D (Angell 2004). After taking on most of the R&D bill, the State often gives away the outputs at a rock-bottom rate. For example, Taxol, the cancer drug discovered by the National Institutes of Health (NIH), is sold by Bristol-Myers Squibb for $20,000 per year's dose, 20 times the manufacturing cost. Yet, the company pays the NIH just 0.5 per cent in royalties for the drug. In most other cases, nothing at all is paid in royalties. It is simply assumed that the public investment is meant to help create profits for the firms in question, with little to no thinking about the obvious distorted distribution of risk and reward this presents.

What to do? I offer some concrete suggestions below.

Golden share of IPR and a national 'innovation fund'

Where an applied technological breakthrough is directly financed by the government, the government should in return be able to extract a royalty from its application. Returns from the royalties, earned across sectors and technologies, should be paid into a national 'innovation fund' which the government can use to fund future innovations. Granting a return to the State should not prohibit the dissemination of new technology throughout the economy, or disincentivize innovators from taking on their share of the risk. Instead it makes the policy of spending taxpayers' money to catalyse radical innovations more sustainable, by enabling part of the financial gains from so doing to be recycled directly back into the programme over time. A first step towards starting this process is increasing the transparency of government investment – by making it easier to track government expenditures in support of industry and by getting companies to report on the content and value of their public–private collaborations in a way that does not compromise proprietary information. The better the information we can glean from the innovation process, the more effective our policy choices can become.

Burlamaqui (2012) argues that this problem cannot be solved through fixing market failures, but must be thought about more broadly in terms of market shaping – through the concept of 'knowledge governance'. He states: 'From a knowledge-governance perspective, the critical question that should be asked here is: when does extended protection cease to work for generating Schumpeterian profits and become a base for rent-seeking and rent extraction?' (Burlamaqui 2012, 5). He argues that a tool for governing publicly funded knowledge would be for the government to retain a golden share of patents that emerge from publicly funded research, making sure that the owner of the patent behaves cooperatively, e.g. licensing the patent *broadly* and *fairly* after an initial period of protection. The first mover should be able to recover their costs but not exclude others from drawing on the innovation.

Income-contingent loans and equity

There are various other possibilities for considering a direct return to the State for its investments in innovation. One is to make sure that loans and guarantees that are handed out by the State to business do not come without strings attached. Loans as well as grants could have conditions, like income-contingent loans, similar to *student loans*. If and when a company makes profits above a certain threshold, after it has received a loan/grant from the State, it should be required to pay back a portion. After Google made billions in profits, shouldn't a small percentage have gone back to fund the public agency that funded its algorithm?

Besides income-contingent loans there is the possibility of the State retaining equity in the companies that it supports. Indeed, this does occur in many countries, such as Finland, where SITRA, one of Finland's public funding agencies, retained equity in its early stage investments in Nokia. The investment is exactly the type of early stage investment that VC has increasingly shied away from. Yet State equity in private companies is feared in countries like the US and the UK (and those countries copying the Anglo-Saxon model) for fear that the next step is... communism. And yet this is pure and plain capitalism: the most successful capitalist economies have had active States, making such risky investments, and we have been too quick to criticize them when things go wrong (e.g. Concorde) and too slow to reward them when things go right (e.g. the Internet).

Development banks

There is of course a more direct tool which is a State investment bank. While many have argued the importance of a State investment bank for the needs of countercyclical lending (Skidelsky, Martin and Wigstrom 2012), another reason why they are important is precisely to reap back a return in order to fund future investments. In 2012 KfW, the German State investment bank, reported $3 billion in profits, while most private banks are in the red, with many experiencing falling profits (KfW 2011). And indeed, if/when the State institution is run by people who not only believe in the power of the State but also have expertise understanding the innovation process, then the result produces a high reward. A good example is the Brazilian State development bank BNDES, which has been actively investing in innovation in both cleantech and biotechnology. In 2010 it made 21 per cent return on equity (ROE). The percentage retained by BNDES was reinvested in key new sectors, focusing specifically on the Death Valley stage of biotechnology in which private VC is so absent. The role of State investment banks can and does go further however, as the China Development Bank (CDB) is not only a substitute for 'private finance' that is too risk averse to invest in its solar manufacturers, but a means of creating opportunities for manufacturers. One such case was the CDB's $3 billion financing of the largest wind project in Argentina using Chinese wind turbines. Argentinean wind developers received the finance unavailable to them through commercial means, and China got sales for one of its wind manufacturers, along with the interest from the loans, which can contribute to future economic ends (Nielsen 2012).

In summary, 'smart', inclusive and sustainable growth will not happen on its own. Specific instruments need to be in place to make that happen. This discussion is just a start.

Chapter 10

CONCLUSION

In seeking to promote innovation-led growth, it is fundamental to understand the important roles that both the public and private sector can play. This requires not only understanding the importance of the innovation 'ecosystem' but especially *what it is that each actor brings to that system*. The assumption that the public sector can at best incentivize private sector–led innovation (through subsidies, tax reductions, carbon pricing, technical standards and so on), especially but not only in the face of the recent crisis, fails to account for the many examples in which the leading entrepreneurial force came from the State rather than from the private sector. Ignoring this role has impacted the types of public–private partnerships that are created (potentially parasitic rather than symbiotic), and has wasted money on ineffective incentives (including different types of tax cuts) that could have been spent more effectively.

To understand the fundamental role of the State in taking on the risks present in modern capitalism, it is important to recognize the 'collective' character of innovation. Different types of firms (large and small), different types of finance and different types of State policies, institutions and departments interact sometimes in unpredictable ways – but surely in ways we can help shape to meet the desired ends. The *systems of innovation* literature, pioneered by Freeman (1995), Lundvall (1992) and Nelson (1993) is especially relevant here. There is increasing reliance on such horizontal systems of diffusion as we move to open innovation systems where barriers between public and private collaboration are reduced.

For years we have known that innovation is not just a result of R&D spending, but about the set of institutions that allow new knowledge to diffuse throughout the economy. Dynamic science–industry links are one way that innovation gets supported, but the examples in this book have shown that the 'links' can go much deeper, and extend back decades.

It becomes much more difficult to continue to visualize the innovation process as one occurring through separate and isolated activities of the State and the firm.

But rather than introducing new trendy words, like *ecosystems* of innovation to describe the innovative process, it is now more important than ever to understand the division of 'innovative' labour between the different actors in these systems, and in particular, the role and commitment of each actor in the context of the very *bumpy risk landscape* within which they are operating. While the State needs to take risks, it should not be simply absorbing (or even 'mitigating') the risk of the private sector, but taking the kind of risks that the private sector is not willing to take, and also reaping returns from that risk taking. Reaping the returns is crucial, because the innovation cycle can thus be sustained over time (with returns from the current round funding the next round – as well as the inevitable losses along the way) and be less susceptible to political and business cycles. Public policies should focus on the specific role the public sector plays, within and between sectors and institutions, in order to allow things to happen *that otherwise would not have* – exactly as Keynes argued in *The End of Laissez Faire* (1926). This is not only about the important countercyclical role that public sector spending should have (and unfortunately is not having today due to the austerity ideology), but also about the types of questions that must be posed to each individual policy instrument: e.g. do R&D tax credits make R&D happen that would otherwise not have?

It is precisely due to its different character (from business) that the State cannot have an 'exact' and 'limited' role in innovation (a sort of balancing point). Accepting this difference means that we need a way to both understand the State's specific area of influence as well as the specific performance indicators that are needed to judge its activities. For example, while funding for the Concorde aeroplane (the usual example that is used to accuse the government of 'picking winners') can be seen as failure, a real understanding of the State's performance in that enterprise should go beyond a simplistic cost–benefit analysis and take into account the full spillovers – tangible and intangible – that the investments in Concorde entailed. Has this ever been done? No, and yet it seems that everyone is in broad agreement that it was a massive failure.

What distinguishes the State is of course not only its mission but also the different tools and means that it has to deploy the mission. In Karl Polanyi's epic book *The Great Transformation* (1944), he argued the

State created – pushing, not only nudging – the most 'capitalist' of all markets, the 'national market' (while local and international ones have predated capitalism). The capitalist economy will always be subordinate to the State and subject to its changes. Thus rather than relying on the false dream that 'markets' will run the world optimally for us 'if we just let them alone', policymakers must better learn how to efficiently use the tools and means to shape and create markets – making things happen that otherwise would not. And making sure those things are things we need. Increasingly this requires growth to be not only 'smart' but also 'inclusive' and 'sustainable'.

It is of course important not to romanticize the State's difference and its ability. The State fearing 'nukes' from the USSR, the sinking of Florida or running out of oil may cause it to do what no one else can – e.g. use its ability to *create money* and risk wasting it on an inane idea/solution, such as war. On the other hand, the State can do this by leveraging a massive national social network of knowledge and business acumen – all with the knowledge that no matter what, tax dollars will keep coming in because, ultimately, the State is an active compulsory force in our lives – which we need, however, to make sure will be controlled with our just, fragmented government structures and election processes.

To rely solely and strictly on Keynes is to accept that the role of the State, in balancing accounts, might as well fund a useless search for banknotes in an abandoned coal mine. Following the wisdom of Steve Jobs, mentioned earlier, it is the State that should 'stay foolish' in its pursuit of technological development and social problem solving. Whether the State is making an investment in the Internet or clean energy in the name of national security (having imagined a new 'threat') or in the name of climate change (or just as often 'energy independence'), it can do so on a scale and with tools not available to businesses (i.e. taxation, regulation). If a central hurdle to business investment in new technology is that it will not make investments that can create benefits for the 'public good' (since it then can't capture the majority of the value created), then it is essential the State do so – and worry about how to transform those investments into new economic growth later. 'Foolish' businesses will not survive, as they all must take calculated risks related to product development and entry into new markets. Apple's success did not hinge on its ability to create novel technologies, it hinged on its organizational capabilities in integrating, marketing and selling those low-hanging technologies. In contrast, the flexibility of the State is an important asset, which should be allowed to make its 'foolish' investments in technology in a targeted and purposeful manner. Who would ever have guessed that technology created to preserve communication abilities during a nuclear war would become the world's go-to platform for knowledge, communication and commerce? How many back then thought the Internet was a 'foolish' way to invest millions in taxpayer dollars?

What is needed today is a 'systems' perspective, but one that is more realistic on the actual – rather than mythological – role of the individual actors, and the linkages between actors, within and along the risk landscape. It must also bridge, as stated earlier, the knowledge gap that exists to explain how State investments catalyse, influence and connect to the growth of business organizations on which we rely, ultimately, to deliver new technologies on a broad scale. It is, for example, unrealistic to think that the highly capital-intensive and high-risk areas in clean technology will be 'led' by venture capital, or 'nudged' by a small and unstructured green investment bank. In the case of clean energy, it's also not just about the willingness of the State to lead, but the willingness to *sustain* support for new and transitional technologies until industry can 'mature' – until the cost and performance meet or exceed those of incumbent technologies (e.g. fossil power). The history of new sectors teaches us that private investments tend to wait for the early high-risk investments to be made first by the State. Indeed, it has often been State spending that has absorbed most of the real risk and uncertainty in the emergence of new sectors, as well as in particular areas of old sectors (e.g. radical new medicines today). Yet the returns from these 'revolutionary' State investments have been almost totally privatized. While this is especially obvious in the pharmaceutical industry, where medicines that are funded from taxpayer money are often too expensive for the taxpayers to buy (Vallas et al. 2011), it is also true in other high-tech areas, with companies like Apple, which have received major benefits from public funds, both direct and indirect, managing to avoid paying their taxes (Mazzucato 2013).

Three key implications arise from this analysis.

First, it is of course not enough to talk about the 'entrepreneurial State', one must build it – paying attention to concrete institutions and organizations in government that are able to create long-run growth strategies and 'welcome' the inevitable failure that this will entail. Indeed, it is not a coincidence that the weakest countries in the eurozone are precisely those that have low spending in areas that seem costly today, but which bring growth in the future: areas like R&D and human capital formation (see Figure 1). Yet we are told they are countries that spent too much. And while 'governance' is often used as a reason to impose market reforms, in reality governance should also be about how to bring expertise together and create willingness to invest in high-growth, high-risk areas. As anyone who has worked in the private sector knows, there are plenty of 'bureaucratic' and inertial businesses. There is nothing in the DNA of the public sector that makes it less innovative than the private sector. But equally, encouraging innovation and creativity in public sector institutions requires thinking about organizational dynamics. Instead, by dismissing the ability of the public sector to be an innovative force from within; most thinkers on *strategic management* and organizational change have focused more on the private sector, leaving the public sector to simply focus on 'creating the conditions' for innovation to happen in the 'revolutionary' private sector. And, as discussed above, this has created a self-fulfilling prophecy, where the smartest young graduates think that it will be more exciting and fun to work at Goldman Sachs or Google rather than a State investment bank or a ministry for innovation. The only way to rebalance this problem is to upgrade, not downgrade, the status of government – and the words and the images used to describe it. There are important implications for the eurozone crisis. The conditions being imposed on the weakest countries, via the 'fiscal compact', should be conditions not about reducing the public sector across the board, but conditions that increase the incentives for governments to spend on key areas like education and R&D, and also to transform the public sector from within so that it is more strategic, meritocratic and dynamic. While this might sound difficult, it is no less difficult than imposing the austerity that is undermining the weaker countries' socioeconomic structure and future competitiveness.

Second, if the State is being asked to engage in the world of uncertainty, with the inevitable wins and losses (which also characterize private venture capital), then it is only right that when the wins arrive (the upside) there is also a return to cover the losses (the downside). That is, while State spending on basic education and health should not necessarily expect a direct return beyond the taxes and supply of skilled and healthy staff, the State's high-risk investments should be thought of differently, and allowed to reap a direct return precisely because the failure rate is so high. Successful 'winning' State investments should be able to cash in so as to cover losses when they arise, as well as fund the investments of the future – still unpredictable today. While the privatization of gains and socialization of losses in the financial sector has been recognized as economically inefficient and socially unjust (Alessandri and Haldane 2009), the same asymmetry that occurs in the real economy, both for new-technology firms and for more mature firms that need external investment in turnaround, has remained unnoticed. A clearer risk–reward relationship will not only increase government revenue – during a time in which public sector budgets are under strain – but also allow taxpayers to see a clearer reward from their investments and hence help increase the political support needed for making investments that lead to long-run future growth.

Third, by focusing on the role that the State plays along the bumpy risk landscape, acting actively and courageously rather than just 'de-risking' the private sector and correcting 'market failures', the analysis provided here has the potential to better inform policies that are directed towards other actors in the 'ecosystem' of innovation. This is important because, as outlined in the section on 'myths' in Chapter 2, part and parcel of having undermined the role of the State has been the 'hyping' up of the role of other actors – from SMEs to venture capital and shareholders. Thus, acknowledging the different roles played in the ecosystem – over time and along the bumpy risk landscape – will make it more difficult for overhyped economic actors that have captured the public imagination to argue for handouts and subsidies. The Appendix contains a list of government savings (using the UK as an example) that could arise by approaching the 'ecosystem' in a more realistic way – with policies based on what we know about the different actors, rather than the associated myths.

We live in an era in which the State is being cut back. Public services are being outsourced, State budgets are being slashed, and fear rather than courage is determining many national strategies. Much of this change is being done in the name of rendering markets more competitive, more dynamic. This book is an open call to change the way we talk about the State, its role in the economy, and the images and ideas we use to describe that role. Only then can we begin to build the kind of society we want to live in, and want our children to live in – in a manner that pushes aside false myths about the State and recognizes how it can, when mission driven and organized in a dynamic way, solve problems as complex as putting a man on the moon, and solving climate change. And we need the courage to insist – through both vision but also specific policy instruments – that the growth that ensues from the underlying investments be not only 'smart', but also 'inclusive'.

APPENDIX

This is a list of policy recommendations, for the UK economy, that appeared at the beginning of the 2011 DEMOS version of *The Entrepreneurial State*.

- Reduce government spending on direct transfers to small firms, such as small business rate relief and inheritance tax relief. This is a cost saving.
- If the Small Business Research Initiative (SBRI)[1] is enhanced, as the government has indicated, it must be done in a way that focuses on how to get SMEs to spend money on new technologies. To do so, it will need to increase the size of the project financing that it administers (too diluted currently), and concentrate on firms that prove they will spend on innovation. This is cost neutral.
- Abandon initiatives to establish a UK patent box (a preferential tax regime for profits arising from patents), which would not increase innovation and according to the Institute for Fiscal Studies would in time lead to greater taxpayer costs. This is a cost saving.
- Review R&D tax credits with a view to ensuring that firms are held accountable for actually spending the money on innovation, and failing that, shift away from blanket R&D tax credits to free up resources towards direct commissioning of the technological advance in question. This is a potential cost saving.
- Enterprise zones, that give regulatory or taxation advantages to firms in a certain area, are a distraction as they do not cause innovation to happen that would not have taken place elsewhere. Best to use the money in other ways. This is a cost saving.

---

1 The UK SBRI programme, run out of the UK Technology Strategy Board (see below), and which targets funding for small and medium enterprises, was modelled around the US SBIR programme discussed in Chapter 4.

- When successful, a part of the return from investments made with significant public support should be returned to government. This is a potential cost saving.
- Use these freed-up resources to engage in a massive expansion of the Technology Strategy Board,[2] structured in line with the model of the US DARPA to directly enable innovation (research, development and commercialization) through a bottom-up, government-directed network of agencies, in line with recommendations of the Confederation of British Industry (CBI 2006). It also requires more transparency about funding decisions and clearer auditing of performance so that failing performance areas are cut off. This would increase expenditure.
- Adopt a more proactive interventionist approach to green technology innovation, drawing on the UK's specific strengths. This would increase expenditure.
- The time any private equity investment must be held before the gains from sale can be exempt from capital gains tax should be raised in the UK to at least five years (currently only two, previously ten in 2002). This would help prevent the 'take the money and run' scenario in green tech, which has characterized investments in biotechnology companies, most of which remain 'product-less'. This is a cost saving.
- Short-termism is especially problematic in contexts in which radical technological change is needed and the reason why venture capital and other forms of private equity are not playing a leading role in green technology. Given the lack of private investments, the UK government should step up and increase its 'green' budget. The Green Investment Bank is not enough. This would increase expenditure.

---

2 The Technology Strategy Board is an innovation agency in the UK government. https://www.innovateuk.org/

BIBLIOGRAPHY

Abbate, J. 1999. *Inventing the Internet*. Cambridge, MA: MIT Press.

Abramovitz, M. 1956. *Resource and Output Trends in the United States since 1870*. New York: National Bureau of Economic Research.

Acemoglu, D. 2002. 'Technical Change, Inequality and the Labor Market'. *Journal of Economic Literature* 40, no. 1: 7–72.

Acuña, R. 1976. *América Ocupada*. Mexico City: Ediciones ERA.

Adner, R. 2012. *The Wide Lens: A New Strategy for Innovation*. New York: Portfolio/ Penguin.

Aghion, P., R. Veugelers and C. Serre. 2009. 'Cold Start for the Green Innovation Machine'. *Bruegel Policy Contribution* 12 (November).

Alessandri, P. and A. Haldane. 2009. 'Banking on the State'. Bank of England, November.

Almus, M. and E. A. Nerlinger. 1999. 'Growth of New Technology-Based Firms: Which Factors Matter?' *Small Business Economics* 13, no. 2: 141–54.

Ambler, T. and K. Boyfield. 2010. 'Reforming the Regulators'. Adam Smith Institute briefing paper, September. Available online at http://www.adamsmith.org/files/ reforming-the-regulators.pdf (accessed 24 January 2013).

Amsden, A. 1989. *Asia's Next Giant: South Korea and Late Industrialization*. Oxford: Oxford University Press.

Andersen, R. 2012. 'The "Silent Green Revolution" Underway at the Department of Energy'. *Atlantic*, 9 September. Available online at http://www.theatlantic. com/technology/archive/2012/09/the-silent-green-revolution-underway-at-the-department-of-energy/261905/ (accessed 22 January 2013).

Anderson, E. 2011. 'Spectra Watt Hopes to Soon Rise Again'. *Times Union*, 27 May. Available online at http://www.timesunion.com/business/article/SpectraWatt-hopes-to-soon-rise-again-1398102.php (accessed 7 July 2012).

Angell, M. 2004. *The Truth about the Drug Companies*. New York: Random House.

Apple. 2012. 'Creating Jobs through Innovation'. Apple.com. Available online at http://www.apple.com/about/job-creation/ (accessed 22 January 2013).

Arora, A. and A. Gambardella. 1994. 'The Changing Technology of Technological Change: General and Abstract Knowledge and the Division of Innovative Labour'. *Research Policy* 23, no. 5: 523–32.

ARPA-E (Advanced Research Projects Agency – Energy). n.d. ARPA-E website. Available online at http://arpa-e.energy.gov/?q=about (accessed 6 June 2011).

Arthur, W. B. 2009. *The Nature of Technology: What It Is and How It Evolves*. New York: Free Press.

Atkinson, A., T. Piketty and E. Saez. 2011. 'Top Incomes in the Long Run of History'. *Journal of Economic Literature* 49, no. 1: 3–71.

Audretsch, D. B. 1995. *Innovation and Industry Evolution*. Cambridge, MA: MIT Press.

———. 2000. 'The Economic Role of Small- and Medium-Sized Enterprises: The United States'. Paper presented at the World Bank workshop on 'Small and Medium Enterprises', Chang Mai, Thailand (August).

———. 2003. 'Standing on the Shoulders of Midgets: The U.S. Small Business Innovation Research Program (SBIR)'. *Small Business Economics* 20: 129–35.

Auerswald, P. E. and L. M. Branscomb. 2003. 'Valleys of Death and Darwinian Seas: Financing the Invention of Innovation Transition in the United States'. *Journal of Technology Transfer* 28, nos. 3–4: 227–39.

Baker, D. R. 2010. 'Funding for Clean-Tech Firms Plunges 33% in '09'. SfGate.com. Available online at http://articles.sfgate.com/2010-01-07/business/17470394_1_venture-funding-cleantech-group-venture-capitalists (accessed 6 June 2011).

Bakewell, S. 2011. 'Chinese Renewable Companies Slow to Tap $47 Billion Credit'. *Bloomberg Business Week*, 16 November. Available online at http://www.businessweek.com/news/2011-11-16/chinese-renewable-companies-slow-to-tap-47-billion-credit.html (accessed 26 January 2012).

Bakewell, S. 2012. 'U.K. "Leading" Vestas Offshore Wind Market, Manager Says'. Bloomberg, 10 July. Available online at http://www.bloomberg.com/news/2012-07-10/u-k-leading-vestas-offshore-wind-market-manager-says.html (accessed 6 March 2013).

Barca, S. 2011. 'Energy, Property, and the Industrial Revolution Narrative'. *Ecological Economics* 70: 1309–15.

Bathon, M. 2012. 'Solyndra Wins Court Approval of Bankruptcy Exit Plan'. Bloomberg, 23 October. Available online at http://www.bloomberg.com/news/2012-10-22/solyndra-wins-court-approval-of-bankruptcy-exit-plan.html (accessed 28 January 2013).

Battelle, J. 2005. *The Search*. New York: Penguin.

Berners-Lee, T. 1989. 'Information Management: A Proposal'. CERN. Available online at http://info.cern.ch/Proposal.html (accessed 22 January 2013).

Block, F. L. 2008. 'Swimming against the Current: The Rise of a Hidden Developmental State in the United States'. *Politics and Society* 36, no. 2 (June): 169–206.

———. 2011. 'Innovation and the Invisible Hand of Government'. In *State of Innovation: The U.S. Government's Role in Technology Development*, edited by F. L. Block and M. R. Keller. Boulder, CO: Paradigm Publishers.

Block, F. L. and M. R. Keller, eds. 2011a. *State of Innovation: The U.S. Government's Role in Technology Development*. Boulder, CO: Paradigm Publishers.

———. 2011b. 'Where do innovations come from?' In *State of Innovation: The U.S. Government's Role in Technology Development*, edited by F. L. Block and M. R. Keller, 154–73. Boulder, CO: Paradigm Publishers.

———. 2012. 'Explaining the Transformation in the US Innovation System: The Impact of a Small Government Program'. *Socio-Economic Review*,

30 September, 1–28. Available online at http://ser.oxfordjournals.org/content/ early/2012/09/30/ser.mws021.full.pdf+html (accessed 13 February 2013).

Blodget, H. 2011. 'Apple's Huge New Data Center in North Carolina Created only 50 Jobs'. 'Daily Ticker', Yahoo Finance, 28 November. Available online at http://finance.yahoo.com/blogs/daily-ticker/apple-huge-data-center-north-carolina-created-only-143852640.html (accessed 22 January 2013).

Bloom, N. and J. van Reenen. 2006. *Measuring and Explaining Management Practices across Firms and Countries*. London: Centre for Economic Performance.

Bottazzi, G., G. Dosi, M. Lippi, F. Pammolli and M. Riccaboni. 2001. 'Innovation and Corporate Growth in the Evolution of the Drug Industry'. *International Journal of Industrial Organization* 19, no. 7: 1161–87.

Bottazzi, L. and M. Da Rin. 2002. 'Venture Capital in Europe and the Financing of Innovative Firms'. Centre for Economic Policy Research, *Economic Policy* 34.

Breakthrough Institute. 2010. *Where Good Technologies Come From: Case Studies in American Innovation*. Oakland, CA: Breakthrough Institute, December. Available online at: http://thebreakthrough.org/blog/Case%20Studies%20in%20American%20 Innovation%20report.pdf (accessed 24 January 2013).

Brodd, R. J. 2005. 'Factors Affecting U.S. Production Decisions: Why are there No Volume Lithium-Ion Battery Manufacturers in the United States?' ATP Working Paper Series, Working Paper 05-01, prepared for the Economic Assessment Office Advanced Technology Program, National Institute of Standards and Technology (NIST), June.

Brouwer, E., A. Kleinknecht and J. O. N. Reijnen. 1993. 'Employment Growth and Innovation at the Firm Level: An Empirical Study'. *Evolutionary Economics* 3: 153–9.

Brown, D. et al., eds. n.d. 'History of Elo'. Elo Touch Solutions. Available online at http://www.elotouch.com/AboutElo/History/default.asp (accessed 22 January 2013).

Bullis, K. 2011. 'Venture Capitalists Back Away from Clean Energy'. Technologyreview. com, 11 August. Available online at http://www.technologyreview.com/ news/424982/venture-capitalists-back-away-from-clean-energy/ (accessed 26 January 2013).

Burlamaqui, L. 2012. 'Knowledge Governance: An Analytical Perspective and its Policy Implications'. In *Knowledge Governance: Reasserting the Public Interest*, edited by L. Burlamaqui, A. C. Castro and R. Kattel, 3–26. London: Anthem Press.

Bush, V. 1945. *Science, the Endless Frontier: A Report to the President*. Washington, DC: US Government Printing Office.

Buxton, B. 2012. 'Multi-touch Systems That I Have Known and Loved'. Microsoft Research. Available online at http://www.billbuxton.com/multitouchOverview. html (accessed 3 October 2012).

CBI (Confederation of British Industry). 2006. 'Innovation and Public Procurement: A New Approach to Stimulating Innovation'. CBI Innovation Brief.

CBO (Congressional Budget Office). 2006. *Research and Development in the Pharmaceutical Industry*. Washington, DC: Congressional Budget Office, Congress of the United States. Available online at http://www.cbo.gov/ftpdocs/76xx/doc7615/10-02-DrugR-D.pdf (accessed 24 January 2013).

CEP (Centre for Economic Performance). 2006. 'Inherited Family Firms and Management Practices: The Case for Modernising the UK's Inheritance Tax'. Available online at www.pa_inherited_family_firms.pdf (accessed 7 June 2011).

CERN. 2010. 'Another of CERN's Many Inventions!' *CERN Bulletin*, 16 March. Available online at http://cds.cern.ch/record/1248908 (accessed 22 January 2013).

Chang, H.-J. 1993. 'The Political Economy of Industrial Policy in Korea'. *Cambridge Journal of Economics* 17, no. 2: 131–57.

———. 2008. *Kicking away the Ladder: The Myth of Free Trade and the Secret History of Capitalism*. New York: Bloomsbury.

Chang, H.-J. and P. Evans. 2000. 'The Role of Institutions in Economic Change'. Paper prepared for 'The Other Canon Meetings', Venice, Italy, 13–14 January and Oslo, Norway, 15–16 August.

Chazan, G. 2013. 'Fossil Fuel Dominance Still Frames R&D Debate'. *Financial Times*, 28 January. Available online at http://www.ft.com/intl/cms/s/0/294650fe-63bd-11e2-84d8-00144feab49a.html#axzz2PGTDXaje (accessed 1 April 2013).

Chesbrough, H. 2003. *Open Innovation: The New Imperative for Creating and Profiting from Technology*. Boston: Harvard Business School Press.

China Briefing. 2011. 'An Overview of China's Renewable Energy Market'. 16 June. Available online at http://www.china-briefing.com/news/2011/06/16/an-overview-of-chinas-renewable-energy-market.html (accessed 12 September 2013).

Chong, F. and D. D. McNicoll. 2006. 'Day in Sun for New Billionaire'. *Weekend Australian*, 11 March.

Choudhury, N. 2012. 'China PV Installations to Experience Surge in 4Q 2012'. Pv-tech.org, 10 October. Available online at http://www.pv-tech.org/news/china_pv_installations_experienced_surge_in_2q_2012 (accessed 25 January 2013).

Christensen, C. M. 1997. *The Innovator's Dilemma: When New Technologies Cause Great Firms to Fail*. Boston: Harvard Business Press.

Chu, K. 2011. 'Solar-Cell Maker Files for Bankruptcy'. *Inside Energy*, 22 August.

———. 2011. 'Solar Firm Says Defective Materials, Chinese Competition Spurred Bankruptcy'. *Inside Energy With Federal Lands*, 29 August.

Citizens for Tax Justice. 2012. 'Press Release: General Electric's Ten Year Tax Rate Only Two Percent'. Ctj.org, 27 February. Available online at http://www.ctj.org/taxjusticedigest/archive/2012/02/press_release_general_electric.php#.UVm3D1fEWyE (accessed 1 April 2013).

Climate Works. 2011. 'China's New Five-Year Plan Aims to Meet Ambitious Climate and Energy Targets'. 13 October. Available online at http://www.climateworks.org/news/item/chinas-new-five-year-plan (accessed 1 December 2012).

Coad, A. and R. Rao. 2008. 'Innovation and Firm Growth in High-Tech Sectors: A Quantile Regression Approach'. *Research Policy* 37, no. 4: 633–48.

Committee on Climate Change (UK). 2010. 'Building a Low-Carbon Economy – the UK's Innovation Challenge'. Available online at http://www.theccc.org.uk/publication/building-a-low-carbon-economy-the-uks-innovation-challenge/ (accessed 1 November 2012).

Coriat, B., F. Orsi and O. Weinstein. 2003. 'Does Biotech Reflect a New Science-Based Innovation Regime?' *Industry and Innovation* 10, no. 3 (September): 231–53.

Cowie, J. 1999. *Capital Moves: RCA's 70-Year Quest for Cheap Labor*. New York: Cornell University Press.

Crouch, B. 2008. '$6bn Empire of the Sun'. *Sunday Mail*, 3 February.

Cullen, S. E. 2009. 'Alternative Energy Powers Up'. Thompson Reuters. Available online at http://lib.sioc.ac.cn/tsg_admin/upload/myupload_4514.pdf (accessed 6 June 2011).

David, P. A. 2004. 'Understanding the Emergence of Open Science Institutions: Functionalist Economics in Historical Context'. *Industrial and Corporate Change* 13, no. 4: 571–89.

Davies, A. 2003. 'Integrated Solutions: The Changing Business of Systems Integration'. In *The Business of Systems Integration*, edited by A. Prencipe, A. Davies and M. Hobday. Oxford: Oxford University Press.

Davies, A. and T. Brady. 1998. 'Policies for a Complex Product System'. *Futures* 30, no. 4: 293–304.

DECC (Department of Energy and Climate Change). 2009. *The UK Low Carbon Transition Plan: National Strategy for Climate and Energy*. London: Department of Energy and Climate Change, 15 July. Available online at http://centralcontent. fco.gov.uk/central-content/campaigns/act-on-copenhagen/resources/en/pdf/ DECC-Low-Carbon-Transition-Plan (accessed 6 June 2011).

Demirel, P. and M. Mazzucato. 2012. 'Innovation and Firm Growth: Is R&D Worth It?' *Industry and Innovation* 19, no. 1: 45–62.

Devlin, K. 2002. 'The Math behind MP3'. *Guardian*, 3 April. Available online at http://www.guardian.co.uk/technology/2002/apr/04/internetnews.maths/ print (accessed 10 October 2012).

DIUS (Department of Innovation, Universities and Skills). 2008. *Innovation Nation*, March. Cm 7345. London: DIUS.

DoD (United States Department of Defense). 2011. *Selected Acquisition Report (SAR): RCS: DD-A&T(Q&A)823-166 : NAVSTAR GPS: Defense Acquisition Management Information Retrieval (DAMIR)*. Los Angeles, 31 December.

DoE (United States Department of Energy). 2007. 'DOE-Supported Researcher Is Co-winner of 2007 Nobel Prize in Physics'. 10 September. Available online at http://science.energy.gov/news/in-the-news/2007/10-09-07/?p=1 (accessed 21 January 2013).

————. 2009. 'DOE Awards $377 Million in Funding for 46 Energy Frontier Research Centers'. Energy.gov, 6 August. Available online at http://energy.gov/ articles/doe-awards-377-million-funding-46-energy-frontier-research-centers (accessed 6 June 2011).

Domar, E. D. 1946. 'Capital Expansion, Rate of Growth, and Employment'. *Econometrica* 14, no. 2 (April): 137–47.

Donahue, J. 2012. 'Walmart to Install Solar on 27 Massachusetts Stores by 2014'. Cleanenergycouncil.org, 15 May. Available online at http://www. cleanenergycouncil.org/blog/2012/05/15/walmart-to-install-solar-on-27-massachusetts-stores-by-2014/ (accessed 25 July 2012).

Dosi, G., P. Llerena and M. S. Labini. 2006. 'The Relationships between Science, Technologies and Their Industrial Exploitation: An Illustration through the Myths and Realities of the So-Called "European Paradox"'. *Research Policy* 35, no. 10: 1450–64.

Dosi, G., F. Malerba O. Marsili and L. Orsenigo. 1997. 'Industrial Structures and Dynamics: Evidence, Interpretation and Puzzles'. *Industrial and Corporate Change* 6, no. 1: 3–24.

Douglas, A. I. and P. J. Klenow. 1996. 'Sematech: Purpose and Performance'. *Proceedings of the National Academy of Sciences of the United States of America* 93, no. 23: 12739–42.

Dowling, S., ed. 2012. 'Apple announces plans to initiate dividend and share repurchase program'. Apple.com, 19 March. Available online at http://www. apple.com/pr/library/2012/03/19Apple-Announces-Plans-to-Initiate-Dividend-and-Share-Repurchase-Program.html (accessed 22 January 2013).

Drucker, P. 1970. *Technology, Management and Society*. Oxford: Butterworth-Heinemann.

Drucker, J. 2010. 'Google 2.4% Rate Shows How $60 Billion Lost to Tax Loopholes'. Bloomberg, 21 October . Available online at http://www.bloomberg.com/news/2010-10-21/google-2-4-rate-shows-how-60-billion-u-s-revenue-lost-to-tax-loopholes.html (accessed 19 July 2012).

Duhigg, C. and K. Bradsher. 2012. 'How the U.S. Lost Out on iPhone Work'. *New York Times*, 'The iEconomy Series', 28 April. Available online at http://www.nytimes.com/2012/01/22/business/apple-america-and-a-squeezed-middle-class.html?_r=1&gwh=CDD8CD36DC4DEF040F857DEB57FA4348 (accessed 21 January 2012).

Duhigg, C. and D. Kocieniewski. 2012. 'How Apple Sidesteps Billions in Taxes'. *New York Times*, 'The iEconomy Series', 28 April. Available online at http://www.nytimes.com/2012/04/29/business/apples-tax-strategy-aims-at-low-tax-states-and-nations.html (accessed 1 July 2012).

Ebeling, A. 2011. 'Get Uncle Sam to Help You Buy an iPad in 2011'. *Forbes*, 'Taxes', 16 August. Available online at http://www.forbes.com/sites/ashleaebeling/2011/08/16/get-uncle-sam-to-help-you-buy-an-ipad-in-2011/ (accessed 3 September 2012).

EC (European Commission). 2010. *Europe 2020: A Strategy for Smart, Sustainable and Inclusive Growth*. Communication from the Commission. Brussels: EC, March. Available online at ec.europa.eu/economy_finance/structural_reforms/europe_2020/index_en.htm. (accessed 24 January 2013).

————· 2012. *The EU Climate and Energy Package*. Available online at http://ec.europa.eu/clima/policies/package/index_en.htm (accessed 24 January 2013).

Economist. 2010a. 'Special Report: The World Economy'. 7 October. Available online at http://www.economist.com/printedition/2010-10-09 (accessed 25 January 2013).

————· 2010b. 'The World in 2011'. 22 November. Available online at http://www. economist.com/theworldin/2011 (accessed 25 January 2013).

————· 2011a. 'Taming Leviathan: How to Slim the State Will Become the Great Political Issue of Our Times'. 17 March. Available online at http://www. economist.com/node/18359896 (accessed 23 May 2013).

————· 2011b. 'Angst in the United States: What's Wrong with America's Economy?' 28 April. Available online at http://www.economist.com/node/18620710 (accessed 25 January 2013).

————· 2012. 'The Third Industrial Revolution'. 21 April. Available online at http://www.economist.com/node/21553017 (accessed 30 April 2012).

Energy and Climate Change Select Committee. 2011. *Energy and Climate Change – Third Report: The Revised Draft National Policy Statements on Energy*. London: House of Commons, 18 January. Available online at http://www.publications.parliament. uk/pa/cm201011/cmselect/cmenergy/648/64802.htm (accessed 2 May 2011).

EPA (United States Environmental Protection Agency). 2011. 'Methane emissions'. Washington, DC: US Environmental Protection Agency, 1 April. Available online at http://www.epa.gov/methane/ (accessed 8 October 2012).

EPIA (European Photovoltaic Industry Association). 2012. *Global Market Outlook for Photovoltaics until 2016*. Brussels: European Photovoltaic Industry Association, May.

Ernst & Young. 2011. 'Cleantech Matters: Seizing Transformational Opportunities'. *Global Cleantech and Trends Report 2011*. Ey.com. Available online at http:// www.ey.com/Publication/vwLUAssets/Cleantech-matters_FW0009/$FILE/ Cleantech-matters_FW0009.pdf (accessed 29 January 2013).

Evans, P. 1995. *Embedded Autonomy: States and Industrial Transformation*. Princeton, NJ: Princeton University Press.

Evans, P. and J. Rauch. 1999. 'Bureaucracy and Growth: A Cross-National Analysis of the Effects of "Weberian" State Structures on Economic Growth'. *American Sociological Review* 64, no. 5: 748–65.

FDA (Food and Drug Association). n.d. Search: 'Orphan Drug Designations and Approvals'. US Department of Health and Human Sciences. Available online at http://www.accessdata.fda.gov/scripts/opdlisting/oopd/index.cfm (accessed 9 January 2013; search results obtained in June 2011).

Fiegerman, S. 2012. 'Here's Why Apple Is Suddenly Laying-Off Employees from Its Retail Store'. *Business Insider*, 16 August. Available online at http://www. businessinsider.com/heres-why-apple-is-suddenly-laying-off-employees-from-its-retail-stores-2012-8 (accessed 22 January 2013).

First Solar. 2011. 'First Solar Sets World Record for CdTe Solar PV Efficiency'. *Firstsolar*, 26 July. Available online at http://investor.firstsolar.com/releasedetail. cfm?releaseid=593994 (accessed 23 July 2012).

Flannery, R. 2006. 'Sun King: Photovoltaics Vendor Zhengrong Shi Is Worth Only $2.2 Billion. If He Could Just Make Solar Power Cost-Effective, He Could Be Really Rich'. *Forbes Asia* 2, no. 5 (27 March).

Florida, R. and D. Browdy. 1991. 'The Invention That Got Away'. *Technology Review* 94, no. 6 (August/September): 42–54.

Flynn, L. 1995. 'Apple Holds School Market, Despite Decline'. *New York Times*, 'Technology', 11 September. Available online at http://www.nytimes. com/1995/09/11/business/apple-holds-school-market-despite-decline. html?pagewanted=print&src=pm (accessed 19 July 2012).

Foray, D., D. C. Mowery and R. R. Nelson. 2012. 'Public R&D and Social Challenges: What Lessons from Mission R&D Programs?' *Research Policy* 41, no. 10 (December): 1697–1702.

Forero-Pineda, C. 2006. 'The Impact of Stronger Intellectual Property Rights Technology in Developing Countries'. *Research Policy* 35, no. 6: 808–24.

Frankfurt School of Finance and Management. 2012. 'Global Trends in Renewable Energy Investment 2012'. Available online at http://fs-unep-centre.org/ publications/global-trends-renewable-energy-investment-2012 (accessed 13 September 2012).

Freel, M. S. and P. J. A. Robson. 2004. 'Small Firm Innovation, Growth and Performance: Evidence from Scotland and Northern England'. *International Small Business Journal* 22, no. 6: 561–75.

Freeman, C. 1995. 'The "National System of Innovation" in Historical Perspective'. *Cambridge Journal of Economics* 19, no. 1: 5–24.

Fried, L., S. Shukla and S. Sawyer, eds. 2012. *Global Wind Report: Annual Market Update 2011*. Global Wind Energy Council (March). Available online at http://gwec. net/wp-content/uploads/2012/06/Annual_report_2011_lowres.pdf (accessed 24 January 2013).

Friedman, B. M. 1979. 'Crowding Out or Crowding In? The Economic Consequences of Financing Government Deficits'. NBER Working Paper no. 284.

Fuchs, E. R. H. 2009. 'Cloning DARPA Successfully: Those Attempting to Copy the Agency's Success in Advancing Technology Development First Better Be Sure They Know How DARPA Actually Works'. *Issues in Science and Technology* 26, no. 9: 65–70.

———. 2010. 'Rethinking the Role of the State in Technology Development: DARPA and the Case for Embedded Network Governance'. *Research Policy* 39: 1133–47.

Gambardella, A. 1995. *Science and Innovation: The US Pharmaceutical Industry during the 1980s*. Cambridge: Cambridge University Press.

Geroski, P. and S. Machin. 1992. 'Do Innovating Firms Outperform Non-innovators?' *Business Strategy Review* 3, no. 2: 79–90.

Geroski, P. A. and M. Mazzucato. 2002a. 'Learning and the Sources of Corporate Growth'. *Industrial and Corporate Change* 11, no. 4: 623–44.

———. 2002b. 'Myopic selection'. *Metroeconomica* 53, no. 2: 181–99.

Geroski, P. A. and S. Toker. 1996. 'The Turnover of Market Leaders in UK Manufacturing Industry, 1979–86'. *International Journal of Industrial Organization* 14, no. 2: 141–58.

Ghosh, S. and R. Nanda. 2010. 'Venture Capital Investment in the Cleantech Sector'. Harvard Business School Working Paper 11-020.

Geller, D. and D. Glodfine, co-directors. 2012. *Something Ventured, Something Gained*. DVD. United States: Miralan Productions.

Gipe, P. 1995. *Wind Energy Comes of Age*. New York: John Wiley & Sons.

Glader, P. 2010. 'GE Chief Slams U.S. on Energy'. *Wall Street Journal*, 24 September. Available online at http://online.wsj.com/article/SB10001424052748703384204575509760331620520.html (accessed on 20 December 2010).

Griffith, R., H. Miller and M. O'Connell. 2010. 'The UK Will Introduce a Patent Box, but to Whose Benefit?' Institute for Fiscal Studies Working Paper 5362.

Griliches, Z., B. H. Hall and A. Pakes. 1991. 'R&D, Patents and Market Value Revisited: Is there a Second (Technological Opportunity) Factor?' *Economics, Innovation and New Technology* 1, no. 3: 183–201.

Grossman, G. and E. Helpman. 1991. *Innovation and Growth in the Global Economy*. Cambridge, MA: MIT Press.

Grindley, P. and D. Teece. 1997. 'Managing Intellectual Capital: Licensing and Cross-Licensing in Semiconductors and Electronics'. *California Management Review* 39, no. 2: 8–41.

Grunwald, M. 2012. *The New New Deal: The Hidden Story of Change in the Obama Era*. New York: Simon & Schuster.

Hall, N. 2011. 'Spending Review 2010: CaSE's Select Committee Response'. Campaign for Science and Engineering, 13 May. Available online at http://sciencecampaign.org.uk/?p=5260 (accessed 13 June 2011).

Haltiwanger, J., R. Jarmin and J. Miranda. 2010. 'Who Creates Jobs? Small vs. Large vs. Young'. NBER Working Paper no. 16300.

Harcourt, G. C. 1972. *Some Cambridge Controversies in the Theory of Capital.* Cambridge: Cambridge University Press.

Harrod, R. F. 1939. 'An Essay in Dynamic Theory'. *Economic Journal* 49, no. 193 (March): 14–33.

Hart, J. and M. Borrus. 1992. 'Display's the Thing: The Real Stakes in the Conflict over High Resolution Displays'. Berkeley Roundtable on the International Economy (BRIE) Working Paper no. 52. Available online at http://brie.berkeley.edu/publications/WP%2052.pdf (accessed 24 January 2013).

Haslam, K. 2012. 'Tim Cook's Disastrous First Appointment as CEO'. *Macworld*, 30 October. Available online at http://www.macworld.co.uk/apple-business/news/?newsid=3407940&pagtype=allchandate (accessed 22 January 2013).

Henderson, J. 2004. 'UT Professor, 81, Is Mired in Patent Lawsuit'. *Houston Chronicle*, 5 June. Available online at http://www.chron.com/default/article/UT-professor-81-is-mired-in-patent-lawsuit-1662323.php (accessed 11 February 2013).

Henderson, N. and M. Schrage. 1984. 'The Roots of Biotechnology: Government R&D Spawns a New Industry'. *Washington Post*, 16 December.

Heymann, M. 1998. 'Signs of Hubris: The Shaping of Wind Technology Styles in Germany, Denmark, and the United States, 1940–1990'. *Technology and Culture* 39, no. 4 (October): 641–70.

Hilton, A. 2012. 'To Be More Like Americans, Europe Should Do What They Do, Not What They Say They Do'. *Independent*, 25 February. Available online at http://www.independent.co.uk/news/business/comment/anthony-hilton-to-be-more-like-americans-europe-should-do-what-they-do-not-what-they-say-they-do-7440626.html (accessed 19 June 2012).

HMRC (Her Majesty's Revenue and Customs). 2011. 'An Evaluation of Research and Development Tax Credits'. Available online at http://www.hmrc.gov.uk/research/report107.pdf (accessed 13 June 2011).

Hobday, M. 1998. 'Product Complexity, Innovation and Industrial Organization'. *Research Policy* 26: 689–710.

Hopkins, M. 2012. 'The Making of a Champion, or, Wind Innovation for Sale: The Wind Industry in the United States 1980–2011'. Airnet working paper. Available online at http://www.theairnet.org/files/research/Hopkins/Hopkins_Wind_20120421.pdf (accessed 28 January 2013).

Hopkins, M. and W. Lazonick. 2011. 'There Went the Sun: Renewable Energy Needs Patient Capital'. Huffington Post, 23 September. Available online at http://www.huffingtonpost.com/william-lazonick/there-went-the-sun-renewa_b_978572.html (accessed 12 July 2012).

————. 2012. 'Soaking Up the Sun and Blowing in the Wind: Renewable Energy Needs Patient Capital.' Working paper. Airnet. Available online at http://www.theairnet.org/files/research/Hopkins/CleanTech_PatientCapital_20121129a.pdf (accessed 1 December 2012).

Hourihan, M. and M. Stepp. 2011. 'A Model for Innovation: ARPA-E Merits Full Funding'. The Information Technology and Innovation Foundation, July. Available online at http://www.itif.org/files/2011-arpa-e-brief.pdf (accessed 24 January 2013).

Hsieh, C. and P. J. Klenow. 2009. 'Misallocation and Manufacturing TFP in China and India'. *Quarterly Journal of Economics* 124, no. 4: 1403–46.

Hughes, A. 2008. 'Entrepreneurship and Innovation Policy: Retrospect and Prospect'. *Political Quarterly* 79, issue supplement s1 (September): 133–52.

Hughes, A. and A. Mina. 2011. 'The UK R&D Landscape'. UK-IRC. Available online at http://ukirc.ac.uk/knowledgeexchange/reports/article/?objid=6403 (accessed 28 January 2013).

Ibele, M. 2003. 'An Overview of California's Research and Development Tax Credit'. Legislative Analyst's Office, November. Available online at http://www.lao.ca.gov/2003/randd_credit/113003_research_development.html (accessed 22 January 2013).

Irwin, D. A. and P. J. Klenow. 1996. 'Sematech: Purpose and Performance'. *Proceedings of the National Academy of Sciences of the United States of America* 93, no. 23: 12739–42.

Isaacson, W. 2011. *Steve Jobs*. New York: Simon & Schuster.

Janeway, W. H. 2012. *Doing Capitalism in the Innovation Economy: Markets, Speculation and the State*. Cambridge: Cambridge University Press.

Jensen, M. 1986. 'Agency Costs of Free Cash Flow, Corporate Finance, and Takeovers'. *American Economic Review* 76, no. 2: 323–9.

Jobs, S., W. Mossberg and K. Swisher. 2010. 'D8: Steve Jobs Onstage: Full-Length Video'. AllthingsD, 7 June. Available online at http://allthingsd.com/video/?video_id=70f7cc1d-ffbf-4be0-bff1-08c300e31e11 (accessed 22 January 2013).

Johansson, B. 2007. 'Award Ceremony Speech'. Nobelprize.org, 28 January 2013, Available online at http://www.nobelprize.org/nobel_prizes/physics/laureates/2007/presentation-speech.html (accessed 24 January 2013).

Johnson, C. 1982. *MITI and the Japanese Miracle: The Growth of Industrial Policy 1925–1975*. Stanford, CA: Stanford University Press.

Judt, T. 2010. *Ill Fares the Land*. New York: Penguin Press.

Kamp, L. 2002. 'Learning in Wind Turbine Development : A Comparison between the Netherlands and Denmark'. Doctoral dissertation, Utrecht University, Denmark. Available online at http://igitur-archive.library.uu.nl/dissertations/2002-1128-170921/inhoud.htm (accessed 28 January 2013).

Kelly, H. 2012. 'How Schools Are Reacting to Apple's Entry into Education'. VentureBeat, 21 January. Available online at http://venturebeat.com/2012/01/21/apple-textbook-public-private-schools/ (accessed 19 July 2012).

Kenney, M. 2003. 'The Growth and Development of the Internet in the United States'. In *The Global Internet Economy*, edited by B. Kogut, 69–108. Cambridge, MA: MIT Press.

Keynes, J. M. 1926. *The End of Laissez-Faire*. London: L & V Woolf.

———. 1934. *The General Theory of Employment, Interest and Money*. New York: Harcourt, Brace & Company.

———. 1937. 'The General Theory of Employment'. *Quarterly Journal of Economics* 51, no. 2 (February): 209–23.

———. 1938. 'Private Letter to Franklin Delano Roosevelt'. 1 February. In *Maynard Keynes: An Economists Biography*, edited by D. E. Moggridge. London: Routledge, 1992.

Kho, J. 2011. 'Clean Tech's Repeat Lesson: Venture Capital Isn't for Factories'. Forbes.com, 30 September. Available online at http://www.forbes.com/sites/jenniferkho/2011/09/30/repeat-lesson-for-vcs-venture-isnt-for-factories/ (accessed 24 January 2013).

Klooster, J. W. 2009. *Icons of Invention: The Makers of the Modern World from Gutenberg to Gates*. Santa Barbara, CA: Greenwood Press.

Knight, F. 1921. *Risk, Uncertainty and Profit*. New York: Augustus M Kelley.

———. 2002. *Risk, Uncertainty and Profit*. Washington, DC: Beard Books.

Kocieniewski, D. 2011. 'G.E.'s Strategies Let It Avoid Taxes Altogether'. *New York Times*, 24 March. Available online at http://www.nytimes.com/2011/03/25/business/economy/25tax.html?_r=1&scp=1&sq=g.e.&st=cse (accessed 25 July 2012).

Korosec, K. 2011. 'Cleantech Saviour: US Military to Spend $10B Annually by 2030'. Smartplanet.com, 13 October. Available online at http://www.smartplanet.com/blog/intelligent-energy/cleantech-savior-us-military-to-spend-10b-annually-by-2030/9593 (accessed 28 January 2013).

Kraemer, K. L., G. Linden and J. Dedrick. 2011. Capturing Value in Global Networks: Apple's iPad and iPhone'. Personal Computer Industry Center, University of California–Irvine. Available online at http://pcic.merage.uci.edu/papers/2007/CapturingValue.pdf (accessed 19 June 2012).

LaMonica, M. 2012. 'Should the Government Support Applied Research?' *MIT Technology Review*, 10 September. Available online at http://www.technologyreview.com/news/428985/should-the-government-support-applied-research/ (accessed 19 June 2012).

Landberg, R. 2012. 'China to Make Regional Adjustments for Solar Power Incentives'. Bloomberg, 19 December. Web. http://www.bloomberg.com/news/2012-12-19/china-to-make-regional-adjustments-for-solar-power-incentives.html (accessed 24 January 2013).

Lauber, V. and L. Mez. 2006. 'Renewable Electricity Policy in Germany, 1974 to 2005'. *Bulletin of Science, Technology & Society* 26, no. 2 (April): 105–20.

Lazonick, W. 2007. 'The US Stock Market and the Governance of Innovative Enterprise'. *Industrial and Corporate Change* 16, no. 6: 983–1035.

———. 2008. 'Entrepreneurial Ventures and the Developmental State: Lessons from the Advanced Economies'. UNU-WIDER. Discussion Paper no. 1 (January).

———. 2009. *Sustainable Prosperity in The New Economy? Business Organization and High-Tech Employment in the United States*. Kalamazoo, MI: W.E. Upjohn Institute for Employment Research.

———. 2011a. 'Apple's Jobs: A Rebirth of Innovation in the US Economy?' *Next New Deal: The Blog of The Roosevelt Institute*. Nextnewdeal.net, 4 August. Available online at http://www.nextnewdeal.net/apples-jobs-rebirth-innovation-us-economy (accessed 12 July 2012).

————. 2011b. 'How Greedy Corporations Are Destroying America's Status as "Innovation Nation"'. Next New Deal: The Blog of The Roosevelt Institute. Nextnewdeal.net, 28 July. Available online at http://www.nextnewdeal.net/how-greedy-corporations-are-destroying-americas-status-innovation-nation (accessed 7 March 2013).

————. 2011c. 'The Innovative Enterprise and the Developmental State'. Academic-Industry Research Network, April. Available online at http://www.theairnet.org/files/research/lazonick/Lazonick%20Innovative%20Enterprise%20and%20Developmental%20State%2020110403.pdf (accessed 7 March 2012).

————. 2012. 'The Innovative Enterprise and the Developmental State: Toward an Economics of "Organizational Success"'. Paper presented at the annual conference of the Institute for New Economic Thinking, Breton Woods, NH, USA, 10 April, 38 (revised November 2012). Available online at http:// fiid.org/?page_id=1660 (accessed 22 January 2013).

————. 2013. 'Strategies for Promoting U.S. Competitiveness in World Markets'. In *Public Economics: The Government's Role in American Economics*, edited by S. Payson. Praeger/ABC-CLIO. Forthcoming.

Lazonick, W. and M. Mazzucato. 2013. 'The Risk-Reward Nexus in the Innovation-Inequality Relationship: Who Takes the Risks? Who Gets the Rewards?' *Industrial and Corporate Change* 22, no. 4. Forthcoming.

Lazonick, W. and O. Tulum. 2011. 'US Biopharmaceutical Finance and the Sustainability of the Biotech Business Model'. *Research Policy* 40, no. 9 (November): 1170–87.

Lee, A. 2012. 'Ralph Nader to Apple CEO Using Texas' Tax Dollars: "Stand on Your Own Two $100 billion Feet"'. AlterNet, 6 April. Available online at http://www.alternet.org/newsandviews/article/877674/ralph_nader_to_apple_ceo_using_texas'_tax_dollars%3A_'stand_on_your_own_two_$100_billion_feet'/ (accessed 22 January 2013).

Lent A. and M. Lockwood. 2010. 'Creative Destruction: Placing Innovation at the Heart of Progressive Economics'. IPPR discussion paper, December.

Lerner, J. 1999. 'The Government as Venture Capitalist: The Long Run Impact of the SBIR Program'. *Journal of Business* 72, no. 3: 285–318.

Leslie, S. W. 2000. 'The Biggest "Angel" of Them All: The Military and the Making of Silicon Valley'. In *Understanding Silicon Valley: The Anatomy of an Entrepreneurial Region*, edited by M. Kenney, 44–67. Stanford, CA: Stanford University Press.

Levine, S. 2009. 'Can the Military Find the Answer to Alternative Energy?' Businessweek.com, 23 July. Available online at http://www.businessweek.com/magazine/content/09_31/b4141032537895.htm (accessed 28 January 2013).

Lewis, J. 2007. 'Technology Acquisition and Innovation in the Developing World: Wind Turbine Development in China and India'. *Studies in Comparative International Development* 32, nos. 3–4: 208–32.

Liedtke, M. 2012. 'Apple Cash: CEO Tim Cook Says Company Has More Than It Needs'. Huffington Post, 23 February. Available online at http://www.huffingtonpost.com/2012/02/23/apple-cash-ceo-tim-cook_n_1297897.html?view=print&comm_ref=false (accessed 19 July 2012).

Lim, B. and S. Rabinovitch. 2010. 'China Mulls $1.5 Trillion Strategic Industries Boost: Sources'. Reuters, 3 December. Available online at http://

www.reuters.com/article/2010/12/03/us-china-economy-investment-idUSTRE6B16U920101203 (accessed 24 July 2012).

Linden, G., K. L. Kraemer and J. Dedrick. 2009. 'Who Captures Value in a Global Innovation Network? The Case of Apple's iPod'. *Communications of the ACM* 52, no. 3: 140–44.

Liu, C. 2011. 'China Uses Feed-In Tariff to Build Domestic Solar Market'. *New York Times*, 14 September. http://www.nytimes.com/cwire/2011/09/14/14climatewire-china-uses-feed-in-tariff-to-build-domestic-25559.html?pagewanted=all (accessed 24 January 2013).

Liu, W. 2011. 'An Unlikely Boost for Chinese Wind'. Chinadialogue, 20 June. Available online at http://www.chinadialogue.net/article/show/single/en/4361-An-unlikely-boost-for-Chinese-wind (accessed 25 April 2012).

Liu, Y. 2012. *China Increases Target for Wind Power Capacity to 1,000 GW by 2050*. Renewableenergyworld.com, 5 January. Available online at http://www.renewableenergyworld.com/rea/news/article/2012/01/china-increases-target-for-wind-power-capacity-to-1000-gw-by-2050 (accessed 14 June 2012).

Lockshin, B. and P. Mohnen. 2012. 'Do R&D Tax Incentives Lead to Higher Wages for R&D Workers? Evidence from the Netherlands'. Maastricht Economic and Social Research Institute on Innovation and Technology (UNU-Merit) Working Paper no. 2012-058, 18 July; revised version of Working Paper no. 2008-034.

Longview Institute. n.d. 'The Birth of the Microchip'. Longviewinstitute.org. Available online at http://www.longviewinstitute.org/projects/marketfundamentalism/microchip/ (accessed 2 July 2012).

Lööf, H. and A. Heshmati. 2006. 'On the Relationship between Innovation and Performance: A Sensitivity Analysis'. *Economics of Innovation and New Technology* 15, nos. 4–5: 317–44.

Lundvall, B.-Å., ed. 1992. *National Innovation Systems: Towards a Theory of Innovation and Interactive Learning*. London: Pinter Publishers.

Lyons, D. 2012. 'Apple Caves on Audits'. The Daily Beast, 13 February. Available online at http://www.thedailybeast.com/newsweek/2012/02/12/apple-s-hypocrisy-on-u-s-jobs.html (accessed 7 July 2012).

Madrigal, A. 2011. *Powering the Dream: The History and Promise of Green Technology*. Cambridge MA: Da Capo Press.

Malakoff, D. 2012. 'Romney, Obama Campaigns Give Clean Tech Research Some Bipartisan Love'. 'Science Insider', sciencemag.org, 11 July. Available online at http://news.sciencemag.org/scienceinsider/2012/07/romney-obama-campaigns-give-clean.html?ref=em (accessed 7 August 2012).

Malone, M. S. 1999. *Infinite Loop: How the World's Most Insanely Great Computer Company Went Insane*. New York: Currency Press.

Markusen, A., P. Hall, S. Campbell and S. Deitrick. 1991. *The Rise of the Gunbelt: The Military Remapping of Industrial America*. New York: Oxford University Press.

Martin, R. and U. Wagner. 2009. 'Climate Change Policy and Innovation'. Centre for Economic Performance conference paper, London School of Economics. Available online at http://cep.lse.ac.uk/conference_papers/18_05_2009/martin.pdf (accessed 7 June 2011).

Martinot, E. 2010. 'Renewable Power for China: Past, Present, and Future'. *Frontiers of Energy and Power Engineering in China* 4, no. 3: 287–94.

————. 2013. 'Renewables Global Futures Report' REN21, January. Available online at http://www.ren21.net/Portals/0/REN21_GFR_2013_print.pdf (accessed 10 March 2013).

Martinot, E. and L. Junfeng. 2007. 'Powering China's Development: The Role of Renewable Energy'. WorldWatch Institute, November. Available online at http://www.worldwatch.org/files/pdf/Powering%20China%27s%20Development. pdf (accessed 20 September 2013).

————. 2010. 'Renewable Energy Policy Update for China'. Renewableenergyworld. com, 21 July. Available online at http://www.renewableenergyworld.com/rea/ news/article/2010/07/renewable-energy-policy-update-for-china (accessed 24 April 2012).

Mason, G., K. Bishop and C. Robinson. 2009. 'Business Growth and Innovation: The Wider Impact of Rapidly-Growing Firms in UK City-Regions'. NESTA research report, October.

Massey, D., P. Quintas and D. Wield. 1992. *High-Tech Fantasies: Science Parks in Society, Science and Space*. London: Routledge.

Mathews, J. et al. 2011. 'China's Move to a Circular Economy as a Development Strategy'. *Asian Business and Management* 10, no. 4: 463–84.

Mazzoleni, R. and R. R. Nelson. 1998. 'The Benefit and Costs of Strong Patent Protection: A Contribution to the Current Debate'. *Research Policy* 27, no. 3: 273–84.

Mazzucato, M. 2000. *Firm Size, Innovation and Market Structure: The Evolution of Market Concentration and Instability*. Northampton, MA: Edward Elgar.

————. 2010. 'US Healthcare Reform Is Not an Act of Meddling'. *Guardian*, 6 April. Available online at http://www.guardianpublic.co.uk/us-healthcare-reform-innovation (accessed 6 June 2011).

————. 2011. *The Entrepreneurial State*. London: DEMOS.

————. 2012a. 'Rebalancing What?' Policy Network discussion paper. Policy-network.net, 24 June. Available online at www.policy-network.net/ publications/4201/Rebalancing-What (accessed 11 February 2013).

————. 2012b. 'The EU Needs More, Not Less Investment, to Get Out of Its Current Economic Predicament'. *European* 34 (October): 4–8. Available online at http://ymlp.com/zm2bu9 (accessed 2 February 2013).

————. 2013. 'Taxpayers Helped Apple but Apple Won't Help Them'. *Harvard Business Review*, 8 March. Available online at http://blogs.hbr.org/cs/2013/03/ taxpayers_helped_apple_but_app.html?utm_source=Socialflow&utm_ medium=Tweet&utm_campaign=Socialflow (accessed 9 April 2013).

Mazzucato, M. and G. Dosi, eds. 2006. *Knowledge Accumulation and Industry Evolution: The Case of Pharma-Biotech*. Cambridge: Cambridge University Press.

Mazzucato, M. and W. Lazonick. 2010. 'The Limits to the 3% R&D Target in Europe 2010: The Roles of Institutions, Industries, and Business – Government Complementarities in Achieving Equitable and Stable Growth'. FINNOV position paper, May. Available online at http://www.finnov-fp7.eu/sites/default/files/FINNOV_POSITION_ PAPER_MAY_2010_3Percent_RD.pdf (accessed 24 January 2013).

Mazzucato, M. and S. Parris. 2011. 'R&D and Growth: When Does Variety Matter?' FINNOV Working Paper 2.8.

McCray, W. P. 2009. 'From Lab to iPod: A Story of Discovery and Commercialization in the post-Cold War era'. *Technology and Culture* 50, no. 1 (January): 58–81.

McIntyre, R. et al. 2011. 'Corporate Taxpayers & Corporate Tax Dodgers 2008–10'. Citizens for Tax Justice and the Institute on Taxation and Economic Policy. Available online at http://www.ctj.org/corporatetaxdodgers/CorporateTaxDodgersReport.pdf (accessed 25 July 2012).

Mia, H. et al. 2010. 'A Survey of China's Renewable Energy Economy'. *Renewable and Sustainable Energy Reviews* 14: 438–45.

Minsky, H. P. 1992. 'The Financial Instability Hypothesis'. Jerome Levy Economics Institute Working Paper no. 74, May.

Mirowski, P. 2011. *Science-Mart*. Cambridge, MA: Harvard University Press.

MIT (Massachusetts Institute of Technology). 2013. A preview of the MIT production in the 'Innovation Economy Report', edited by Richard M. Locke and Rachel Wellhausen, mit.edu, 22 February. Available from http://web.mit.edu/press/images/documents/pie-report.pdf (accessed 25 February 2013).

Motoyama, Y., R. Appelbaum and R. Parker. 2011. 'The National Nanotechnology Initiative: Federal Support for Science and Technology, or Hidden Industrial Policy?' *Technology in Society* 33, nos. 1–2 (February–May): 109–18. Available online at http://ac.els-cdn.com/S0160791X1100011X/1-s2.0-S0160791X1100011X-main.pdf?_tid=fdf274f8-71ce-11e2-82ef-00000aab0f02&acdnat=1360314641_02c6c7c82b80f38f77571a611ab9305c (accessed 8 February 2013).

Mowery, D. C. 2010. 'Military R&D and Innovation'. In *Handbook of the Economics of Innovation*, edited by B. H. Hall and N. Rosenberg. Amsterdam: North-Holland.

NAS (United States National Academy of Sciences). 2010. *Rising Above the Gathering Storm, Revisited: Rapidly Approaching Category 5*. Washington, DC: National Academies Press.

Nelson, R., ed. 1993. *National Innovation Systems: A Comparative Analysis*. Oxford and New York: Oxford University Press.

Nelson, R. and S. Winter. 1982. *An Evolutionary Theory of Economic Change*. Cambridge, MA: Harvard University Press.

NESTA (National Endowment for Science Technology and the Arts). 2006. 'The Innovation Gap: Why Policy Needs to Reflect the Reality of Innovation in the UK'. Policy briefing, October. Available online at http://www.nesta.org.uk/library/documents/innovation-gap-pb.pdf (accessed 7 June 2011).

———. 2009a. 'The Vital 6 Per Cent: How High Growth Innovative Businesses Generate Prosperity and Jobs'. Research summary.

———. 2009b. From Funding Gaps to Thin Markets: UK Government Support for Early-Stage Venture Capital'. Research report. Available online at http://www.nesta.org.uk/library/documents/Thin-Markets-v9.pdf (accessed 7 June 2011).

———. 2011. 'Vital Growth: The Importance of High Growth Businesses to Recovery'. Research summary, March.

National Research Council. 1999. *Funding a Revolution: Government Support for Computing Research*. Washington, DC: National Academies Press.

Nielsen, K. H. 2010. 'Technological Trajectories in the Making: Two Studies from the Contemporary History of Wind Power'. *Centaurus* 52, no. 3: 175–205.

Nielsen, S. 2012. 'Argentina Plans Biggest Wind Project with Loan from China'. Bloomberg, 5 July. Available online at http://www.bloomberg.com/news/2012-07-05/argentina-plans-biggest-wind-project-with-loan-from-china.html (accessed 24 July 2012).

Nightingale, P. 2004. 'Technological Capabilities, Invisible Infrastructure and the Un-social Construction of Predictability: The Overlooked Fixed Costs of Useful Research'. *Research Policy* 33, no. 9: 1259–84.

———. 2012. Evidence provided on the 'Valley of Death' to Science and Technology Committee, UK House of Commons, 28 April. Available online at http://www.publications.parliament.uk/pa/cm201012/cmselect/cmsctech/uc1936-i/uc193601.htm (accessed 1 January 2013).

NIH (National Institutes of Health). n.d. 'Home', US Department of Health and Human Sciences website. Available online at http://www.nih.gov/ (accessed 25 January 2013).

Nordhaus, T. and M. Shellenberger, eds. 2011. *Breakthrough Journal* 1 (Summer).

NREL (National Renewable Energy Laboratory). 2010. *Rapid Deposition Technology Holds the key for the World's Largest Solar Manufacturer.* Golden, CO: NREL, United States Department of Energy, October.

———. 2012. 'Thin Film Photovoltaic Partnership Project'. Available online at http://www.nrel.gov/pv/thin_film_partnership.html (accessed 23 July 2012).

NSB (National Science Board). 2012. 'Science and Engineering Indicators 2012'. National Science Foundation. Available online at http://www.nsf.gov/statistics/seind12/start.htm (accessed 18 January 2013).

NSF (National Science Foundation). 2010. 'National Patterns of R&D Resources: 2008 Data Update'. NSF 10-314, March.

OECD (Organisation for Economic Co-operation and Development). 2005. *Main Science and Technology Indicators*, volume 2005, issue 2. Paris: OECD.

Office of the Budget, National Institutes of Health. 2011. 'Appropriations History by Institute/Center (1938 to Present)'. Available online at http://officeofbudget.od.nih.gov/approp_hist.html (accessed 15 November 2012). Adapted from W. Lazonick and O. Tulum, 'US Biopharmaceutical Finance and the Sustainability of the Biotech Business Model,' *Research Policy* 40, no. 9 (2011): 1170–87.

Ogg, E. 2012. *How Apple Gets Away with Lower R&D Spending.* GIGaom, 30 January. Available online at http://gigaom.com/apple/how-apple-gets-away-with-lower-rd-spending/ (accessed 19 July 2012).

OSTI (Office of Science and Technical Information). 2009. 'John B. Goodenough, Cathode Materials, and Rechargeable Lithium-ion Batteries. DoE R&D Accomplishments'. 17 September. Available online at http://www.osti.gov/accomplishments/goodenough.html (accessed 14 February 2012).

OSTP (Office of Science and Technology Policy). 2006. 'American Competitiveness Initiative: Leading the World in Innovation'. Domestic Policy Council, Office of Science and Technology Policy, February.

OTA (US Congress Office of Technology Assessment). 1995. *Flat Panel Displays in Perspective.* OTA-ITC-631. Washington, DC: US Government Printing Office. Available online at http://www.fas.org/ota/reports/9520.pdf (accessed 29 January 2013).

OTP (Office of Tax Policy). 2011. 'Investing in U.S. Competitiveness: The Benefits of Enhancing the Research and Experimentation (R&E) Tax Credit'. A report from the Office of Tax Policy, United States Department of the Treasury, 25 March.

Overbye, D. 2007. 'Physics of Hard Drives Wins Nobel'. *New York Times*, 10 October. Available online at http://www.nytimes.com/2007/10/10/world/10nobel.html?pagewanted=print (accessed 10 October 2012).

Parris, S. and P. Demirel. 2010. 'Innovation in Venture Capital Backed Clean-Technology Firms in the UK'. *Strategic Change* 19, nos. 7–8: 343–57.

Patton, D. 2012. 'Further Huge Boost to Solar Target "Not on China's Agenda"'. Recharge News, 12 September . Available online at http://www.rechargenews.com/business_area/politics/article322558.ece (accessed 22 January 2013).

Pavitt, K. 1984. 'Sectoral Patterns of Technical Change: Towards a Taxonomy and a Theory'. *Research Policy* 13, no. 6: 343–73.

Pentland, W. 2011. 'China's Coming Solyndra Crisis'. *Forbes*, 27 September. Available online at http://www.forbes.com/sites/williampentland/2011/09/27/chinas-coming-solyndra-crisis/ (accessed 23 July 2012).

Perez, C. 2002. *Technological Revolutions and Financial Capital: The Dynamics of Bubbles and Golden Ages*. Cheltenham: Edward Elgar.

———. 2012. 'Financial Crises, Bubbles and the Role of Government in Unleashing Golden Ages'. FINNOV Discussion Paper D2.12.

Perlin, J. 1999. *From Space to Earth: The Story of Solar Electricity*. Michigan: Aatec Publications.

Pernick, R., C. Wilde and T. Winnie. 2012. 'Clean Energy Trends 2012.' Clean Edge, March. Available online at http://www.cleanedge.com/reports (accessed 17 April 2012).

Perrons, D. and A. Plomien. 2010. *Why Socio-economic Inequalities Increase?: Facts and Policy Responses in Europe*. EUR (Series) 24471. Luxembourg : Publications Office of the European Union.

Pew Charitable Trusts. 2012. *Who's Winning the Clean Energy Race? 2011 Edition*. Philadelphia and Washington, DC: The Pew Charitable Trusts. Available online at http://www.pewenvironment.org/uploadedFiles/PEG/Publications/Report/FINAL_forweb_WhoIsWinningTheCleanEnergyRace-REPORT-2012.pdf (accessed 25 January 2013).

Pierrakis, Y. 2010. 'Venture Capital: Now and after the Dotcom Crash'. NESTA research report, July 2010. Available online at http://www.nesta.org.uk/library/documents/Venture_Capital.pdf (accessed 25 January 2013).

PIRC (Public Interest Research Centre). 2011. *The Green Investment Gap: An Audit of Green Investment in the UK*. Machynlleth: Public Interest Research Centre, March.

Pisano, G. P. 2006. 'Can Science be a Business? Lessons from Biotech'. *Harvard Business Review* 84, no. 10: 114–25.

Polanyi, K. 2001 [1944]. *The Great Transformation: The Political and Economic Origins of Our Time*. Boston: Beacon.

Politi, J. 2012. 'The Future of Development Banks'. *Financial Times Special Reports*, 24 September, 1–4. Available online at http://www.ft.com/intl/cms/c1628ce2-03a3-11e2-bad2-00144feabdc0.pdf (accessed 1 April 2013).

Prestowitz, C. 2012. 'Apple Makes Good Products but Flawed Arguments'. *Foreign Policy*, 23 January.

Proebstel, D. and W. Clint. 2011. 'Renewable Energy for Military Applications'. I.bnet.com, Pikes Research. Available online at http://i.bnet.com/blogs/rema-11-executive-summary.pdf (accessed 28 January 2013).

RAND. 2011. 'Paul Baran and the Origins of the Internet'. Rand.org, 23 December. Available online at http://www.rand.org/about/history/baran.html (accessed 11 July 2012).

Randerson, J. 2010. 'Cameron: I Want Coalition to Be "Greenest Government Ever"'. *Guardian*, 14 May. Available online at http://www.guardian.co.uk/environment/2010/may/14/cameron-wants-greenest-government-ever (accessed 4 January 2013).

Rao, A. and P. Scaruffi. 2011. *A History of Silicon Valley: The Largest Creation of Wealth in the History of the Planet: A Moral Tale.* Palo Alto, CA: Omniware Group.

Reinert, E. 2007. *How Rich Countries Got Rich and Why Poor Countries Stay Poor.* London: Constable.

Reinganum, J. F. 1984. 'Practical Implications of Game Theoretic Models of R&D'. *American Economic Review* 74, no. 2: 61–6.

REN21 (Renewable Energy Policy Network for the 21st Century). 2012. 'Renewables 2012: Global Status Report'. REN21.net, 11 June. Available online at http://www.map.ren21.net/GSR/GSR2012_low.pdf (accessed 25 January 2013).

Reuters. 2012. 'Hanwha SolarOne to Beat US Tariffs with Q-Cells Buy'. Reuters, 11 September. Available online at http://in.reuters.com/article/2012/09/11/hanwhasolarone-results-idINL3E8KB44G20120911 (accessed 24 January 2013).

Richard, D. 2008. 'Small Business and Government: The Richard Report'. Submission to the Shadow Cabinet. Available online at http://www.bl.uk/bipc/pdfs/richardreport2008.pdf (accessed 6 June 2011).

Robinson, J. 1953–54. 'The Production Function and the Theory of Capital'. *Review of Economic Studies* 21, no. 2: 81–106.

————. 1978. 'Obstacles to Full Employment'. In *Contributions to Modern Economics.* New York, San Francisco: Academic Press.

Rodrik, D. 2004. 'Industrial Policy for the 21st Century'. CEPR Discussion Paper 4767.

Rogoff, K. and C. Reinhart. 2010. 'Growth in a Time of Debt'. *American Economic Review* 100, no. 2: 573–8.

Roland, A. and P. Shiman. 2002. *Strategic Computing: DARPA and the Quest for Machine Intelligence, 1983–1993.* Cambridge, MA: MIT Press.

Roush, W. 2010. 'The Story of Siri, from Birth at SRI to Acquisition by Apple – Virtual Personal Assistants Go Mobile'. Xconomy.com, 14 June. Available online at http://www.xconomy.com/san-francisco/2010/06/14/the-story-of-siri-from-birth-at-sri-to-acquisition-by-apple-virtual-personal-assistants-go-mobile/ (accessed 2 July 2012).

Ruegg, R. and P. Thomas. 2009. 'Linkages from DOE's Wind Energy Program R&D to Commercial Renewable Power Generation'. United States Department of Energy, Office of Energy Efficiency and Renewable Energy, September. Available online at http://www1.eere.energy.gov/analysis/pdfs/wind_energy_r_and_d_linkages.pdf (accessed 7 March 2013).

————. 2011. 'Linkages from DOE's Solar Photovoltaic R&D to Commercial Renewable Power from Solar Energy'. United States Department of Energy, Office of Energy Efficiency and Renewable Energy, April. Available online at http://www1.eere.energy.gov/ba/pba/program_evaluation/pdfs/solar_rd_linkages_report7.18.11.pdf (accessed 25 January 2013).

Ruttan, V. 2006. *Is War Necessary for Economic Growth?: Military Procurement and Technology Development.* New York: Oxford University Press.

Salter, A., P. D'Este, B. Martin, A. Geuna, A. Scott, K. Pavitt and P. Nightingale. 2000. *Talent, Not Technology: Publicly Funded Research and Innovation in the UK.* London: CVCP.

Sande, S. 2012. 'Reno City Council Approves Tax Break for Data Center'. TUAW, 28 June. Available online at http://www.tuaw.com/2012/06/28/reno-city-council-approves-apple-tax-break-for-data-center/ (accessed 22 January 2013).

Sanderson, H. and M. Forsythe. 2012. *China's Superbank: Debt, Oil and Influence – How China Development Bank is Rewriting the Rules of Finance.* Singapore: John Wiley & Sons.

Sapolsky, H. M. 2003. 'Inventing Systems Integration'. In *The Business of Systems Integration*, edited by A. Prencipe, A. Davies and M. Hobday. Oxford: Oxford University Press.

Sato, H. 2011. 'Can US Factories Take on China?' *Lowell Sun*, Chinasubsidies.com, 1 March. Available online at http://www.chinasubsidies.com/Lowell-Sun-Mar-2011.pdf (accessed 5 February 2013).

Schmidt, H. D. D. 2012. *You Cannot Buy Innovation.* Asymco, 30 January. Available online at http://www.asymco.com/2012/01/30/you-cannot-buy-innovation/?utm_source=feedburner&utm_medium=feed&utm_campaign=Feed%3A+Asymco+%about 28asymco%29 (accessed 12 June 2012).

Schumpeter, J. 1949. 'Economic Theory and Entrepreneurial History'. In Research Center in Entrepreneurial History, Harvard University, *Change and the Entrepreneur: Postulates and the Patterns for Entrepreneurial History*. Cambridge, MA: Harvard University Press.

————. 2003 [1942]. *Capitalism, Socialism and Democracy.* New York: Routledge.

Segal, D. 2012. 'Apple's Retail Army, Long on Loyalty but Short on Pay'. *New York Times*, 23 June. Available online at http://www.nytimes.com/2012/06/24/business/apple-store-workers-loyal-but-short-on-pay.html?gwh=7D59E115E4CC232BCFF56011281AF183 (accessed 7 July 2012).

Shapiro, I. 2012. 'Comparing the Pay of Apple's Top Executives to the Pay of the Workers Making Its Products'. Economic Policy Institute, 30 April. Available online at http://www.epi.org/publication/apple-executives-pay-foxconn-workers/ (accessed 19 July 2012).

Sherlock, M. 2011. 'Energy Tax Policy: Historical Perspectives on and Current Status of Energy Tax Expenditures'. Congressional Research Service, 2 May. Available online at http://www.leahy.senate.gov/imo/media/doc/R41227EnergyLegReport.pdf (accessed 19 July 2012).

Singer, A. 2012. 'General Electric's Ten Year Tax Rate Only Two Percent'. Citizens for Tax Justice (CTJ) press release, 27 February. Available online at http://www.ctj.org/taxjusticedigest/archive/2012/02/press_release_general_electric.php (accessed 25 July 2012).

Skidelsky, R., F. Martin and C. Wigstrom. 2012. *Blueprint for a British Investment Bank.* eBook. Available online at http://www.skidelskyr.com/site/article/blueprint-for-a-british-investment-bank/ (accessed 15 February 2013).

Slater, K. 1983. 'Banks Seek Profit in Venture Capital Arena; High-Risk, High-Reward Business Is Attracting More Adherents'. *American Banker*, 31 October.

Smith, A. 1904 [1776] *An Inquiry into the Nature and Causes of the Wealth of Nations*, edited by E. Cannan. 5th edition. London: Methuen & Co.

Solow, R. M. 1956. 'A Contribution to the Theory of Economic Growth'. *Quarterly Journal of Economics* 70, no. 1 (February 1956): 65–94. Available online at http://qje. oxfordjournals.org/content/70/1/65.full.pdf+html (accessed 29 January 2013).

———. 1987. 'We'd Better Watch Out'. *New York Times*, 12 July, 36. Available online at http://www.standupeconomist.com/pdf/misc/solow-computer-productivity. pdf (accessed 29 January 2013).

Soppe, B. 2009. 'How Countries Matter to Technological Change: Comparison of German and U.S. Wind Energy Industry'. Unpublished paper presented at DRUID-DIME Academy winter conference, Denmark, January, 22–4. Information available from http://epub.uni-regensburg.de/6478/ (accessed 14 February 2013).

Southwick, K. 1999. *Silicon Gold Rush: The Next Generation of High-Tech Stars Rewrites the Rules of Business*. New York: John Wiley & Sons.

St John, J. 2011. 'China's Solar Loans Still Mostly Untapped'. Greentech Media, 17 November. Available online at http://www.greentechmedia.com/articles/read/ chinas-solar-loans-still-mostly-untapped/ (accessed 23 July 2011).

Storey, D. 2006. 'Evaluating SME Policies and Programmes: Technical and Political Dimensions'. In *The Oxford Handbook of Entrepreneurship*, edited by M. Casson, B. Yeung, A. Basu and N. Wadeson, 248–79. New York: Oxford University Press.

Strategic Environmental Research and Development Program (SERDP) and Environmental Security Technology Certification Program (ESTCP). n.d. 'Installation Energy Test Bed'. Serdp.org. Available online at http://www.serdp. org/Featured-Initiatives/Installation-Energy (accessed 28 January 2013).

Sullivan, M. A. 2012. 'Apple Reports High Rate but Saves Billions on Taxes'. *Tax Analysts*, 13 February, 777–8. Available online at http://taxprof.typepad.com/ files/134tn0777.pdf (accessed 1 July 2012).

Sweet, C. 2011. 'Google Invests $75 Million in Home Solar Venture'. *Wall Street Journal*, 28 September. Available online at http://online.wsj.com/article/SB10001 424052970204831304576596833595375002.html (accessed 31 October 2012).

Tassey, G. 2012. 'Beyond the Business Cycle: The Need for a Technology-Based Growth Strategy'. Economic Analysis Office working paper, US National Institute of Standards and Technology (NIST), February. Available online at http://www.nist.gov/director/planning/upload/beyond-business-cycle.pdf (accessed 29 January 2013).

Telegraph. 2010. 'David Cameron Pledges Greenest Government Ever'. Video, 14 May. Available online at http://www.telegraph.co.uk/news/newsvideo/ uk-politics-video/7723996/David-Cameron-pledges-greenest-government-ever.html (accessed 2 May 2011).

Tracy, R. 2011. 'US Offers $150m Loan Guarantee to Solar-Wafer Manufacturer'. *Dow Jones International News*, 17 June.

Unruh, G. C. 2000. 'Understanding Carbon Lock-In'. *Energy Policy* 28, no. 12: 817–30.

Usha, H. and D. Schuler. 2011. 'Government Policy and Firm Strategy in the Solar Photovoltaic Industry'. *California Management Review* 54, no. 1: 17–38.

US Department of the Treasury. 2012. 'Overview and Status Update of the 1603 Program'. Treasury.gov, 20 July. Available online at http://www.treasury.gov/initiatives/recovery/ Documents/Status%20overview.pdf (accessed 25 January 2013).

US Government Accountability Office. 2012. 'Advanced Research Projects Agency – Energy Could Benefit from Information on Applicants' Prior Funding'.

13 January. Available online at http://www.gao.gov/products/GAO-12-112 (accessed 9 February 2013).

Vallas, S. P., D. L. Kleinman and D. Biscotti. 2009. 'Political Structures and the Making of US Biotechnology'. In *State of Innovation: The U.S. Government's Role in Technology Development*, edited by F. L. Block and M. R. Keller, 57–76. Boulder, CO: Paradigm Publishers.

Vascellaro, J. E. 2012. 'Tech Industry Rebuts Critics on Outsourcing'. *Wall Street Journal*, 6 June. Available online at http://online.wsj.com/article/SB100014240 52702303830204577446492207816330.html (accessed 17 July 2012).

Wade, R. 1990. *Governing the Market: Economic Theory and the Role of Government in Taiwan's Industrialization*. Princeton, NJ: Princeton University Press.

Wald, M. 2011. 'Energy Firms Aided by U.S. Find Backers'. *New York Times*, 2 February. Available online at http://www.nytimes.com/2011/02/03/business/energy-environment/03energy.html?pagewanted=all&_r=0

Walker, R. 2003. 'The Guts of a New Machine'. *New York Times*, 30 November. Available online at http://www.nytimes.com/2003/11/30/magazine/30IPOD.html?pagewanted=all&pagewanted=print (accessed 10 October 2012).

Westerman, W. 1999. '"About" Wayne Westerman'. Available online at http://www.eecis.udel.edu/~westerma/About_Wayne.html (accessed 22 January 2013).

Wheeler, B. 2011. 'David Cameron Says Enterprise Is Only Hope for Growth'. BBC News, 6 March. Available online at http://www.bbc.co.uk/news/uk-politics-12657524 (accessed 7 June 2011).

WIPO (World Intellectual Property Organization). 2009. 'Patent Co-operation Treaty Applications Relating to Environmental Technologies (2001–05 Average)'. In P. Aghion, R. Veugelers and C. Serre, 'Cold Start for the Green Innovation Machine', *Bruegel Policy Contribution* 12 (November).

Wiser, R., M. Bolinger and G. Barbose. 2007. 'Using the Federal Production Tax Credit to Build a Durable Market for Wind Power In the United States'. Lawrence Berkeley National Laboratory, Environmental Energy Technologies Division, (November. Preprint of article submitted to the *Electricity Journal*. Available online: http://eetd.lbl.gov/ea/emp/reports/63583.pdf (accessed 25 January 2013).

Woo-Cumings, M., ed. 1999. *The Developmental State*. Ithaca, NY: Cornell University Press.

Wood, R. 2012. 'Fallen Solyndra Won Bankruptcy Battle but Faces Tax War'. *Forbes*, 11 June. Available online at http://www.forbes.com/sites/robertwood/2012/11/06/fallen-solyndra-won-bankruptcy-battle-but-faces-tax-war/ (accessed 29 January 2013).

Wright, R. 1997. 'The Man Who Invented the Web: Tim Berners-Lee Started a Revolution, But It Didn't Go Exactly as Planned'. *TIME* 149, no. 20 (19 May).

Yasuda, T. 2005. 'Firm Growth, Size, Age and Behavior in Japanese Manufacturing'. *Small Business Economics* 24, no. 1: 1–15.

Zenghelis, D. 2011. 'A Macroeconomic Plan for a Green Recovery'. Centre for Climate Change Economics and Policy, Grantham Research Institute on Climate Change and the Environment policy paper, January. Available online at http://www2.lse.ac.uk/GranthamInstitute/publications/Policy/docs/PP_macroeconomic-green-recovery_Jan11.pdf (accessed 14 February 2012).

INDEX

Information from tables and figures is indicated by bold page numbers.

CPSIA information can be obtained at www.ICGtesting.com
Printed in the USA
BVOW08s2328100913

330866BV00004B/170/P

9 780857 282521